Withdrawn

Lessons Without Limit

Lessons Without Limit
How Free-Choice Learning is Transforming Education

JOHN H. FALK AND LYNN D. DIERKING

ALTAMIRA
PRESS

A Division of
ROWMAN & LITTLEFIELD PUBLISHERS, INC.
Walnut Creek • *Lanham* • *New York* • *Oxford*

ALTAMIRA PRESS
A Division of Rowman & Littlefield Publishers, Inc.
1630 North Main Street, #367
Walnut Creek, CA 94596
www.altamirapress.com

Rowman & Littlefield Publishers, Inc.
A Member of the Rowman & Littlefield Publishing Group
4720 Boston Way
Lanham, MD 20706

PO Box 317
Oxford
OX2 9RU, UK

British Library Cataloguing in Publication Information Available

Library of Contress Cataloging-in-Publication Data

Falk, John H. (John Howard), 1948–
    Lessons without limit : how free-choice learning is transforming education / John H. Falk and Lynn D. Dierking.
    p. cm.
    Includes bibliographical references (p.   ).
    ISBN 0-7591-0160-4 (pbk. : alk. paper)
    1. Continuing education—United States. 2. Non-formal education—United States.
I. Dierking, Lynn D. (Lynn Diane), 1956–

LC5251 .F35 2002
374'.973—dc21

                                2002001570

Printed in the United States of America

♾™ The paper used in this publication meets the minimum requirements of American National Standard for Information Sciences—Permanence of Paper for Printed Library Materials, ANSI/NISO Z39.48–1992.

TABLE OF CONTENTS

ACKNOWLEDGMENTS

We would like to acknowledge and thank the many people who have contributed to this book and encouraged us on our free-choice learning journey. We feel an enduring gratitude to the staff and board of the Institute for Learning Innovation, current and past. Their counsel, commentary, insights and support aided us not just in the writing of this book, but through many years of up-hill efforts to define and understand the realm of free-choice learning. Also, we wish to thank a wide assortment of colleagues, especially Desmond Griffin and Dennis Schatz, who reviewed and commented on this book. We are particularly grateful to Mitch Allen and Susan Walters of AltaMira Press for believing in us and this topic. We can not begin to thank all of the many, many people over the years who shared with us personal stories of their free-choice learning experiences. We only wish we had the room to include all of their stories, in full. Finally, we wish to thank our mothers Edith and Joan who began us on the path to lifelong learning, and our children, Joshua, Daniel and Lara, who continue to inspire us to keep on pushing down that path.

John H. Falk, Ph.D.
Lynn D. Dierking, Ph.D.
Annapolis, Maryland

FOREWORD

As local school boards and national political leaders debate how to improve America's schools, a far greater transformation of learning in America is well underway. In this landmark publication, John Falk and Lynn Dierking have boldly described the essence of a learning society. Their provocative term, *free-choice learning*, challenges us to redefine traditional notions of education. They invite us to move past our limited focus on a "school system" to imagine the stunning potential of a "learning system"—a system that utilizes all of the educational resources of our communities to connect and extend learning opportunities across a lifetime.

Our new age of information and global competition demands attention to all of the ways in which we invest in the intellect and creativity of people. To participate in the knowledge-based revolution of our century, lifelong learning is increasingly essential. It supports a healthy and productive society and develops individual achievement and self-actualization. As this book so clearly details, free-choice learning accompanies all ages and stages in an individual's development. Yet, though we are in the midst of a learning society, Americans have little public rhetoric to define the educational activity that takes place outside of our formal education system. As a nation, we have even less recognition of the need to support education beyond the school years.

Leadership toward a new learning agenda, however, is gradually appearing in disparate sectors. Museums, libraries, and archives, the repositories of rich learning resources, are deeply engaged in conversations at the national level to establish educational partnerships. Public broadcasting has initiated an intensive examination of new opportunities for public service in a digital age. Higher education is likewise exploring how its resources can be more widely accessible to a broad public. As Falk and Dierking emphasize, connecting and building access to such entities could be a major step in supporting an infrastructure for free-choice learning.

Technology adds a new dimension of urgency to the learning community. The digital revolution has raced into all facets of our lives from how we do business to how we communicate with family and friends. Harnessing the power of digital technology to promote learning and improve public life is a stunning challenge. Not only must the libraries, museums, archives, universities, and other repositories of learning compete in an aggressive commercial environment, they must also do so in a manner that provides access for all. The digital divide must not become a learning divide as well.

Falk and Dierking's inventive *Free-Choice Learner's Bill of Rights* and their bold ideas for building a national awareness of and commitment to promoting lifelong learning make this book must reading in our changing world. They outline with clarity and insight the necessity to connect the dots between school-based, workplace, and free-choice learning and to consider what such an infrastructure might look like. Though free-choice learning is driven by individual choice and need, the power of this book is that it argues for collective action to support individual lives. The ultimate winner is the community itself, strengthened through knowledge, purpose, and an informed citizenry.

Beverly Sheppard

*Nothing, not all the armies in the world,
can stop an idea whose time has come.*

Victor Hugo

Learning about the American Civil War (Photo by [clockwise from top left] John H. Falk; Deanna Voight; New Jersey Civil War Association; and New Jersey Civil War Association; Joe Crocetta, The Harold-Mail Company)

CHAPTER 1

INTRODUCTION:
IN SEARCH OF LIFELONG LEARNING

"Well," said Pooh, "we keep looking for Home and not finding it,
so I thought if we looked for this Pit, we'd be sure not to find it,
which would be a Good Thing, because then we might find something that we
weren't looking for, which might be just what we were looking for really."

—A. A. Milne, *Winnie the Pooh*

The two soldiers charged down the hill, the wind flapping their blue coats. To their right flowed Antietam Creek, to their left what remained of the Union battery. Every few minutes, one of them, and then the next, was cut down by Confederate rifle fire. They tumbled in apparent agony onto the grass. Then, miraculously, they would rise to their feet and again charge down the hill. Up on high, the generals watched their descent into the valley. The only sound was the screaming of the young soldiers.

In a desperate effort to keep up with her "men," Clara Barton was also charging down the hill. It was a difficult task, tending to the wounded soldiers and trying to make them well again. And every now and then, the men actually cooperated and waited long enough for her to do her job. But most of the time, the two soldiers were too focused on their task of single-handedly winning the Civil War for the Union Cause. And that summer afternoon at Antietam National Battlefield, they came close to succeeding.

After more than an hour of "war," exhausted and hot, we, the generals, retreated with 9-year-old Joshua, 7-year-old Daniel, and 3-year-old Lara to the air-conditioned comfort of the visitor center. We watched a wonderful film depicting the events of the battle of Antietam. We cruised the museum, admired the old guns and uniforms, and learned more about the soldiers who fought there 125 years earlier. We picked up a few brochures and chatted with the rangers.

That evening we camped along the banks of the Potomac River, just downstream from where Robert E. Lee and his troops fled the Union Army in September of 1862. We cooked hot dogs and beans over an open fire, we sang Civil War-era songs, we slept in tents in the dark, listening to the sounds of the night. Fortunately for us, there were no sounds of injured and dying soldiers, only nighthawks, crickets, and cicadas. The next morning we broke camp, ate flapjacks at a real restaurant, and drove back home.

Over the years, we took many trips like this, visiting battlefields, museums, and reenactments. We watched movies like *Glory*, the PBS series on the Civil War, and checked out dozens of library books. We cooked Civil War meals and listened to Civil War-era music, all of us dressed up like Civil War soldiers. And we did all of this because our two young sons, for some reason none of us can remember anymore, got interested in a particular period of American history.

As a family we were committed to learning. And learn we did. Our classroom was anywhere we could find something relevant to the Civil War, which, in the Washington, D.C., area, included a lot of places. We took advantage of any and every educational opportunity and resource we could find to aid us in our learning quest and, like most Americans, we were lucky to have a wealth of such opportunities and resources available to us. This was a very special time in our lives, and for all of us a series of very special learning experiences—experiences we have never forgotten, experiences that we believe directly affected the lives of our children and without question directly affected the lives of us adults as well. All of us grew in our understanding of the Civil War and nineteenth-century American history. Perhaps equally important, all five of us also developed and refined our capabilities using community resources to pursue our lifelong learning interests. We became frequent users of the public library, local museums, and nearby national parks. We also kept a watchful eye out for the occasional newspaper article or public television special on our topic of interest. All of these sources we regularly exploited in order to fulfill our family's personal learning agenda. The more we practiced at lifelong learning, the better we became at it.

Lifelong learning—possessing the skills, commitment, and capacity to learn across an entire lifetime—has long been the "holy grail" of public education in America. Perhaps this sentiment was best summarized by Beverly Sheppard, acting director of the Institute for Museum and Library Services (IMLS), the primary federal agency charged with supporting America's museums and libraries:

> The profound changes of the twenty-first century are transforming America into what must become a learning society. We enter this century in the midst of a bewildering mix of opportunity, uncertainty, challenge and change, all moving at unprecedented speed. Fueled by dazzling new technologies, increasing social diversity and divide, and radical shifts in industry and labor markets, accelerating change has become a way of life. To navigate the changes, minimize the risks and participate in shaping a new order, all Americans need access to learning throughout their lifetimes.

The Learning Society

Our society is in the midst of changes as great as any experienced thus far, changes that are affecting everyone. These changes are directly and profoundly influencing all facets of our lives, and are tied to the shifting of the American economy from one that is industrially based to one that is information and knowledge based. Princeton economist Fritz Machlup suggested in the late 1950s that knowledge and information (which he felt were functionally the same) were rapidly becoming the major economic products of society. Whereas in an earlier age goods were viewed as the ultimate product, today services, ideas, and increasingly *experiences* are the products of choice. Even everyday goods such as computers and pizza are economically viable to the extent that they are marketed and delivered in a personal and information-rich manner. No longer is it sufficient to market a mass-produced computer or pizza. Today's computer is custom-built and even offers options for custom colors and personalized features. The traditional pizza parlor is being replaced by the restaurant that offers an increasingly knowledgeable and discriminating diner the opportunity to personally design the perfect pizza, which comes complete with Italian music and language tapes playing in the restrooms, table cloths, and imported Chianti bottles.

This transformation, though driven by economics, is fueled by the increasing learning needs of society. Just as futurists were beginning to herald the coming of the knowledge economy, a number of forward-thinking educators were talking about the transition of America into a *Learning Society*. They suggested that if America was to fully transition into a knowledge-based economy, where information and ideas were paramount, learning across the life span would need to become central to the society as never before. And in fact, this is exactly what is happening.

America is rapidly evolving into a Learning Society. The new knowledge economy is being constructed with ideas, and creating these new ideas, not to mention keeping up with all of them, is a challenging task. It takes information and experience to generate a new and innovative idea. The best route to new information, more refined knowledge, and relevant cutting-edge experience is learning. Creating an innovative idea, above all, requires openness to new information and a commitment to learning all the time. Lifelong learning, long a utopian educational goal of our society, is increasingly becoming not just a necessity, but a way of life. As our society is increasingly inundated with information, each individual finds it necessary to develop better strategies with which to analyze the increasing quantity of information in order to select that of high quality and broad utility. In a myriad of subtle and not-so-subtle ways, this necessity has resulted in America becoming a nation of lifelong learners.

But wait a moment. How can this be possible? A day does not go by without someone telling us about the educational crisis in our schools. How can we be achieving the utopian goal of lifelong learning when people tell us our schools are failing? Maybe the answer is that lifelong learning, in fact learning in general, is not totally dependent upon schooling. Schooling represents one building block of a learning society, but perhaps not the only or even the most important one. Perhaps, like Winnie the Pooh suggests in the opening quote, if we focus instead on something we *weren't* looking for, it might just be what we *were* looking for all along.

Learning in America

It has often been said that people commonly perceive their times to be filled with more rapid change than usual and to assume that the pace of change is quickening. At least from the days of the sixteenth-century English Puritans, there has been a pervasive assumption that one's parents' lives were different and that one's children will have a still more uncertain and challenging time of it. These ideas seem to be fundamental to American culture, and thus, too, the long-held belief in the importance of educating children. Learning, it was believed, not only helped one to "make something of oneself," but also promoted flexibility, adaptability, and the development of strategies to survive and even prosper in a chancy world.

It has only been within the last one hundred years or so that the words *learning, education,* and *schooling* came to be treated as synonyms. In fact, learning in America has always drawn from many different sources, including, but not limited to, schooling. For most of our history, schools were very short-term experiences in our life—five to eight years at most, and then for only six months out of the year. Most of our lives were spent outside of school. Despite the expansion of schooling to as many as twenty years, each year now filling nine or even ten months, schooling still represents a relatively small percentage of our lives. As a society, we have had a long-standing perception that knowledge is available from many, many sources—what America's most distinguished educational historian Lawrence Cremin called the "configurations of education." For example, in the early nineteenth century, Americans relied upon such diverse resources as farming almanacs for tips on agriculture and the evangelical movement for early versions of "self-help" courses. By the early twentieth century, Americans could turn to a wealth of resources in order to gain more and better knowledge; daily newspapers were in abundance, as were periodicals on everything from advertising to plumbing. Libraries, museums, and the increasingly popular encyclopedias were also available. Now, at the beginning of the twenty-first century, the information resources available to Americans are truly staggering. For the first time in human history, the problem is not that there is too little information available, but too much!

In the new Learning Society, learning is something that happens not just during the school day, or even just at work, but throughout the day and across our life span. More and more of our time, at work and play, is invested in learning. And it goes without saying that there is a growing awareness of the importance of nonschool sources of information and education that extend learning before and after the years of schooling.

Before we proceed further, though, it is very important that we clarify what we mean when we use the term *learning*. Our idea of learning is very broad, as epitomized by our Civil War example. It includes the typical notions of learning ideas, facts, and concepts, most often expressed in words. For instance, in the case of the Civil War, learning would include knowing the names of battles, generals, or the reasons the war began. But our definition of learning also encompasses shifts in attitude, values, and beliefs such as an appreciation for how passionately many Civil War soldiers felt about the cause they were fighting for—whether protection of homeland, preservation of the Union or a way of life, or abolition of slavery. Our definition of learning also includes aesthetic understanding—the beauty of the Maryland countryside, and psychomotor skills—understanding how it felt to cook over an open fire. Learning also includes sociocultural dimensions—understanding what makes one's parents happy and what makes them mad—and learning includes how to think critically and refine one's learning skills—discovering that the American Civil War was actually a very complex struggle involving tangible benefits and unthinkable atrocities. This broader definition of learning means that as we immersed ourselves in the time period, listening to Civil War-era music, preparing the food, and dressing up like nineteenth-century soldiers and women, we learned much more than the mere facts of the war. We learned as much as we could about what it felt like to live at that time and experienced, in small ways, the triumphs and tragedies of that period. We also learned a great deal about one another as learners and people, how to support and facilitate one another's interests, and how to use our community's learning resources. All of these things, some of which are not easily expressed in words, are important parts of lifelong learning.

Learning, as we have broadly defined it, has become so pervasive that it is rapidly becoming the single largest leisure activity. For the first time in history, learning is what most Americans choose to do for enjoyment! And like everything else in our changing economy, the public wants their leisure learning to be a personalized, non-mass-produced experience—learning experiences that meet the individual's own unique requirements, interests, and needs. This is not the type of learning we were used to getting in school, but it is the type of learning we now expect to receive during our leisure time.

Evidence for this shift is everywhere you look, but the most scientific evidence comes from research conducted just north of the United States in Canada. Fortunately, Canadian leisure behavior is quite similar to U.S. leisure behavior, and the Canadians have had the prescience to track this behavior. A Toronto-based Canadian research institute has been polling the public for more than a quarter century in order to determine how adults spend their leisure time. The most recent survey shows that, on average, Canadian adults spend about 18 hours each week engaged in some type of learning activity. This represents a 50-percent increase in time spent on such learning when compared with similar data collected in the 1970s. The vast majority of this learning time, nearly 95 percent, was not for work or in order to earn a degree; this was learning freely engaged in for leisure purposes. Adults in the survey spent their free time learning everything from how to use a computer to keep track of their personal finances to learning better strategies and techniques for home renovations. Virtually all of the learning in which adults participated occurred outside of school. As we enter the twenty-first century, learning, broadly defined, is not only something children do when they are in school, it is more and more what all people, children and adults, do every day of their lives. Learning today is much, much more than schooling.

Free-Choice Learning

Let us return briefly to our family's American Civil War learning. What we did as a family to learn together was very special, but not that unique. In myriad ways, every day, Americans in every corner of the country learn as we did, using similar resources, sometimes with friends and family and sometimes alone. Every day, millions of Americans partake in what we call *free-choice learning* and, in the process, make lifelong learning a reality. Free-choice learning is the single, most dominant form of learning. Free-choice learning is the learning people do when they get to control what to learn, when to learn, where to learn, and with whom to learn. Young people and old people participate in free-choice learning; they do so through various media—television, books, radio, museum exhibitions, through conversations with friends and family, and in ever-increasing numbers on the Internet. Because of free-choice learning, Americans are learning more things, more often, than at any other time in human history. Learning on demand, anywhere, any time—learning 24/7! There is a revolution going on in America and it is all about learning. Yes, lifelong learning is alive and well. The vehicle propelling this long-sought-after societal goal is free-choice learning. Ironically, this all-important learning vehicle is largely unrecognized and widely undervalued. How could something so important be so underappreciated? Perhaps, we've been looking too long and hard at the wrong thing; perhaps we need to follow Winnie the Pooh's advice. So saying, let's explore something that we *weren't* looking for—free-choice learning—so that we can discover something we *were* hoping to find—lifelong learning in America. Let us explore the what, why, where, and when of free-choice learning.

Part I
THE HOWS AND WHYS OF LEARNING

Learning science at the museum (Photo by The Children's Museum, Indianapolis)

CHAPTER 2
A THIRST FOR LEARNING

The purpose of life after all, is to live it, to taste experience to the utmost, to reach out eagerly and without fear for newer and richer experience.

—Eleanor Roosevelt

One recent summer day we paid a visit to our local public library. The library was full of people—young and old, affluent and poor, black and white, Asian and Latino. What were these people doing, we wondered. So we took the time to actually talk to a number of them to find out. One middle-aged man told us he was planning a trip to Europe with his wife and children and was using the library to research accommodations and travel tips. A teenage girl said she was interested in backpacking and was trying to see if there were any books that would help her learn more about the subject (as she so far had not been successful, we suggested she ask the reference librarian). A woman of about thirty told us she was here with her two children, helping them pick out good books to read over the summer. An elderly man was reading a newspaper in the corner and informed us he comes to the library every day to read the New York *Times*. Two people we talked to said they were doing genealogical research by using the library's Internet access. Not surprisingly, several people we talked to indicated that they were just here to find an interesting book to read. All of these people, each in his or her own way, were engaged in free-choice learning.

What Is Free-Choice Learning?

Free-choice learning is the most common type of learning in which people engage. It is self-directed, voluntary, and guided by individual needs and interests—learning that we will engage in throughout our lives. Since it is the learning that we do when we want to, by definition it involves a strong measure of choice—choice over what, why, where, when, and how we will learn. The fact that free-choice learning happens for the most part outside of the imposed structure and requirements of schools, universities, or workplaces makes it at once extremely interesting and chronically underrecognized.

As we have already suggested, we are learning all the time, throughout our lifetime; in school, at home, in classrooms, in workplaces, in museums, while watching television, playing sports, and talking with friends. People learn both through formal instruction and on their own. Some of what we learn, we learn because we have to learn it. If we want to drive a car, we learn the rules of the road; if we want to practice medicine, we learn about the human body and how it functions; and if we want to please others in our lives, we learn what makes them happy or unhappy. However, most of what we learn in our lives we learn not because we have to, but because we choose to. We choose not only what we will learn, but also where, when, and with whom we will learn. This is free-choice learning.

Learning can often be facilitated by a teacher, but a teacher is not always an authority figure standing at the front of a classroom. Parents are teachers; so are youth and religious leaders and native elders; and some of our best teachers are our friends. Even our pets can be teachers, as we appreciate that napping in the sun is a pretty good way to spend a weekend afternoon! Often, our teachers are objects, such as books, Web sites, television shows, or exhibitions. What we learn from these teachers may be what they intended, but just as likely the lessons learned are different, unique to our own particular needs and interests. This, too, is free-choice learning.

There is no single right way to learn things, and no single place or even moment in which we learn. All of our learning happens continuously, from many different sources and in many different ways. We are not born knowing what is important to learn, but as a society, as a community of learners, we must be guided to discover what is important to learn. There are three main places in our society where we receive this guidance—schools and universities, the workplace, and the free-choice learning sector. All three are important; all three are essential for lifelong learning.

There is a need in our lives for formal education. Formal education is the place where professionals help guide us in the development of basic skills and help introduce us to new realms of knowledge. There is also a need in our lives for career-directed learning. The workplace is where we learn the skills and abilities necessary to do productive work, and in the process earn the money we need to sustain our lives. But so, too, there is a need for free-choice learning. The free-choice learning sector is where we can tap into a vast array of resources, where we are provided an opportunity to explore the thousands of topics, whether shallowly or deeply, occasionally or frequently, that lead us to understand ourselves, our families, our society, and our world a little better. All of these educational sectors currently exist, all are large and vibrant, but one of these, the free-choice learning sector, has been largely ignored and underappreciated for the profound impact it has on American learning. As a society, we have developed this bad habit of assuming that learning is only that thing we do in school. Now, as well as historically, most Americans acquire most of the knowledge, understanding, and information they require for their daily lives outside of school. This is one of those statements that seems at once obvious and yet profoundly surprising and, dare we suggest, radical.

If you don't believe this is true, take a moment and do a little thought experiment with us. Think of five topics that you know something about—any five topics. Say, for example, cooking, biology, politics, movies, or sports. How did you come to know something about these topics? Where did you first begin to learn about these topics? Why did you learn about them? How do you stay current in these topics? If you are like most people, at least one of the topics you picked was related to your work. Hence, much of what you know about that topic you learned as part of "on the job training." But what about the others? Our research would suggest that the majority of the topics you listed represents a range of subjects relating to personal and avocational interests. Some of these may be topics traditionally taught in school, but many are not. Your interest in these various topics likely developed early in life, maybe initially from friends or perhaps your family. Although you may have even gained some basic information about some of these topics in school, over time, because of your interest in the topics, you maintained and extended your knowledge by reading articles in magazines and newspapers. You also probably watched television shows on these topics, continued to talk about them with friends and family, perhaps saw exhibitions about them at a museum, and maybe checked out a book or two on the topics from the library somewhere along the way. Well, you say, of course I learned how to cook and discriminate between movies outside of school. But the real substantive knowledge I possess—knowledge of history, literature, and science— that knowledge I most certainly acquired in school. Perhaps.

Let's take science as an example. Ever since Sputnik, billions of dollars have been poured into America's schools to enhance the quantity and quality of science education. Science is a subject taught in every school in America, not once, but repeatedly from elementary through high school and college. However, on national tests of science knowledge most adult Americans fare poorly. Only those with college-level courses in science do well on these tests. Of course, what should we expect? The questions asked on these tests are typically multiple choice, many drawn straight from school textbooks. Does every American really need to know how a laser works or be able to define *radiation* in order to be a productive, informed, and competent citizen? We certainly do not think so. However, given the importance of science in modern life, shouldn't every American know something about science? Of course, the answer is yes. Our suspicion, though, is that Americans actually do know quite a bit about science, but it is not a generalized, "textbook" type of knowledge. Rather, Americans' knowledge of science is likely to vary widely and be very topic specific. Depending upon need and interest, one American is likely to know a lot about tropical fish biology and another about computers; few are likely to know a lot about all areas of science. Just for the record, most scientists do not know a lot about the branches of science outside their specialization, either.

Recently we launched an investigation to help determine how, when, where, and why people learn science. To do this we conducted two separate scientific telephone surveys. In each study, we randomly called close to two thousand Los Angeles residents and asked questions about their science knowledge. These were average folks—some were poor, some were affluent, some had graduate degrees, some had not completed high school. They represented young and old individuals of virtually every imaginable race, ethnicity, and background. We asked these people if they were interested in science—overwhelmingly they said they were. Interest in science seemed to be universal, true of virtually all individuals, regardless of education, race, ethnicity, or gender. We asked them if they felt they were knowledgeable in science—by and large they thought they were "sort of knowledgeable." Then we asked each person to describe some area of science in which they felt they knew more than the average person. We then asked people to tell us why they felt they had a greater-than-average knowledge in that area of science and from what source they acquired that knowledge. First of all, virtually everyone we talked to felt that there was at least one area of science they had some reasonable knowledge of, a knowledge that exceeded the norm. The areas described ranged from astronomy to zoology. Some people described very specific areas of scientific knowledge such as the physics of the internal combustion engine or the physiological basis of depression; others gave more general categories of knowledge such as health or the environment. Most people claimed that the motivation behind their knowledge was simply interest and curiosity, although occasionally the motivation to learn about a topic was a personal crisis such as the need to learn about the disease of an ill relative. Professional and work-related reasons were also commonly given. Across the board, though, at some point in each individual's life, something about the science topic they claimed a special knowledge of had piqued their curiosity. And it was this curiosity for the subject that had primarily prompted them to continue pursuing greater knowledge and understanding of the subject.

Most fascinating of all were the sources of scientific knowledge that the public identified. Roughly a third of the people surveyed claimed to have primarily learned their favored science topic in school. Just under a quarter of respondents said they learned their science on the job, as part of their work. However, the largest number of people, approximately half of all those surveyed, claimed to have learned their science during their leisure time, through some kind of free-choice learning experience. People described learning science from using the Internet, reading magazines and books, going to museums, zoos, and aquariums, and participating in special-interest clubs and groups. Although schooling was an important source of scientific learning for some, it was not the primary source for most.

A recent study by the National Science Board found that 50 percent of American adults read a daily newspaper including articles on science, 15 percent read one or more science magazines each month, and a majority of Americans watched one or more science television shows each month. Approximately two-thirds of adults visited a science or natural history museum at least once a year and a third of Americans reported that they had purchased one or more science books during the preceding year. These studies lend tremendous support to the important role non-school sources play in sustaining lifelong learning in general and science learning in particular. The data would suggest that even a traditional school subject such as science is not exclusively, or even primarily, learned in school. Similar investigations have been conducted to determine where the public learns history. And similar to our study of science, it was found that the majority of Americans attributed their knowledge and understanding of history to free-choice learning sources such as family members and television, and not to school or university. Certainly this has been true for us, as evidenced by our Civil War–learning experiences.

The above is not intended as a condemnation of school-based learning, but rather to emphasize the fundamental role played by non-school-based learning. Each of America's three educational sectors significantly contributes to public learning. But of the three, the free-choice sector is far and away responsible for providing more people, more educational opportunities, more of the time, than the other two combined. Of the three, the free-choice sector is also the most diverse, the fastest growing, and arguably the most innovative. Already, most of the learning in America occurs within the free-choice sector, and this will become even more true in the years to come.

Why Do We Engage in Free-Choice Learning?

Six-year-old Molly was very excited.[1] Her dad was taking her to the Science Museum today. Molly had heard from her friends that it was a lot of fun and she couldn't wait to go. All during the car trip, Molly peppered her dad with questions about the museum, most of which her dad couldn't answer. "How big is the museum?" "How many things are there to do?" "What will we do first?" "What do you think will be the most fun thing there?" Finally, there was one question he could answer, "How much longer 'til we get there?" Mr. Kennedy said, "Just a couple more minutes. Look, there it is now!" Sure enough, the tall yellow building emerged into view at just that moment.

It took a few minutes to park the car and walk into the lobby of the building. Although it was still early on a Saturday morning, already the building was teeming with people. The ticket seller gave them a map of the building and a friendly smile, and they were all set. Mr. Kennedy started looking at the map, but Molly was already running ahead into the museum. Catching up with her, Mr. Kennedy wisely decided to just go with the moment, and Molly. Thus began an incredibly fun, but very whirlwind visit to the Science Museum.

Dead ahead, and their first stop of the day, was the physics playground. Molly pulled on ropes with pulleys, jumped on boards with fulcrums, and cranked on handles that made wheels turn. Her favorite was a huge bubble-making device that she and her dad must have spent fifteen minutes or more playing with together, making the most humungous bubbles imaginable.

Next stop was an area that had exhibits on the human body. Molly peered into microscopes; her curiosity seemed to be boundless. She asked her dad endless questions about what she was seeing, and Mr. Kennedy gamely did his best to answer her. Satisfactory explanation or not, Molly seemed to be having a great time.

On and on they went. They walked through a child-sized maze. They visited a temporary exhibition on aging, which Mr. Kennedy wished he had more time to view but Molly found pretty boring. They briefly played with some puzzles. And they spent some time looking at a miniature railroad exhibition. Molly seemed to really enjoy watching the trains and seeing all the tiny, scaled-down buildings, trees, and farm animals.

Before they knew it, it was time for lunch. Map in hand, they navigated their way to the Science Museum cafeteria. The food was not particularly good, but Molly was happy as a clam. After lunch, it was time for the IMAX show. Neither Molly nor her dad had ever been to an IMAX film, and the size of the screen and theater were truly impressive. Plus, this was a 3-D IMAX show to boot. Mr. Kennedy helped Molly adjust the funny oversized glasses on her face and then they settled back to watch a film on the Galapagos Islands. It lasted about twenty minutes and there was some really neat footage of lizards and tortoises, including some spectacular underwater shots. Molly particularly liked seeing all the sharks swimming around. Mr. Kennedy was totally blown away by the IMAX experience.

Exiting at the top of the museum, Molly and her dad zipped through a few more exhibition halls, but by that time, both seemed to appreciate that they had had enough. They left after a quick stop in the gift shop, where Mr. Kennedy was delighted to find a family activity guide based on the Galapagos film that he and Molly could use to explore evolution and biodiversity together at home. In total, they had spent close to three hours at the museum and both of them were really tired. Once in the car, Molly fell asleep almost immediately. As he drove home, Mr. Kennedy wished that he, too, could just curl up and take a nap, but he felt very pleased with the day. Molly had really enjoyed herself and she had been exposed to a lot of neat stuff. He resolved to bring her back again soon, maybe next time with a friend.

Scenes like this are played out every day in museums all over America. Hundreds of millions of people visit museums, science centers, zoos, aquariums, historic homes, and parks and natural areas every year. In almost every case, people go to see new things and discover more about art, science, history, nature, or people. These visits are not compelled by some outside need. There are no tests to pass, grades to receive, or bosses to impress. Rather, hundreds of millions of people visit museums and similar settings every year motivated by nothing more "serious" than general curiosity. Throughout our lives, we find that there are things and events that seem worth finding out more about—learning just for the sheer joy of learning.

Motivation

Curiosity about the world, and the joy that comes from satisfying that curiosity, is actually quite basic. It comes as standard equipment on all human beings. Humans learn many things, and for many reasons. Just because someone is instructed to learn to read, multiply fractions, or memorize the parts of a cell or historical chronology, does not mean it *will* happen. And just because someone is not required to learn something, does not mean that it will *not* happen. For many years psychologists have appreciated the important relationship between motivation and learning.

Most human learning is self-motivated, emotionally satisfying, and very personally rewarding. Researchers have found that humans are highly motivated to learn when:

1. they are in supporting environments;

2. they are engaged in meaningful activities;

3. they are freed from anxiety, fear, and other negative mental states;

4. they have choices and control over their learning; and

5. the challenges of the task meet their skills.

When in the right context, adults as well as children, find learning fun and easy.

This joy for learning can manifest itself differently in different individuals. Reading an engaging book, fixing a broken machine, watching a good movie, having a stimulating conversation with a friend, playing sports, successfully preparing food with a new recipe, or solving a challenging crossword puzzle can be fun for some, boring for others. However, what all these tasks have in common is that they require learning. They require the application of prior knowledge and experience to new circumstances and come with the expectation that new knowledge and experience will be useful in completing similar tasks in the future. This is learning freed from the external reward system of society; it is learning for the sake of learning. Within this context, it is easy to imagine Molly and her father readily learning about fulcrums, levers, the human body, and life on the Galapagos Islands.

Over forty years ago, psychologists realized that a basic dichotomy existed in learning: People either learned when they felt they wanted to or learned because they felt they had to. The outcomes of learning, it seemed, differed significantly depending upon which of these two motivations existed. The terms used to distinguish between these two types of motivation were *intrinsic* and *extrinsic* motivation.

Learning is extrinsically motivated when the anticipated benefits are external to the activity. For example, extrinsic rewards might include getting good grades or a high salary, or the "benefit" could be avoiding punishment, like not being ticketed for driving faster than the posted speed limit. By contrast, learning that is intrinsically motivated is done for its own sake, even in the absence of some external reward. Adult participation in evening arts and crafts, exercise and relaxation classes, visiting a historic monument or theater while on vacation, and learning to play sports and games after school are examples of intrinsically motivated learning activities. Except for the few professionals who derive an income from these activities, the people who engage in these types of learning experiences receive no rewards other than the joy of the experience itself. People are intrinsically motivated when they are freely learning something purely for the joy of learning it.

These two types of motivation are not mutually exclusive nor good or bad in and of themselves. The professional dancer or athlete can thoroughly enjoy what he or she does. Many children enjoy learning in school. It is not uncommon for people to strive for situations that combine both types of motivation. For example, most college students try to sign up for classes in subjects they enjoy. In this way they can derive personal, academic, and potentially even professional benefit from performing a single task. Combining "pleasure and necessity" is clearly an ideal solution. However, not all people enjoy their formal education, and therefore they pursue what interests them during their free time. For these people, there is a clear separation between extrinsically and intrinsically motivated learning activities. Of importance here, though, is that research has consistently shown that when learning occurs for intrinsic reasons, it is highly effective learning. Free-choice learning is intrinsically motivated, highly effective learning.

For many people free-choice learning is motivated not so much for the purpose of learning facts and concepts, but out of a desire for personal self-satisfaction and relaxation. This is still learning. Often what is learned during free-choice learning is more about yourself as an individual, or perhaps more about the significant others around you. Free-choice learning may also involve reminiscing and finding comfort in recollections stimulated by experiences in the world or interactions with others. These types of learning are deeply motivating because they may rekindle memories, embellish previous knowledge, and reinforce identity, extending understanding in personal, idiosyncratic ways.

At its most basic level, all learning is about affirming *self*. In particular, free-choice learning is the way we find out more about who we are and how we fit into our physical, social, and cultural world. Perhaps no researcher has done more for our understanding of the interaction between self, motivation, and learning than a University of Chicago psychologist named Mihalyi Csikzentmihalyi. Csikzentmihalyi even coined a term to describe this special kind of self-fulfilling, intrinsically motivated learning—*flow*.

Flow

Csikzentmihalyi and his colleagues discovered that people appear to exhibit a common set of behaviors and outcomes when engaged in free-choice tasks for which extrinsic rewards are absent. Chess players, rock climbers, dancers, painters, and musicians use similar explanations when describing the attraction of the activities they enjoy doing. They stress the fact that what keeps them involved in these demanding activities is an inherent quality to the experience. Csikzentmihalyi called this common experiential quality the *flow experience*, because it is generally described as a state of mind that is spontaneous, almost automatic, like the flow of a strong current. A general characteristic of activities that produce flow is that they have clear goals and appropriate rules. In a game of tennis, or of chess, or playing a musical instrument, one knows every second what one would like to accomplish, even if it cannot always be accomplished. In addition to clear goals, flow activities usually provide immediate and unambiguous feedback. One always knows whether one is doing well or not. Musicians find out immediately if they hit a wrong note, tennis players if they hit the ball badly. According to Csikzentmihalyi, this constant accountability is a major reason individuals get so completely immersed in a flow activity.

Another universally mentioned characteristic of flow experiences is that they tend to occur when the opportunities for action in a situation are in balance with the person's abilities. In other words, the challenges of the activity must match or be attainable through the skills of the individual or group. If the challenges are greater than the skill levels, anxiety results and if skills are greater than challenges, the result is boredom. This phenomenon appears to hold true across a wide array of skills, including physical, mental, artistic, and musical. The more one does an activity, the greater one's skill. The greater one's skill, the greater the challenges required in order to continue enjoying the activity and remaining in a state of flow. All of this equally applies to learning.

Successful free-choice learning experiences, whether they be museum exhibitions, performances, films, programs, or Web sites, all share this flow quality for the learner. A good medium of communication permits the participant to seek the level of engagement and understanding appropriate to the individual. It is often said that a good exhibition, performance, film, or other experience can be understood at many different levels and from many different perspectives. By this is meant that the learner can engage via many entry points, and can be challenged at a variety of different skill levels. Thus, engagement, a flow experience, can result because there is sufficient depth to permit appropriate levels of challenge for a wide range of users. In free-choice learning situations, the learner can self-select the challenge they wish, rather than having it imposed upon them. This element of control emerges as another fundamental component of motivation. For example, in our Kennedys visiting the museum example, this was evidenced by the high degree of control that the Kennedys exercised over which exhibits to view and/or utilize, and in which order. The ones selected were the ones that Molly and/or her father thought would be interesting. If they seemed to provide an appropriate level of intellectual, physical, and emotional challenge, they were chosen. If they did not meet these criteria, they were rejected. Choice and control are at the heart of free-choice learning. When choice and control exist, the experience is free-choice learning; when they are absent, the learning experience falls somewhat short of being free-choice.

It is important to note that flow learning experiences, like all free-choice learning experiences, are not just mental experiences, but rather whole body experiences involving all the senses. As Csikzentmihalyi states, "When goals are clear, feedback is unambiguous, challenges and skills are well matched, then all of one's mind and body become completely involved in the activity." In this state, the person becomes unaware of fatigue or the passing of time. It is truly an exhilarating experience, physically, emotionally, and cognitively. Accordingly, it is also extremely pleasurable. People who experience something even approaching a flow experience desire to do it over and over again. At some level, all of us can think of a flow free-choice learning experience we have had at some time in our lives. These are the experiences in which we felt a deep sense of intrinsic reward and pleasure. No wonder these were the experiences we wanted to keep going back to again and again.[2]

Of course, not all free-choice learning experiences are flow experiences. However, many, if not most, have the potential for being so for some segment of the population. Somewhere out there is a flow experience for you, just waiting to happen! So, where does one go to find free-choice learning opportunities, be they potential flow-generating experiences or not? The possibilities are so endless it's hard to know where to even begin.

Notes

1. To protect privacy, we have used pseudonyms for all individuals described in this book, except our immediate family.

2. As we will explore more fully in a subsequent book, flow experiences represent part of an elaborate evolutionary feedback system for building and extending self.

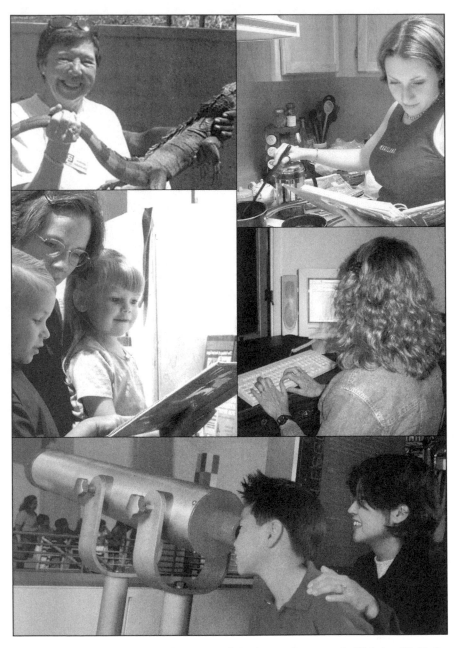

Free-Choice learning sampler (Photo by [clockwise from top left] John H. Falk; Janette Griffin, University of Technology Sydney; Leslie Kim, Stanford Alumni Association; California Science Center; Leslie Kim, Stanford Alumni Association; Janette Griffin, University of Technology Sydney)

CHAPTER 3

THE FREE-CHOICE LEARNING LANDSCAPE

This is the hardest stuff in the world to photograph. You need a three-hundred-and-sixty-degree lens, or something. You see it, and then, you look down in the ground glass and it's just nothing. As soon as you put a border on it, it's gone.

—Robert M. Pirsig, *Zen and the Art of Motorcycle Maintenance*

Lifelong learning is a vibrant reality in America. It is everywhere to be seen, as long as you know how to look. We were over at our twenty-five-year-old son Josh's house one day and began chatting with two of his friends. Not surprisingly, the topic got around to what we do for a living and we told them about free-choice learning. Also not surprisingly, we were curious to learn what free-choice learning experiences they engage in. This is what they told us.

Kevin and Lee said they first heard about the wine festival on the radio. The alternative music station they listened to played an ad for the festival and it sounded really cool. Not only would there be wine distributors from fifty different vineyards there, but there would be wine tastings, information on appropriate glasses to use for different types of wines, tips on wine storage and buying, and of course, there would be good music. Their favorite local group was scheduled to play, along with some group they'd never heard of. They said they were just beginning to discover the joys of wine drinking but felt like total fools whenever they went to a wine store. So, all in all, it sounded like just the ticket for a Saturday afternoon in June.

Confirming our suspicions, they said they bought their tickets over the Internet. They had even managed to convince their friends Rex and Margie to come with them. So the whole event was quite a twenty-something social happening.

The actual event lived up to their expectations. The music, we were told later, was awesome, and the wine was pretty decent, too. They ended up buying a case of this really inexpensive but great-tasting Australian Shiraz and a set of four glasses specially designed for this type of medium-bodied red. They thought we might also enjoy the festival and told us to keep our ears open for the ads next June.

Americans are devoting huge chunks of their life to learning, and examples are everywhere. However, if you think learning looks like rows of students sitting in a classroom being lectured by a teacher, then you won't see it. You won't see it, either, if your concept of learning is a bearded scholar sitting alone in the musty bowels of a library. Lifelong learning in America is Kevin and Lee, learning about wine at a festival. It is dozens of earnest folks sitting in on a seminar at Home Depot about how to lay a tile floor, and people cupping their cappuccinos in their hands in an upscale bookstore while listening to a poetry reading. It is also hordes of ten-year-olds at a computer camp, forty-year-olds at a tennis camp, and teenagers on the Internet swapping software solutions. It is also an older man watching a cooking show on television so that he can find a good recipe for the dinner he is cooking for his girlfriend tomorrow. These are all free-choice learning. It is everywhere you look.

However, trying to describe the length and breadth of the free-choice learning sector is a little like trying to capture the vastness of Grand Canyon in a photograph. No matter how you try to frame the picture, you can't quite encapsulate the full panorama. So, accepting the limitations, we'll provide a snapshot. Our lens will be the leisure marketplace, since so much of what currently constitutes the free-choice learning sector is oriented toward the public's leisure time. The reader should be cautioned, however, that this is only one way to approach describing free-choice learning experiences, and like any approach we could have taken, this one leaves out as much as it includes.

The Leisure Free-Choice Learning Market

Free-choice learning is hot! The demand for leisure-time free-choice learning is at an all-time high. As demand for free-choice learning increases, so also do efforts to satisfy that demand. Kevin and Lee, like most of us today, live busy, hectic lives. Our days, and particularly, it seems, our leisure time, are filled to capacity with potential activities. When Kevin and Lee began the process of deciding what to do on that particular summer day, the wine festival was clearly not the only choice available to them. If they had actually stopped to list all of their leisure options, the choices, even just the learning-oriented choices, would have been vast. The fastest growing segment of the leisure market is what is known as value-added leisure experiences. Out-of-home experiences such as festivals, museum-going, themed restaurants and shopping areas, and eco-and cultural tourism, represent the areas of greatest expansion. Large toy companies are buying up small educational toy and software companies because, as David Miller, former president of the Toy Manufacturers of America, was recently quoted as saying, "Family entertainment and education is where the business is." A vast world of free-choice learning opportunities beckons, and these days we don't even have to leave the comfort of our homes to access this world.

Fred Schwartz told us it was the sound of the mail falling through the mail slot that broke his concentration and finally caused him to realize that he needed to get back to paying the bills. Fred had been home paying his bills on-line when, on a whim, he typed volcano into his search engine. Fred then proceeded to spend nearly an hour surfing the Internet on the topic. Up popped hundreds of listings. The top ten were:

1. Volcano World

2. Dartmouth College—Electronic Volcano, The

3. Public Broadcasting Service—Savage Earth

4. Index of U.S.G.S. Servers

5. U.S. Volcanic Parks and Monuments

6. Volcanic Hazard Program

7. Active Tectonics

8. As an Earth Scientist

9. Mount St. Helens

10. Society for Interdisciplinary Studies.

Fred clicked on "Volcano World," the self-proclaimed premier Web site about volcanoes on the Net. Whether it was the premier Web site, Fred found much to occupy his time. On this site Fred discovered that on average every week there is at least one volcanic eruption somewhere in the world. In fact, according to volcanologists at the Smithsonian Institution, there are roughly 1,500 active volcanoes world-wide. He clicked on "eruption of the week" and learned about Maly Semiachik, a volcano located in Kamchatka, Russia. Maly Semiachik was described as a caldera-type volcano located inside another caldera, which has erupted 23 times. The biggest of these eruptions was in 1804 and the last one was in 1952. Next Fred clicked on "Ask a volcanologist." He found lots and lots of questions. He read through all the questions and clicked on several of the answers.

As we talked to Fred, an electrician, further about this voyage into the world of volcanoes, he said that he had been fascinated by volcanoes ever since he was a child. However, one day the previous week while clicking through the television channels, he stumbled upon "Savage Earth," a Public Broadcasting show on volcanoes. Fred said, "Watching that show is really what prompted me to try and find more information on the Web." Even though he had missed the first few minutes of the program, "something about these huge mountains spewing hot, molten rock" grabbed his attention. He watched the entire show. He particularly enjoyed catching up on all the new ideas about how and why volcanoes form. Back when he was in school they hadn't talked much about plate tectonics and hot spots and such, since the research was so new and exploratory. Based on this latest venture into the topic, Fred said that he was planning on trying to find a book on the topic next time he goes to the library or bookstore. "Who knows," he said, "maybe I'll just see if I can't find a good book on-line and order one that way."

How unique is Fred? How many electricians try to bone up on volcanoes in their free time? In fact, there are millions of Fred Schwartzes all over America, maybe not volcano-loving electricians, but certainly bird-watching plumbers, racecar-enthusiast physical therapists, and gourmet-cooking steelworkers. It seems there are nearly as many leisure free-choice learning options as there are free-choice learning interests.

This Internet example and the wine festival example are but two of literally thousands we could have chosen. Free-choice learning resources include such diverse offerings as a television special on whales, a new book about the presidents, a special course offered by the local community group, a compelling Web site, or a special demonstration on planting perennials at the local nursery. A visit to the Elderhostel Web site revealed this testimonial from Arthur H. Michaels of Indianapolis, Indiana:

> I recently returned from a trip to Alaska, with a two-week Elderhostel program as the key element of the trip. There could not have been a better way to come to an understanding of Alaska, especially the people of Alaska, than by coming face-to-face with the history and present day life of a bush community. The authenticity of the experience came from a wide range of people who lectured to us or demonstrated for us. We learned about the life of a fur trapper who spends six months a year with his wife and son in a cabin 40 miles from other people. We learned about mining in Alaska in recent decades from a resident who has been a commercial miner for many years. We visited the headquarters of a sled dog operation and met a family that is engaged in breeding and racing. We spent time in an original sod house and learned how people existed there during all seasons of the year. In all, the week was a lesson on how people in an isolated village earned their living, overcame obstacles, survived, arrived and enjoyed community life.

And, there is something for everyone. The free-choice learning sector is composed of a diverse array of organizations, and in some cases individuals, in increasing competition for the minds and time of a learning-hungry citizenry. The result is a mind-boggling smorgasbord of experiences and opportunities catering to the increasingly refined and narrowly defined tastes of the masses. The major free-choice learning players include:

- broadcast media (radio, television, and film);

- print media (newspapers, magazines, and books);

- libraries;

- museums of all kinds (art museums and galleries, natural history museums, history centers, science centers, zoos, aquariums, botanical gardens, arboretums, historic houses and parks, and environmental centers);

- performing arts organizations (dance, theater, and music);

- community-based organizations serving youth, adults, and families; and

- faith-based organizations.

All of these organizations communicate to the public through a wide array of media, including television, film, video, radio, print, exhibitions, performance, and, most recently, via the Internet.

In fact, a staggering array of free-choice educational offerings are available to every citizen, twenty-four hours a day, seven days a week, 365 days a year. But there is not only a vast assortment of free-choice learning media from which to select, but also a vast sea of topics from which to choose. Take one single medium—magazines, for example. A quick perusal of any bookstore reveals hundreds of magazines, on virtually any topic imaginable, and a few on topics that aren't imaginable! Each magazine appeals to its unique readership by presenting a dozen or more stories specifically designed to satisfy the curiosity, needs, and interests of its special interest readers. A sampling from just one recent day included:

Mademoiselle: "The 25 best places to work in America"

American Heritage: "Building the transcontinental railroad"

Seventeen: "Beauty traumas—47 solutions"

Mothering: "Ultrasound: Weighing the risks"

Wired: "The truth, the whole truth and nothing but the truth. The untold story of the Microsoft anti-trust case"

Business Week: "Managed Care—Employees seek new solution"

Sports Illustrated: "Scouting Report: The Avalanche and the Maple Leafs will emerge to meet in the Stanley Cup finals"

Outdoor World: "Take great hunting photos"

Snowboard Life: "What the pros ride"

Muscle & Fitness: "100 best exercises: Plus programs, tips and techniques to get lean and hard now"

Freshwater & Marine Aquarium: "25% more light for less than $10.00"

Want to explore a topic more deeply? Try a book. Despite public laments about the decline in literacy, the number of book titles published—50,000 a year in the United States—has remained stable for years. The number of users of libraries has increased 13 percent in the last twenty years, with more than 80 percent of these visitors checking out books. The number of library books in circulation continues to grow every year. Not only are people reading more, but they are also talking about it more. The biggest phenomenon in the book world is book discussion groups. It is estimated that 60 percent of all public libraries in America offer book discussions and author presentations, as do nearly all bookstores. Perhaps the most famous book group promoter of all was Oprah Winfrey, but in communities large and small, book groups are flourishing and attracting members from all walks of life.

Not much of a reader? How about learning from television? A perusal of our local public television station's offerings for just one day included offerings such as:

PBS Kids Bookworm Bunch: Corduroy, Elliot Moose, 7 Little Monsters, more.

Motor Week: "Type S" Road tests: 2002 Acura 3 2TL Type-S, 2001 Panoz Esperante, After fender-bender

Ciao Italia: Eat Pasta!

Sew Young, Sew Fun: Skirt Level II

Victory Garden: Sunday House, Florida

This Old House: Santa Barbara Architectures

Joy of Painting: First snow

In the Mix: Activism

Antiques Roadshow: Madison, Wisconsin Part 2/3 Tailesin; parasol from Queen Victoria, incense burner

And how about Antiques Roadshow! Who would have guessed that a show with a bunch of experts talking about antiques would become the most popular show on public television, a show with the unabashed aim of educating the public about the nuances of old furniture, paintings, jewelry, and every type of assorted oddity! Thousands of people wait for hours in line for the opportunity to learn how to appraise the value of all the stuff hanging around in their homes, closets, and garages. They hope against hope that the treasure they discovered buried in Aunt Mildred's attic ten years ago is truly a treasure and not a worthless fake. Thousands of people are there in person, and millions more watch at home. What a phenomenon! Our favorite segment, and perhaps the show's producers, also, was the one featuring the ten-year-old girl who brought in a valuable painting that she and her grandfather had found in a garage sale and then proceeded to wow the appraiser by telling him all about it. When the amazed expert asked her how she had learned so much about furniture, she calmly stated, "I learned it by watching Antiques Roadshow." Clearly, the show was accomplishing its free-choice learning objectives!

Shows like these can be seen every day in America, and not just on public television. The Learning Channel, The History Channel, Discovery, Animal Planet, Life Channel, ESPN, The Family Channel, and many more offer round-the-clock learning opportunities. Even the seeming wasteland of daytime soaps, talk shows, and cops and robbers shows provides learning opportunities. A recent article in *Time* magazine on the courts and law stated that daytime talk shows like *Oprah!* have forever changed the nature of trials in this country. The prevalence of discussions about early childhood trauma and abuse, and the consequent heightened awareness by jurors of these issues, has made this a favorite and increasingly successful plea by all kinds of accused criminals.

Learning is rapidly becoming the single most important leisure commodity in our society, and the free-choice learning sector has emerged as the primary vehicle for facilitating such learning. The free-choice learning sector has emerged as a flexible, innovative, and efficient device for facilitating the learning that the public craves. This is why more and more television stations find it profitable to air educational programming; why faith-based organizations run evening educational programs on nonreligious topics; why museums are investing significantly greater resources in the development and mounting of exhibitions than they are in the acquisition, storage, and study of collections; why retail chains now sponsor courses for the public and develop public education newsletters; and why the Internet is being touted as potentially the greatest educational tool ever devised. And these primarily nonprofit organizations have been joined by an array of commercial educational vendors. They offer learning-oriented experiences through such vehicles as educational theme parks, for example, Disney's Animal Kingdom; retail outlets such as Home Depot and Michael's craft stores, offering workshops and seminars; educational toy and computer games; and even themed shopping experiences and vacations. Even HMOs and doctors' offices are entering the free-choice learning arena, providing classes on stress reduction and weight loss. We live in an Information Society and learning and knowledge are the keys to the realm. It is also why "education" has now become the strategy of choice when trying to sell goods or promote an idea.

The Use of Free-Choice Learning in Marketing

Once a month we get a newsletter from our local realtor, which always includes decorating tips, ideas for how to maximize the resale value of your home, and a recipe for a great dinner or dessert. Slipped in-between the pages is a pitch to make sure you keep the realtor in mind should you decide to sell your house. This is a national service available to any realtor willing to spend his or her marketing dollars in this way. Given the current technology, it is easy enough to customize the newsletter to include the name and picture of the specific realtor and make it appear as if the newsletter was being generated by the individual realtor, exclusively for his own personal list of key clients. In America today, selling homes is about free-choice learning!

We also receive a newsletter from our accountant, which counsels us on how to manage our money. The newsletter includes articles about mutual funds, the new tax laws, and how to save for retirement. Of course, there is also a reminder that tax time is sooner than you think so don't forget to call and make an appointment early.

Everyone's got a pitch, and for every pitch there's a newsletter or a seminar. For the investment-minded, the local brokerage house conducts free seminars on how to secure your future through financial planning. For the culinary-minded, the kitchen appliance emporium runs continuous demonstrations on new techniques in cooking, of course using only the latest in cookware. The bridal shop runs workshops on wedding planning. The grocery store chain has seminars on nutrition and food storage tips. The building supply store has demonstrations on building techniques and tools. And the garden store runs demonstrations on how to build and maintain a water garden. The goal is sales, but the promotional strategy of choice in today's market is free-choice learning.

Even when the pitch is not so much sales but public awareness, the strategy of choice seems to be free-choice learning. For example, among our collection of newsletters is one from our local hospital, which includes tips on preventative medicine—the five signs of high blood pressure, tips on smoking cessation, the dos and don'ts for pregnant women. Our HMO also sends us a newsletter discussing health issues and we have been told that, for a fee, we can get a monthly newsletter from any of a number of medical schools; to date, we've been contacted by Harvard, Johns Hopkins, Georgetown, and UCLA medical schools. These medical school-sponsored newsletters are touted as being much more informative, and of course authoritative, than your run-of-the-mill health and medicine newsletter. The newsletter will provide us with the most up-to-date information in the health field. If we want, we can even get our health newsletter gender-specific—one for women and one for men.

The local police department runs seminars for the public on child safety and home safety; the local YWCA on spousal abuse prevention; the local government on proper disposal of toxic wastes; and the American Lung Association on asthma awareness and prevention. These are all "quick hits" for a busy, knowledge-hungry society. Tiny bites of knowledge are coming at us fast and furious, but what happens if you're really hungry? A small bite won't do. Where do you go if you want a whole meal?

In-Depth Free-Choice Learning

Camps

The campers got off the bus and sorted through the collection of bags and luggage in search of their belongings. Double-checking their cabin assignments, they dragged their luggage to their cabins, selected a bunk, and began unpacking. Lunch was being served in the lodge in twenty minutes. So began another typical day at summer camp. But in this case, the campers were not children, but adults, and the camp not a typical summer camp, but a camp for individuals interested in learning about building better family relations. Every summer, this erstwhile children's summer camp runs intensive training programs for parents eager to learn more about raising and supporting their families. For an entire week, surrounded by the smells and sights of the forest, professional counselors and psychologists hold workshops, conduct role-playing exercises, and provide eager parents with strategies and tools necessary to facilitate and maintain good rapport with spouses and children. This particular camp happens to be sponsored by a Methodist church, but the course is open to all and is largely areligious. The goal is in-depth, immersive training.

There are sports camps featuring football, baseball, soccer, golf, tennis, sailing, volleyball, and basketball; camps for wilderness training and survival skills; outward bound-type camps to build self-esteem and self-reliance; computer camps, finance camps, cooking camps, and business camps; camps for children, adolescents, adults, and seniors; camps focused on specific minority or ethnic groups; and camps for women only, and for men only. There seem to be camps now for learning virtually any topic imaginable, and for virtually any age or group category definable.

Vacations

Camps not your thing? How about a learning vacation? Eco- and cultural tourism are the fastest growing sector of the tourist industry. Take a cruise and make stops with guided tours at exotic locales; while on board enjoy evening slide shows and seminars by experts. Ships are leaving daily for the Amazon, the Greek Islands, Alaska, and even Antarctica. Want something that won't make you seasick? Sign up for a bus tour of the historic homes of Pennsylvania, the vineyards of California, the fishing communities of New England, or the National Parks of the western United States. How about a museum-sponsored trip to the Galapagos Islands or East Africa? The tour includes all accommodations, travel, connections, and knowledgeable guides and discussions in the evening. For the more adventurous, there are scuba-diving trips to The Seychelles or Thailand, trekking trips to the Australian Outback or Tibet, whitewater rafting trips to Costa Rica or Mexico, or mountain climbing trips in the Andes, Alps, or Rockies. All include adventure and learning; one-week, two-week, and three-week packages are available.

Classes

Camps and tour packages are not the only avenue for in-depth experiences. The tried-and-true models are classes, and there are classes aplenty in the land. A trip through the yellow pages reveals organizations offering lessons in acting, American sign language, bookkeeping, computer, cooking, driving, foreign language, golfing, hair-styling, homeopathic medicine, jewelry-making, Karate and other martial arts, landscaping, meditation, music, painting, piano, photography, retriever training, sailing, tap-dancing, voice, water safety, and Zen Buddhism. And these were just the courses for adults; there's a whole youth-course industry aimed at training the next generation of Olympic and professional athletes, performing artists, and academic geniuses. What is it you want to become better at? the arts? the sciences? sports? food? fashion? history? antique collecting? literature? automobile maintenance? finance? public speaking? social skills? spirituality? You name it! There's a course somewhere for you or the one you love. Most of these courses are aimed at the amateur, but increasingly the professional, too, can find training through the free-choice learning world.

On-Line

As the boundaries of where and when learning can and should occur continue to erode, free-choice learning increasingly is being seen in the other two educational sectors as well—the schools and the workplace. Fueled by the communication revolution of the Internet, more and more courses and training programs are being put on-line and the criteria for who can or cannot take these courses becomes less restricted. Once enrollment in educational programs was tightly controlled by institutions, and limited by the availability of teachers and classroom space. In cyberspace, these limits become boundless and unfettered. In an increasingly competitive education marketplace, schools, universities, and workplace educational programming are being driven more and more by the needs and interests of the learners, rather than exclusively by institutional needs and interests. The University of Phoenix led the way, but many universities are heading into the e-learning fray, eager to attract larger and more diverse student bodies than ever before. As this happens credentials, testing, and control over enrollment become less important than the motivation and commitment of the learners. This is the transition to the free-choice model of learning. And increasingly, free-choice learning is becoming the prevailing model for most of the learning that occurs in America. As we've seen, though, the model is not about how learning gets delivered, but why people choose to engage in such learning. It is the transition to a true learning society where learning is something people do continuously, not because they have to but because they want to.

It is not, however, that the *how* of learning is unimportant. It is wonderful that everyone wants to be a learner, and inevitable, given this reality, that everyone with something to sell or say wants to get into the act and become an educator. However, to be a successful free-choice learner, it helps if the information is presented in ways that truly facilitate learning. In other words, to be a successful free-choice educator, it helps to know something about how people learn. And given how fundamental learning is to our present-day lives, knowing how people learn is something that is useful for everyone to understand. So, how do people learn? Let's take a look.

Visiting the National Air and Space Museum (Photo by Carolyn Russo, National Air and Space Museum)

CHAPTER 4
LEARNING FROM THE INSIDE OUT

We see things not as they are, but as we are.
—Henry M. Tomlinson, British novelist (1873–1958)

Planes, aviation, air and space, things like that, always have fascinated me," said Hernando Sanchez, a computer expert in his late thirties living and working in Des Moines, Iowa. "Ever since I was a boy, I've loved to learn about these things. It all started with my brothers. They would get these model airplanes, mostly WW II planes, and build them. I was only seven at the time. But like my three older brothers, I just loved to learn about the planes, wars, and things like that. My interests just took off from there.

I grew up in Mexico, in the town of Torreo, in Coahuila State. There we could get all kinds of models—Japanese, American, Russian, German. At first, I couldn't read the stuff on the boxes, so my brothers would tell me about the planes. Later, I could read the boxes myself and I would find out about the engines, how many machine guns they had, and what the planes could and couldn't do. Also, I had a group of five friends, and we would go to this place that sold used magazines. We'd buy all the magazines we could find about planes and stuff. Some of them were in English, some of them were in Spanish. We'd also go to the movies, and see films like *Tora! Tora! Tora!*, *Battle of Midway*, and *Flying Machines*.

When I was older, one of my brothers took me flying sometimes. That was fantastic. When I was in high school, I got a job at the airport, so I got to fly then sometimes too. In the army, I flew in helicopters and that was really something. I went to college in El Paso, Texas. I wanted to try and get my pilot's license, but it was too expensive for me, otherwise I probably would have pursued flying as a career. But I did go to my first air show there. They have a big two-day air show called the Amigo Air Show. I used to go every year.

These days, I pretty much continue to be interested in these things, but between my job and family I don't have that much time. I always try to watch any television specials on air and space kind of things that I can find. Like recently there were specials on the start of aviation, and one on the discovery and rescuing of a World War II airplane they found covered by ice. The plane had crashed way up north, but because of the ice it was still really well preserved. Just the other day I recorded the *Nova* special on the Apollo 13, which was about the real thing, not the movie. When I go to the library with the kids I occasionally pick out a book on the subject, like a biography on Charles Lindbergh. Near where I live, a couple of hours away, there's a Strategic Air Command museum which I've visited with my family a number of times. I also got to go to the Air and Space Museum in Washington. That was fabulous. I spent a half a day there. My favorite part was the Apollo Lunar Module, and of course the World War II exhibition. They had three planes that were the same as the ones I built models of as a child—the German Messerschmitt, a U.S. Navy bomber like the one that George Bush (senior) had flown in the war, and a Japanese Zero.

Not just me, but my brothers too, are still interested in aviation. Whenever we go back to Mexico, my brothers always ask, "Have you flown lately?" or "Have you been to any air shows recently?" It's always a major topic of conversation in my family. Thanks to airplanes, I now know a lot of facts about WWI and WWII, and just history in general.

At the time Hernando related this story to us, we had known him for several years and knew that, besides his family and his job as a computer expert for a large insurance firm, he had a third passion: air, space, and aviation. So, being the curious types, we asked him to tell us how he had become so interested and knowledgeable about these topics. Hernando's lifelong interest in air and space is not only a fascinating story, but also provides a useful vehicle for understanding more about how all of us come to know what we know about ourselves, others and the physical world around us. For embedded within Hernando's very personal story are important insights about how all people learn and make meaning in their lives; insights into the cumulative, personal, and social/cultural nature of learning and the important role played by real world experience.

What is Learning?

Learning is such a profoundly human experience that all of us assume we have some basic understanding of what it is and how it occurs, yet few human processes are so poorly understood. Our lack of understanding is not because scientists, philosophers, and psychologists have never tried to understand learning, quite the contrary. It has been a topic of inquiry for well over 2,500 years. The reason it has been so difficult to understand is that learning is actually an extremely complex process, involving many counterintuitive components and activities.

Take the case of Hernando learning about airplanes. How would you begin to characterize what Hernando knows about planes? As we talked together, more and more pieces of his story, and his knowledge, came together. Hernando's knowledge was only revealed over the course of our conversation; the longer we talked the more the conversation revealed what he knew and why and how he knew it. Learning is not a product we store as a whole in our heads, but actually is more a process, in fact a never-ending process. Although many non-Western peoples have intuitively appreciated the holistic nature of learning, Western science has only recently begun to recognize that learning is a whole series of complex processes woven together, which in turn are intertwined with nearly all other parts of our being. And it is because of this very complexity that learning, more than virtually any other life activity, has been slow to reveal its underlying secrets to many scientists. Within the last ten to twenty years, hastened in part by new imaging techniques that allow scientists to literally "see" inside the brain, the secrets of learning have begun to emerge. As a result we have learned more about learning within the past dozen years or so than was discovered in the previous 2,500 years.

Perhaps the most important finding of the past dozen years or so is that, despite the fact that the general process of learning is comparable in all humans, the products of learning are anything but comparable. In one of those strange, ironic twists of nature, it is as if everyone starts off driving down the very same road but ends up in a different place. So it is with learning. It turns out that learning is a uniquely individual, dare we say idiosyncratic, event. No two people ever learn exactly the same thing in quite the same way. The key to understanding this irony revolves around context, a fact that was either missed or avoided for nearly a hundred years.

For most of the twentieth century, learning was not viewed by scientists as either uniquely individual or contextual. Quite the contrary, the prevailing view was that learning was a totally generalizable, linear, and predictable accumulation of knowledge. In other words, everyone learned in the same way, and as long as the same information was presented, they learned the same things. This is like saying that everyone who had experiences similar to Hernando's would know exactly the same things, but this is not true. What Hernando knows about air and space might be similar to others, but in many ways Hernando's knowledge is very unique and highly personal. The essence of learning is the ability to combine past experience with the present moment in order to meaningfully understand and, to a degree, predict and control the future.

Learning researchers have come to appreciate that the human mind uniquely "constructs meaning." In other words, all human knowledge—in fact, all memories—are not permanent, "whole-cloth" features of the mind. Knowledge is not stored like a collection of widgets in the brain, each on its particular shelf. Rather, all of our knowledge and experience is stored as bits and pieces, and the bits and pieces are distributed throughout our brains. These bits and pieces of "memory" are assembled, on an as-needed basis, to quite literally *construct* a memory or an idea as we need it. More often than not, what determines what we "require" are events in the world; the knowledge of the world an individual constructs is virtually always tightly connected to the unique and specific social, cultural, and physical contexts in which it was constructed. For example, the traumatic events of September 11, 2001, forever embedded images and associations in our minds for the words *Pentagon, World Trade Center, Afghanistan, terrorist, box cutter,* and others; prior to this date these words held little or no association for us. In other words, most human knowledge is very context-specific and only poorly generalizable beyond the situation in which it was learned. Learning is a uniquely personal, contextual experience, constructed from both internal (head and body) and external (physical world and sociocultural contacts) experience. It is rarely linear and is almost always highly idiosyncratic.

Additionally, learning researchers have come to more fully appreciate that learning is rarely an instantaneous event, but rather an unfolding, cumulative process. Typically, individuals acquire an understanding of the world through a continuous accumulation of experiences, deriving from many different sources at many different times. Thus, year by year, event by event, over a lifetime, Hernando has constructed his knowledge about air and space from, not one, but literally hundreds if not thousands of experiences. For example, working at an airport affected all of Hernando's subsequent learning, as did the fact that he could not afford to take flying lessons. Hernando's knowledge of things aeronautical has accumulated over many years, but more importantly, that knowledge is fed by his interests and experiences; and his interests and experiences are, in turn, fed by his knowledge.

Much of what constitutes learning is going on inside our brains; we refer to this as learning from the inside out. However, learning is not entirely an inside-out process. As the famous American educator and philosopher John Dewey said in 1938, "The history of educational theory is marked by opposition between the idea that [learning] is development from within and that it is formation from without." Although this debate continues to rage at some level, the evidence increasingly confirms that learning is probably not exclusively a process formed from within or from without, but a combination of the two. Learning is strongly influenced by the outside world, a world that comes in two basic flavors, the outside world as dictated and interpreted by other humans in our lives and the sights, sounds, tastes, and sensations of that world as perceived directly through our own senses. We call this learning from the outside in. Recognizing that there is a risk in oversimplifying the complexity of the learning process, we would suggest that the nature of learning can be described in three simple statements:

- Learning begins with the individual.

- Learning involves others.

- Learning takes place somewhere.

To put it poetically, we can think of these as the three major streams of influence on learning and meaning-making. Meaningful learning is constructed by each person at the confluence of these three streams—the contexts of the individual, the society and culture of the individual, and the physical environment in which the individual resides—what we have called the Contextual Model of Learning (figure 1). Mindful of the fact that whole books have been written on each of these topics, we would like to briefly consider each of these "streams" or contexts further. And given the complexity of the streams and their influence we will explore them in two chapters, in this chapter exploring learning from the inside-out and in the next chapter learning from the outside-in.

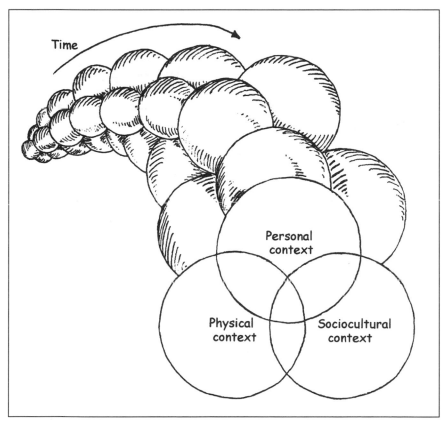

Figure 1. The Contextual Model of Learning

Learning Begins with the Individual

In order to explore learning from the inside out, let's think for a moment how Hernando has come to understand the concept of flight. First, he very tactilely learned about the shape and sweep of a wing by watching and then building model airplanes. Then in school, when other children might have found lessons on Bernouli's principle boring and not relevant to their daily experience,

Hernando was attentive and very primed to understand how the shape of the wing creates lift. Driven by his strong interest in aviation, Hernando continued to have more and more experiences with flight throughout his childhood and adulthood. He flew in planes, first with his brothers and then alone, hung out with pilots and mechanics while working at the airport, watched movies and television shows, visited air and space museums and air shows and talked with friends, relatives and anyone else he met passionate about the subject. All of these experiences were ultimately intertwined as Hernando constructed a personal, rich and highly individualized understanding of flight. Importantly, no one source of information was sufficient in the construction of his understanding, nor one single educational entity solely responsible for it. And in one of the most intriguing idiosyncrasies of human learning and memory, functionally two sides of the same coin, the resulting knowledge gleaned from these many different sources is woven together in Hernando's mind and perceived by him as a single, seamless whole. It would be next to impossible for him to identify the primary source of his learning on flight. As in the above example, Hernando's knowledge of flight was constructed from many different sources, all of them highly contextual, and all combined within his mind to create a single, comprehensive understanding.

Any discussion of learning must somehow accommodate this unique, personally constructed nature of learning. What an individual learns on any given day and in any particular situation is determined first and foremost by the individual's prior experiences, knowledge, and interests. The fact that Hernando chose to get a job at an airport in high school was not an accident. He chose this opportunity because of his childhood passion for airplanes. Learning is strongly influenced by each individual learner's interests and motivations, and by prior experience, knowledge, and the unique learning preferences, capacities, and styles of the learner.

Motivation and Interest

In order to understand the personal nature of learning, we first have to appreciate that learning evolved long before there was language or mathematics, in fact, before there were humans or other mammals at all. At the most basic level, learning is the process/product of a complex series of electrochemical interactions in the brain and body. These processes/products have evolved over many hundreds of millions of years (for reference, humans in any form have been around on this planet for less than ten million years and modern humans for considerably less than one million years). Learning, even twenty-first century human learning, is built upon a very ancient, whole-body, biological base. It is profoundly important to appreciate the long evolutionary history of human learning; learning is not just a recent cultural overlay unique to "modern humans."

A very important and relatively unappreciated by-product of this long evolutionary history are the feedback loops that exist between emotional states and learning processes. In large part these feedback loops are mediated by one of the oldest parts of the brain, the area known as the limbic system. Located in the middle of the brain and made up of a number of discrete structures, the limbic area was early on recognized as the major center in the brain for emotional and geographical memory. But as we have begun to appreciate that the brain is highly integrated and only loosely specialized, it is clear that the limbic system is extensively connected in looped circuits to all parts of the brain and, besides regulating emotions and geography, seems to also regulate memory. Every memory seems to get an emotional "stamp" after journeying through the limbic system. The stronger the emotional "value," the more likely the sensory information becomes a part of memory, and not surprisingly, given what we have said about this system, pleasant experiences are strongly favored over unpleasant ones. Evolution has thus insured a dependency between learning and survival by making the process of constructing meaning both very thorough and, more often than not, a pleasurable and rewarding experience.

Clearly, humans are genetically programmed to learn and we do so all the time, learning much of what we know outside of formal schooling. However, it is not enough to understand the biological and evolutionary basis of learning. We also need to understand what influences the emotional stamping process of the limbic system. Why are some topics or activities chosen as areas of interest by some people and not others? Two important factors seem to influence what people choose to learn at a very personal level: motivation and interest.

Motivation was discussed in great detail in chapter 2 so we will not do so again, but we will highlight a few aspects of motivation, in the context of Hernando's experience. Remember that we discussed two types of motivation, *intrinsic* and *extrinsic*. Learning is extrinsically motivated when the anticipated benefits are external to the activity, such as trying to please someone or reach some externally imposed goal. By contrast, learning that is intrinsically motivated is done for its own sake, even in the absence of external reward. People are intrinsically motivated to learn when they are freely learning for the pure joy and inherent benefits of doing so. Think back to our friend Hernando. No one forced him to learn about aviation. Throughout his life he has freely chosen to pursue this interest in his free time. Even though under other circumstances he might have tried to get a degree in the area or turn his interest into a profession, events dictated otherwise and Hernando chose to continue to enjoy learning about aviation for intrinsic reasons. We know many others who pursue chosen interests, such as astronomy, sewing, and biking, all because of intrinsic motivation.

Not all intrinsically motivated activities involve learning, but a surprisingly high percentage of them do. When learning occurs for intrinsic reasons, it has been shown time and again to be highly effective. Students in schools who are intrinsically motivated tend to have higher achievement scores, and tend to more successfully make the most of their abilities. Intrinsic enjoyment of learning also appears to be associated with higher creativity, and under certain conditions, external rewards even appear to undermine intrinsic motivation and one's ability to do well.

The wonder, and as it turns out the power, of free-choice learning is that by definition it is intrinsically motivated. Perhaps this is why, more than any other reason, free-choice learning—learning in which the individual gets to have choice and control over what, when, where, and how to learn—emerges as such a powerful and important form of learning. An increasingly compelling body of research is emerging which shows that choice and control are fundamental constituents of all learning. It is really nothing more than the learning version of the old saying, "You can lead a horse to water, but you can't make him drink." Time and again, we and other researchers have found that what makes the proverbial horse "drink" from the trough of learning is some knowledge of the *personal* benefits of drinking and some positive prior experiences with the contents of the trough.

As we suggested earlier, motivation has been a largely ignored aspect of learning, often described in vague, everyday terms; and interest, a component of motivation, has been even less recognized. Psychologist Ulrich Schiefele has pointed out that motivation, in general, and interest, in particular, are complex, multidimensional states. As humans we are bombarded with stimulation all the time. The human brain is designed to sift through this abundance of information to selectively determine what to attend to and what to ignore. One important filter for this selection process is *interest*. If we had no interests, our senses would be deluged with information and total mental chaos would result. As pioneering psychologist William James suggested one hundred years ago, "Millions of items in the outward order are present to my senses which never properly enter into my experience. Why? Because they have no *interest* for me. *My experience is what I agree to attend to.* Only those items which I *notice* shape my mind—without selective interest, experience is an utter chaos."

We should clarify that when we use the term *interest* we do not merely refer to what someone likes or dislikes. We refer to a complex, multidimensional psychological construct that includes a number of behaviors that directly influence learning—attention to the topic or idea, persistence in tasks associated with it, and continued curiosity about it. These are all factors that are important to understanding what might motivate someone to learn something, to become fully engaged in learning about it.

Individuals tend to engage in and enjoy learning when the learning relates to their personal, often subject-specific interests. For example, throughout his lifetime Hernando has sought out resources for learning about aviation—visiting museums and air shows, reading books, and watching television. His focus has been very specific, and the intrinsic motivation to learn more in this area has not extended much beyond aviation, although he clearly feels that he has learned a great deal about history pursuing this personal interest.

Interests are influenced by a range of variables—some universal, some the result of individual experiences, and some because of personal history. For example, most people are interested in food, in sex, in whatever gives them power and acclaim, and in babies and pets. Beyond these universals, though, interests diverge tremendously. Some people are interested in sports, some people enjoy fashion, and still others find ancient Roman history particularly fascinating. When people like something, they attribute positive feelings and values to it; it is highly probable that they will choose to follow up on that interest with action. Hernando's interests clearly are an important part of his personal history—closely connected to the experiences he shared with his brothers in Mexico.

Knowledge, Experience, and Learning Style

With great expectation and excitement, we recently attended a public lecture by Jared Diamond, author of the award-winning book *Guns, Germs and Steel*. The lecture was quite well attended, one hundred or more individuals of all ages and backgrounds showed up on this particular Sunday afternoon. Dr. Diamond spoke for nearly an hour; his talk was an engaging and thought-provoking summary of the ideas presented in his book. So, what did people learn from this lecture? Our historic ideas of learning would suggest that this is a pretty straightforward question. However, as we have attempted to make clear, what was learned that afternoon would have been as widely varied and unique as the audience itself. If there were one hundred people in the audience, than there were one hundred different versions of the learning that occurred.

The capacity to learn is always dependent upon prior knowledge and experience, as well as upon interest, motivation, and expectations. The attendees of Dr. Diamond's lecture all arrived as unique, highly varied individuals. Some of the audience had read Dr. Diamond's book prior to the lecture and some had not. Some had a reasonably good idea of what he was going to say. Many, if not most, probably had virtually no idea what he was going to say. Some of the audience had backgrounds in biology and/or the social sciences, which enabled them to immediately grasp many of the concepts and ideas presented by Dr. Diamond. Others knew very little about biology, anthropology, or the scientific method, thus limiting their comprehension of much of what was said. Some in the audience were big fans of Dr. Diamond, bringing along copies of his current and past books in hopes of obtaining an autograph. Others had never heard of Dr. Diamond before, and came to the lecture only because of a recommendation by a friend or perhaps in the company of an interested spouse. Still others attended purely by accident—one individual we met at the reception afterward said that he had been visiting this venue for another reason and discovered there was a free lecture by some guy from UCLA and decided to pop in and see what it was all about! These prior conditions dramatically affected what and how much an individual learned at this lecture. Dr. Diamond may have *said* the same thing to all hundred people in the audience, but what was *heard* would have been different for each. If each audience member had been asked to summarize the lecture, there would have been as many versions as attendees. This is not bad or good, it is just the reality of learning.

All learning represents a cumulative, usually incremental growth in understanding over time, both a construction upward and outward by the learner and also a consolidation of prior knowledge and experience. Quite literally, our brains are constantly constructing and reconstructing patterns of relationships between our previous experiences as "recorded" in our brains and the new experiences our senses continuously deliver to us. This construction of relationships between the old and the new is the essence of learning. Our brains can only make sense of our current experience in reference to preexisting patterns in our brains. Those patterns derive either from things learned in the past or from patterns inherited over the course of evolutionary time, or often from both. Knowing that soda is a thirst-quenching drink is an example of cultural learning, knowing that we should drink when we are thirsty is an example of genetic learning, and wanting to drink a soda when we are thirsty is a combination of both. Thus, when the individual who had already read *Guns, Germs and Steel* listened to Dr. Diamond's lecture, she was able to use the lecture as a way to reinforce her prior understanding of Diamond's basic premise that the course of human cultural evolution has been strongly shaped by the environment. By contrast, the attendee hearing Diamond's ideas for the first time may have found the complexity of the thesis too much to totally grasp during the brief exposure. He very well may have walked away thinking that it was all very interesting, but did not really understand what Diamond's main thesis was. The person who came in believing that Diamond was a genius likely left still believing that Diamond was a genius. The individual who arrived skeptical about the role biology and environment play in the development of human culture and inventiveness likely departed still skeptical. Rarely do our experiences dramatically change our conception of the world; rather, they tend to merely reinforce and confirm, incrementally adding to our understanding. Occasionally an experience creates an epiphany, some dramatic shift or change in our understanding of the world, but such events are exceedingly rare.

Most educators have traditionally viewed educational experiences as isolated singular events in people's lives. Whether the educational experience was a school lesson, a visit to a museum exhibition, or a public lecture, the prevailing model has been to think of each of these educational experiences as distinct, separable learning events. With this model in mind, educators would regularly ask, what did the child learn from this lesson? What did the visitor learn after visiting this exhibition? Or in our example, what did the public learn at the Jared Diamond lecture? Everything we now know about how the mind constructs meaning from the world tells us this is an inaccurate model and these are not the right questions. Since learning is a continuous, almost seamless process of developing and elaborating our understanding of the world, we should be asking how did this school lesson, museum exhibition, or public lecture *contribute* to what someone knows and understands about a topic? Again, the key is in appreciating that virtually no one learns anything in one moment or in one place. Rather, learning is a constant, lifelong process of building and refining our understanding of the world. The meaning we make of the world is constantly changing and shifting; although the basic form of our understandings, beliefs, and abilities may remain in place for a while, the details and specifics are always in flux. Even the things we think we know and understand, even the most fundamental skills we possess, vary from day to day, moment to moment. The mind is a dynamic entity, not a fixed one. Learning, and by extension the behaviors influenced by it, is a continuous process, not a stable product. This is why even Albert Einstein and Tiger Woods had off days!

No one is exactly like anyone else, not even identical twins. Certainly, Albert Einstein and Tiger Woods, two exceedingly bright and talented individuals, are not exact clones of one another. The learning styles and aptitudes of these two talents are very different. Although Einstein might have been able to play golf, it is fair to say that from what we know of him, this was unlikely to ever be his strong suit. Tiger probably has a pretty good gut sense of the physics of motion because of his years of hitting golf balls, but, without in any way denigrating his intellect, it is probably fair to say that he is unlikely to be long remembered for his achievements in theoretical physics. Why is this true? Is it just that no one ever taught Einstein how to play golf and that Tiger was never encouraged to study physics? Probably not. Both possessed rare gifts, but different gifts with different potentials for expression.

Another way of describing these differences is in terms of *aptitudes* or *intelligences*. A wide variety of investigators have explored individual differences in these terms, perhaps none better known than the educational psychologist Howard Gardner. Gardner has developed a theory of learning styles that proposes that people are born with the potential to develop a multiplicity of "intelligences," rather than the limited notion of intelligence as measured by the standard I.Q. test. Gardner's original model included seven intelligences; he has subsequently added others. The original seven were:

1. *Linguistic intelligence,* seen in the highly verbal person, who likes to write and read and has a good memory for detail.

2. *Logical-mathematical intelligence,* seen in those who can conceptualize mathematical and logic problems quickly in their heads and who often win at chess.

3. *Spatial intelligence,* seen in those who have good visual memory and can easily read maps, charts, and visual displays.

4. *Musical intelligence,* seen in those who play musical instruments, remember melodies, and like to work with music on to concentrate.

5. *Bodily/kinesthetic intelligence,* exhibited in those who perform well in sports and crafts.

6. *Interpersonal intelligence,* possessed by those who have many friends, like to socialize, and enjoy group games.

7. *Intrapersonal intelligence*, seen in those who are independent, like to work alone, and have initiative.

Gardner notes that schools have traditionally focused on three of these: verbal, logical, and intrapersonal intelligence. One of the strengths of the free-choice learning sector is that individuals get to pick those situations and experiences that best meet their own personal learning styles. Hence, some people like to learn by watching films or television, others prefer to read, and still others prefer to actively engage in learning through hands-on experiences; the majority of folks like to do some combination of the above. In any case, free-choice learning emerges as a powerful vehicle for supporting diversity in learning styles.

Howard Gardner is not the only educational psychologist who has talked about "intelligences." For example, a number of investigators have recently drawn attention to the varying abilities of individuals to communicate and work in teams. Some individuals seem to innately possess these skills, while others struggle all their lives to master them. Collectively, these skills have come to be known as emotional intelligence. The proponents of emotional intelligence claim that this highly important way of approaching the world has been neglected in traditional school-based educational programming.

Psychologist and author Daniel Goleman popularized the term "emotional intelligence" in his best-selling book of the same name. What emotional intelligence is, says Goleman, "is the capacity for recognizing our own feelings and those of others, for motivating ourselves, and for managing emotions well in ourselves and in our relationships." Or, as Maurice Elias, Rutgers University psychology professor, puts it, "It's the set of abilities that helps us get along in life with other people in all kinds of life situations." He calls it the "missing piece" in American education. Emotionally intelligent individuals stand out. Their ability to empathize, persevere, control impulses, communicate clearly, make thoughtful decisions, solve problems, and work with others earns them friends and success. They tend to lead happier lives, with more satisfying relationships. At work they are more productive, and they spur productivity in others. At school they do better on standardized tests and help create a safe, comfortable classroom atmosphere that makes it easier to learn. Like most of the intelligences described above, there is considerable debate on how readily these can be enhanced by instruction, or even facilitated through experience and practice. One thing is clear, though: Individuals vary considerably in their individual aptitudes and abilities, and these differences manifest themselves in both how and to what degree they benefit from specific educational experiences. Although to our knowledge this has never been studied, we would assume that free-choice learning experiences would be rich places to support and facilitate emotional intelligence.

If we think back to Hernando, it is significant that much of his learning about aviation occurred not from a book or lecture, but at museums and air shows and while making model airplanes and playing with his brothers; at its very roots it is deeply personal and emotional learning. Many investigators have remarked on the importance of "affect" (feelings, attitudes, and emotions) in free-choice learning. As theorized by neuroscientist Gerald Edelman, learning is a whole-body experience, involving the emotions, the senses, the physical, and the mental. Sigmund Freud appreciated this fact over a hundred years ago when he observed that memories unattended by emotion were unrecognizable. Emotion is clearly an important component of all human learning.

Learning and Human Development

Up to this point we have described the basic mechanisms of learning as if they were similar in all humans. As a gross generalization this is true; however, the greatest exception to this premise is when thinking about learning in people of different ages. Some of the strongest influences on learning are predictable outgrowths of the changes in the human condition that occur over the life span of an individual, the products of human biological and social development. All this suggests that some aspects of the learning of a three-year-old are determined by the fact that the learner is physically, mentally, and socially three years old. Less appreciated, but equally true, some of the aspects of the way a thirty-three-year-old learns are determined by the fact the learner is physically, mentally and socially thirty-three. Over the years a number of investigators have taken this developmental approach to understanding learning, perhaps most notably the German psychologist Erik Erikson, the Swiss psychologist Jean Piaget, and the American educator Malcolm Knowles. Some of the conclusions of these men have now been disputed; for example, most learning researchers, ourselves including, question the rigid developmental schedule originally suggested by Piaget. Still there is no question that the basic thesis of these pioneers is true: Age makes a difference! Young children really do see and respond to the world differently than adolescents, and young adults differently than older adults. These differences are in large part shaped by the needs and realities of their respective environments, but some part of the difference is also shaped by their stage of biological and psychological development. We will explore these developmental stages in more detail in subsequent chapters when we highlight the nature of free-choice learning experiences for infants and children, adolescents and young adults, and middle-aged adults and seniors.

In conclusion, although our understanding of the learning process remains incomplete, we currently understand quite a bit about how humans learn on an individual level. It is clear that learning is highly personal, contextual, and strongly influenced by development. However, even though individual differences between people—whether genetic, experiential, or developmental—account for quite a bit of the variability in what and how people learn, fully half of the variability is accounted for not by the individual person, but by the social and physical world they inhabit.

Among the shoppers at the market in Samarkand, Uzbekistan (Photo by Mike Harrison, Stanford Alumni Association)

CHAPTER 5
LEARNING FROM THE OUTSIDE IN

There are stories. . . . There are songs also that are taught. . . . Everything I know is through teachings, by word of mouth, either by song or by legends.
—Terrance Honvantewa, Hopi

The band played a rollicking version of a catchy Cajun tune, while dozens of dancers of all ages danced to the zydeco beat. The experienced, many of them elderly like Uncle Stanley, assisted the less experienced ones, as they made their way around the dance floor. Some neophytes picked up the zydeco form quickly, while others struggled, stepping on their partners' toes as they tried to keep up with the tricky beat. Uncle Stanley was one of the best. He had grown up in this small Bayou town and had been dancing to zydeco music since he was a small boy. He proudly watched his grandson Len move gracefully around the floor with one of the prettiest girls in the room, chuckling to himself as Len danced by, winking. Len had not always appreciated his granddad's efforts to pass along his dancing skills, but on this night with every girl clamoring for a dance, perhaps he was a bit more grateful! It was a real town and family affair. There were babes in arms, toddlers running about, preteens making awkward attempts to dance, experienced dancers like Stanley in their seventies and eighties, and couples enjoying a few moments alone from the kids. At a table in the back of the room, Stanley's wife, Claudine, and her sister, Cecilia, watched the dancing but never paused from the particularly difficult baby blanket they were knitting together for Claudine's new grandbaby. In another corner people were gathered around a table intently playing pinochle. Sam's best friend, Ernie, not much of a dancer, huddled in the corner talking business and fishing with several friends from town.

At first glance one might assume that this social gathering is merely that, an opportunity for family and friends to gather and enjoy one another's company. However, everyone at the dance, in one way or another, is learning. Learning is not something restricted to high-level cogitations on nuclear physics, world religion, or Aristotelian philosophy. Appropriate for a biological process that has been evolving and developing for hundreds of millions of years (long before humans conceived physics, religion, or philosophy), learning is a process and way of responding to the day-to-day experiences of our lives. The primary teacher in our lives is the world in which we live—the music, the books, the television and radio, and especially our friends and relatives. Learning is strongly influenced by other humans.

Think back to our friend Hernando in a previous chapter. The inside-out dimensions of his learning are very clear, but without question his fascination and understanding of things related to aviation and air and space were also tremendously influenced by outside-in factors. Hernando attributes his passion for aviation and air and space to the influence of his brothers. To this day, his siblings play a role in his interest and knowledge of flight; they were the ones who first introduced him to the topic and they continue to support and reinforce his interest. Starting with the construction of model airplanes and later flying with his brothers, then talking with pilots and mechanics at the airport and in the army, and finally attending air shows, movies, and museums with friends and family, Hernando's understanding and even reasons for pursuing this interest were and continue to be strongly affected by his social interactions.

As we suggested, learning is not just about facts and concepts, either. One can picture Len's efforts over the years to learn to zydeco dance and Claudine and Cecilia's efforts to master a particularly difficult knitting stitch as they work together on the baby blanket. Such learning is far more whole-body, but nonetheless valid and important, strongly influenced by social and cultural dimensions. Think of all the dances Len attended and the series of partners that helped him reach his current skill level. Social interaction enhanced, sustained, and consolidated his knowledge, appreciation, and ability to zydeco dance. And at each new dance, the memories of the steps and cadence will be refreshed, elaborated on, and consolidated as he becomes an even more masterful dancer.

Learning Involves Others

Humans are social creatures. We live in societies, among other humans, and the other humans we interact with to a greater or lesser extent play a role in shaping our ideas, our beliefs, and our behaviors. In turn, we help to shape the ideas, beliefs, and behaviors of others. So it has been for millions of years. As we suggested in the previous chapter, learning has developed and evolved in response to the social and cultural world. Many scientists believe that the primary driving force behind the evolution of our enlarged brains and advanced intelligence was social interaction—first in response to living in primate social groups and subsequently in response to the demands of a communal hunting and gathering life style. Consequently, learning is directly influenced, in fact filtered, through cultural and social interactions. Humans have developed an exceptionally strong ability, in fact desire, to learn from others, in particular from more skilled and knowledgeable individuals.

Social Interaction and Collaborative Learning

We can discover much about the important role social interaction plays in learning by observing even brief interactions between people. Take for example a conversation we recorded in Los Angeles as part of a study of learning at the California Science Center. A father and his six-year-old daughter enter a life science exhibition and approach an exhibit on the size and capacities of different kinds of animal hearts.

The girl shouts, "Oh look, look over there," as she runs toward the exhibit. "Look at all those things in jars. What are they, Daddy?"

Her father responds, "Those are hearts of different kinds of animals." Reading the labels, he continues, "See, there's a heart of an elephant, a cow, a dog, a rat, and a mouse." The girl looks closely at the hearts. Then her father asks, "Honey, do you know how big your heart is?" She shrugs her shoulders. "Well, do you think it is bigger or smaller than this elephant's heart?"

"Silly," the girl answers, "It's smaller."

"Okay," says the father, "that's right. Is it bigger or smaller than this cow's heart?"

"Smaller."

"Is it bigger or smaller than this dog's heart?"

"Bigger," she says, "because I'm bigger than Scamp (the family beagle). Scamp's okay, isn't he?" she asks, referring to Scamp's visit that morning to the vet.

"Yes, Scamp is a very healthy dog for his age."

"Good," she says, "I wouldn't want Scamp to be sick. He's such a silly."

"Yes he is, isn't he?" replies the father.

Dad then attempts to get her back to looking at the exhibit. "Look how tiny the mouse heart is."

"Oooh, it's so tiny," she says in a tiny voice.

"So," says dad, "isn't it interesting that your heart is smaller than the cow's heart and bigger than Scamp's heart, because you are in between the size of a cow and a dog like Scamp?"

"Yep," says the girl.

The father then asks: "So, show me how big your heart is." The little girl then holds up her hands and says about this big, fairly accurately indicating the size of her heart, a size between that of the cow and the dog.

This brief conversation provides a rich window through which to begin to understand the social and cultural context of learning. Apparent in this conversation are the obvious social bonds between father and daughter, as well as the role parents in our society play in teaching as well as "enculturating" their children. The conversation helps to demonstrate the role that conversations play in our day-to-day life, helping to build the bonds of shared meanings between individuals that are fundamental to relationships. Finally, this episode between father and daughter also provides a glimpse into the ways humans construct knowledge and understanding through conversation.

The very first learning group that an individual collaborates with is her family. Family learning is a process that incorporates the social bonds that exist between relatives, their construction of knowledge, and understanding through conversation and observation, all developed into a family narrative, a set of shared stories and meanings between family members. But this does not only happen with family and close friends, but also with people less well known. Much of the way humans make sense of the world is through such social/cultural interaction with others.

In many ways, the content of any conversation is secondary to the fact that it took place at all. The positive benefits that flow from these shared moments often overwhelm the specifics. In our example, father and daughter reinforced their respect and enjoyment for each other as they built a reservoir of satisfying and enjoyable experiences together. In a sense they were creating an "account of quality interactions" that can be drawn upon for years to come; both father and daughter derived benefit from being in a learning situation together, regardless of where. This family "value" comes from continuous discourse, from a lifetime of shared family conversations. Even the seemingly tangential discussion of the family dog Scamp collectively created shared meanings between family members, and in the process generated a collection of shared values and interests.

Recent neuroscience research reinforces these ideas suggesting that the human brain is actually constructed to gather and process information in meaningful social/cultural ways, which is why stories, songs, poems, dance, and music are such powerful facilitators of learning. Although this research particularly pertains to children, it is probably relevant for adults as well. There is a great deal of evidence that stories help build mature, long-term memory, as people use them to make meaning and find significance in the events they experience. These stories become a part of the family's narrative. Rich narratives and stories also have an emotional impact, a vital component of learning we discussed in the previous chapter. Fun, excitement, joy, mystery, surprise, and sadness are all emotions that can and should be considered fundamental constituents of learning, components that help create an indelible emotional stamp on our memories.

It is fair to say that for most of the twentieth century this view of learning was not a mainstream perspective within the fields of psychology, philosophy, medicine, or biology. However, as early as the nineteenth century, there were individuals who suggested that social processes affected individual learning. In the early part of the twentieth century, a Russian psychologist, Lev Semanovich Vygotsky, and his students in Russia argued that learning developed as a result of interactions in the social life of the individual. Although ignored and for all intents forgotten by a generation of social scientists, today Vygotsky's ideas enjoy a rebirth in interest and popularity.

Mentors and Facilitators

The ideas of Vygotsky are not easily summarized; however, the example we used of father and daughter in the museum provides a concrete example of his approach to thinking about learning. Vygotsky was particularly fascinated by the fundamental role that others, particularly those more knowledgeable, play in mentoring and facilitating learning.

According to Vygotsky, all learning is built upon previous learning, not just the learning of the individual, but the learning of the entire society in which that individual lives. In our example, the daughter's knowledge was formed by an interaction between her and her father, within the context of a learning institution, the museum. Much of the way humans make sense of the world is through such social interaction with others, through what social psychologists call "distributed meaning-making." We have long argued that you cannot truly understand learning if you merely focus on the individual; you could not fully understand the learning in this example by focusing exclusively on either the father or daughter. In isolation, their experiences would make no sense. By the end of the conversation, the daughter had achieved a level of knowledge that exceeded what she would have been capable of acquiring all by herself. Importantly, though, it was not that her father "taught" her about the sizes of hearts, but rather through the verbal guidance and assistance of her father she was able to construct her own understanding. This process, what Vygotsky called "scaffolding," is a process that involves the creation of mental processes and ideas that begin as an interaction between two or more individuals, but which can become internalized by the individual. In the conversation, the father provided social support or scaffolding for the child's investigation about the size of her heart, assisting her in developing a strategy for figuring out how large her own heart was by relating it concretely to a family pet. The father assisted her in solving a problem that she alone would have struggled to solve, helping her forge the divide between her vague knowledge of the relative sizes of various animal hearts and her subsequent knowledge constructed in conversation with her father. Her father also helped her develop a strategy for inferring the heart size of other animals she might encounter. In other words, if internalized, the daughter not only learned about the heart sizes of animals, but potentially a problem-solving strategy that could become a permanent part of her mental repertoire, helping her solve similar problems in the future. Vygotsky argued that examples like this are the rule in learning situations, rather than the exception. He believed that humans virtually always learn through such dialogues, whether explicitly, as in this case, or implicitly, as would be the case if the child used this logical strategy in the future to help her estimate the size of another animal heart, or perhaps a brain or lung. In this sense, most learning develops as a series of experiences facilitated by others, which is then boot-strapped into new learning in comparable situations. But equally important, learning is shown to be a shared social experience. Although the daughter could not be said to have fully known how big her heart was upon entering the museum, in the presence of her father she did know the answer. In other words, her knowledge and her learning were a shared, or "distributed," process, a process that was significantly facilitated by the presence of a more knowledgeable individual.

Despite the billions of dollars spent on training programs in schools, and billions more spent in the business sector, the single most efficient way to learn a new skill, particularly a complex or challenging one, is to apprentice with someone who already possesses the required skills. Mentors and apprenticeships, not classrooms, have been the mainstays of human learning for the entirety of human history.

It is not that there is no role for "book learning" in our world, particularly in the increasingly knowledge-driven world of the Information Age. It is just that learning by watching and following a mentor has proven to be a far more powerful strategy. Examples in the free-choice sector, where we have the opportunity to choose our learning situations, bear this out. Individuals wanting to learn how to take good photographs, learn Tai Chi, repot petunias, master a golf swing, cook a soufflé, as well as those just wanting to learn a new dance step or improve their return in the stock market, find that learning from a mentor is far more effective than trying to just read it in a book. Fortunately, the number of opportunities for such learning is exploding—courses and services fill phonebooks and catalogues, how-to courses at garden stores, hardware stores, and housewares stores. Classes for kids, classes for adults, classes for seniors—all are available within the free-choice sector. Since the 1970s, the prevalence of free-choice options and participation in those options by the public has doubled. But no matter what the task, it is not just someone telling you how to do it, learning requires practice. Ideally this practice takes place under the watchful eye of someone more skilled than you, often someone older, but not necessarily (think of all the young children so facile with technology who are teaching parents and grandparents how to use computers and VCRs). This form of learning has evolved over millions of years, and although the details vary from culture to culture, the basics are the same—basics that have worked for the majority of learning the majority of the time. At the end of the day, learning is most efficiently accomplished when it occurs in an appropriate context; a context that includes both an experienced mentor and an appropriate setting. The environment in which learning occurs is also critical to learning.

Learning Takes Place Somewhere

We live in unusual times, certainly by comparison with the vast majority of the past five million or so years of human history. For most of our history as a species, humans lived exposed to the sun, the rain, the wind, and the cold. We lived according to the seasons, not just for holidays, but for the sustenance of our very lives. To a large degree, we were at the mercy of the rhythms and vagaries of temperature, light, and humidity. Today, we live in climatically controlled buildings, illuminated day and night by artificial lights. We easily, and relatively comfortably, travel long distances with hardly a thought about the historical novelty of it all. Hence, it is perhaps no surprise that the investigations of learning, virtually all of which were conducted within the last one hundred or so years, have consistently operated as if these physical novelties are in fact normal to the human condition. Roughly 99 percent of all investigations into learning have been conducted in either a classroom or a laboratory setting, and well over 99 percent of all those investigations assumed that the physical setting was largely irrelevant to the outcome of the investigation. Truth be known, where you are does affect how and what you learn.

Appropriate Settings

Cary Hansen had always loved learning about the culture and lives of other people. As an adolescent she would read novels like James Michener's *Hawaii* or Pearl Buck's *The Good Earth*. In college, she had studied anthropology and history and then had been in Indonesia briefly, working for the Peace Corps there before marrying her college sweetheart. However, life has a way of taking strange turns. Throughout much of her adulthood, necessity had pushed her in different directions. After marrying she had children and raised a family. In part due to necessity, she had worked throughout her adult life, and the work opportunities that had opened up for her were in the business world. She became a loan officer at a bank, a job she enjoyed and became good at. Although banking did permit her to meet lots of interesting people, circumstances had dictated against her actively pursuing her real passion. All that changed when she retired. By that time she was without a husband or children at home, but fortunately possessed of good health and a reasonable income. So armed, Cary set out to pursue her lifelong passion to study other peoples and other cultures.

Of course she could have satisfied this passion by reading books and watching travelogues on television. But this was not enough for Cary. If she was going to really find out how other people lived and thought, she decided that she really needed to go there, to experience firsthand. She needed to be with other people, to see the way the people lived their lives, and, as best she could, she needed to talk to them. So off she went. During the first part of the trip, her daughter Linden traveled with her, the first time they had traveled together as adults. Cary and Linden visited Europe, and through a mutual friend, they were able to arrange to live with a couple in France for over a month. Later, Cary traveled alone to Spain and Italy, Switzerland and Germany. Then she went to Asia. In Asia, Cary visited India and Thailand, Indonesia and Taiwan, China and Japan. Six months after departing, Cary returned home, tired but enriched. Hers was a firsthand learning experience, an unabashed effort to place herself within the suitable social, cultural, and, most particularly, physical context in which to learn about others—their home, their city, their country. In so doing, Cary was able to actually immerse herself in the lives of other people, to learn by doing, to discover by seeing, touching, tasting, and feeling the world of other people.

The influence of physical setting on learning occurs at the most basic levels. For example, humans evolved as biological creatures adapted to thrive only within a relatively limited range of environmental conditions. Our learning is optimal within these ranges, and suffers significantly outside these ranges. If you don't believe us, try reading this book while sitting in a walk-in freezer. You'll quickly discover that temperature directly affects learning, so too the space if you happen to be even a little bit claustrophobic. But environmental conditions do not have to be extreme to affect learning. Every day, in every way, our learning is influenced by the physical environments we live in. Sometimes the effects are subtle and subconscious.

Take color for example. Nature has evolved an entire signaling system that most animals seem to respond to, even we highly civilized humans. There is a reason why stop and yield signs, McDonald's and Burger King signs, and Campbell's and Knorr's soup containers are red and yellow. Red and yellow are colors in nature that mean ATTENTION! Something is going on here. Plants advertise their ripe fruits with red and yellow coloration, as do poisonous and stinging insects and frogs that want to warn other creatures to leave them alone. Meanwhile, the colors blue and purple are soothing colors, evoking calm and composure in us. Blue and purple are the colors of the sky, water, and faraway mountains, all permanent and important features that instill a sense of security, permanence, and serenity. So deeply embedded in our psyche is this knowledge of color that we do not have to be consciously aware of a color for it to affect us. Advertisers, on the other hand, became conscious of this knowledge nearly a century ago and have tried to use color to influence our purchasing decisions ever since.

Spaces, too, have a way of affecting our behavior and learning. Why do well-lit buildings with large, vaulted ceilings or huge atriums inspire us while dark buildings with low ceilings and walls crowding in frighten us? These feelings can also be unconscious, but normally we are acutely aware of these feelings, even if we cannot immediately verbalize them. It is the feeling we get when we view an amazing natural sight like Grand Canyon. Humans, in particular architects, have intuitively understood these feelings for hundreds of years. The great monuments of the ancient and present-day world, as well as the world's great cathedrals, mosques, and temples, and more recently shopping malls and hotels, have consistently attempted to create human-made structures that mimic the scale and grandeur of nature. When successful, these structures evoke the same feelings of awe and inspiration that large spaces in nature have always evoked in us humans.

Certainly at the level of continents and cultures, setting makes a difference, but does this really hold true at the small, everyday level of most people's lives? The answer is yes. Many of the environmental effects on learning are not on this grand scale; much of what influences our learning occurs at smaller, more mundane levels. For example, when you are channel surfing on your television, what is it that makes you pause and watch one program and not another? Sometimes it is discovering something familiar, something you know you are interested in, such as a favorite sporting event or screen personality. But just as frequently, what gets you to stop is an image or juxtaposition of images grabbing your attention and piquing your curiosity. Today's television is highly crafted and scripted, not just in the dialogue, but in the visual vocabulary and presentation as well. Television producers know that they are competing for the time and attention of an increasingly sophisticated, and fickle, public. Few of us appreciate just how visually discriminating we have become in the last decade or two. All you need to do to convince yourself of this is to watch reruns of television programming from the 1950s or early 1960s. A few minutes of viewing will make you appreciate just how sophisticated both the producers and consumers of today's television have become. Unless you were motivated for nostalgic reasons to watch such early favorites as *Dragnet* or *Gunsmoke*, you would soon find them visually drab, slow, and unimaginative. Not because the stories were uninteresting, but because the production values were so poor compared with those used today.

Learning depends upon our ability to experience the world, but more importantly, learning is enhanced when the quality of the environment is maximized. In other words, the more appropriate the physical setting to what is being learned, the more meaningful the learning that results. Yes, Cary Hansen could have learned about Europe and Asia by reading or watching television, but her learning would have been but a shadow of what it was when she actually went to those places. Why do we take young children to zoos and aquariums? Why do we think it is useful for children to go on field trips to museums, concerts, and historic sites? Why do we enjoy going someplace novel on vacation? All for the same reason: By placing ourselves within an appropriate physical context, learning is significantly facilitated. We do not have to imagine what an elephant looks and smells like; we can actually see and smell it. We do not have to imagine what a Mozart string quartet sounds like; we can actually hear it performed. We do not have to imagine what a tropical paradise might be like; we can actually experience it ourselves. Context matters, both because it enriches and strengthens learning, and because it makes learning easier. Remember Hernando from a previous chapter. The real world of planes was always a part of his learning, starting with the construction of airplane models, and then, as he got older, exposure to real planes. He observed planes at air shows, movies, and museums, read about planes, and even flew in them. All of these experiences built upon, sustained, and enhanced his knowledge, appreciation for, and interest in aviation. All of these impressions were stored in memory, refreshed, elaborated, and consolidated each time a new experience with the topic presented itself.

Interestingly, the group of educators who most fully seem to grasp the benefits of setting includes many home-schoolers. Freed from the constraints of the classroom, thousands of parents are utilizing the entire community as their children's learning laboratory. They take children to museums, zoos, aquariums, monuments and historic sites, malls and festivals; they visit farms and forests, take trips to distant cities, plant gardens, and buy pets. In short, they appreciate that it is not only easier, but more successful, to bring their little Mohammeds to the mountains rather than trying to reduce the mountain to a textbook so it will fit into a single room in the home.

Toward a Model of How We Learn

Although our understanding of learning remains incomplete, hopefully these two chapters have demonstrated that we actually understand quite a bit about how humans learn in general, and how they learn in free-choice situations in particular. We know that learning is highly personal, and strongly influenced by our social/cultural and physical context, as well as by development. To summarize:

- All learning begins, and ends, with the individual's unique interests, motivations, prior knowledge, and experience.

- Learning is both an individual experience and a group experience. What someone learns, let alone why someone learns, is inextricably bound to the social, cultural, and historical context in which that learning takes place.

- Learning is facilitated by appropriate physical contexts and by well thought-out and built designs—the outdoors or an immersive zoo for learning about animals, an art museum or studio for learning about the visual arts, a historic site or reenactment for learning about history.

- Learning is influenced by the developmental stage that the person is at.

To maximize free-choice learning is to bring all of these factors to bear at just the right time in a learner's life. Yes, timing does matter. Learning occurs in a series of cycles—cycles in which these few fundamentals of learning are equally relevant, but where the application of these fundamentals varies because of the differing needs and expectations of the learner. There are many ways these cycles could be described, but our personal favorite is to think about lifelong learning as a series of never-ending explorations, interspersed with periods of intense focus, or mastery. Mastery prompts further exploration, and so on.

Exploration and Mastery

Constance had always enjoyed music, but then, who didn't? It wasn't until Constance was twenty-eight and already well established in her life that she began to explore her interest in music more deeply. She started listening to music on the radio more closely. She started talking to friends she knew who played musical instruments. She went to concerts in her community. And then one day, she decided that she needed to learn how to play the piano. She looked in the classified ads and found a person who taught piano lessons in the evenings. She called and signed up that day.

Over the next several months Constance took piano lessons. She bought a book on music theory and read through it in her spare time. And she practiced, and practiced and practiced. The more she played, the more she realized how important music was to her and how important playing music was to her sense of well-being and fulfillment. Over time, the hours of practice, as well as the coaching, reading, and listening to others, began to prepare Constance for what it took to actually play music.

By the time Constance was in her mid-thirties, she had developed into quite an accomplished pianist. She started performing at a local coffeehouse and began getting requests for performances elsewhere. By her fortieth birthday, Constance was a master pianist, graced with a fine understanding of both the technical and emotional nuances of the art. Although she never earned her living by piano playing, piano playing was her life. Although she always found her greatest pleasure in contemporary music, the better she got, the more Constance derived enjoyment in exploring other musical forms, from classical to modern jazz. She even went to Vienna with a fellow group of musicians to attend an international piano competition there. In time, she started teaching piano to others. In the process, she passed on what she had learned to other aspiring pianists; she particularly sought out those who, like herself, wished to start playing the piano later in life. Exploration and mastery—an ongoing cycle of learning throughout our lifetimes.

Exploration

At the heart of lifelong learning is the never-ending exploration of new ideas, new skills, new experiences, and new relationships. In some cases the exploration can lead to areas of interest that the person decides to focus on, develop, and master, for either professional or personal reasons. Think of Constance's pursuit of music. In other cases these interests are explored for a time, and for whatever reasons, not pursued further, unless at some later point they are reintroduced and reawakened.

Exploration is an important and, unfortunately, often-neglected ingredient in any educational process. Humans are naturally inquisitive and curious animals. From the moment we are born, we make sense of the world through observation, inquiry, and social interaction with others. This is no accident. As we have suggested, learning has evolved over a long period and consequently the human brain contains a rich collection of dedicated, functionally specialized, interrelated mechanisms organized to guide exploration and inquiry. Exploration is a fundamental building block of learning, an activity that we continue to engage in throughout our lives.

Each human possesses both a long evolutionary history of exploration and a long personal history. From cradle to grave we are constantly exploring our physical and social environments. There is no time in our lives when exploration is unimportant, but there are several critical time periods when exploration seems essential—early childhood, adolescence, and again during the early senior years. The free-choice learning sector is particularly well suited to facilitating such exploration.

Mastery

Moving beyond the surface is the essence of mastery. Every day we are bombarded with information. We watch or listen to the news on television and radio; each day there are dozens of stories that compete for our attention. Most we deal with at only the most superficial level. However, some pique our interest or affect us closely, and these we choose to pursue more deeply. Alternatively, like Constance, we decide to dabble in some new skill or topic. Most we leave at that, dabbling, but a few are worthy of our time and effort to actually try and figure out what it takes to actually learn them well. This is the essence of mastery.

All of us learn and master many things over the course of our lives. All healthy individuals master such challenging feats as walking, talking, running, jumping, skipping, and clapping. We master complex, culturally specific social skills such as knowing when to laugh, when and how to show appreciation, when to talk, and when to remain silent. Most Americans master complex cognitive tasks such as reading and writing, balancing a checkbook, and utilizing a computer. We learn complex physical skills such as swimming, bicycle riding, and driving an automobile. Although few of us master these things at a world-class level, we nearly all master them at a surprisingly high level of proficiency. There are gradations in mastery; in fact, mastery is not really a destination, but a process. Take Constance, for example. She was one of those few who possessed both the talent and commitment to not only become proficient, but to truly excel at a demanding art form. Achieving this level of mastery, even for someone with the talent and determination of Constance, does not just happen. Attaining the highest levels of mastery requires a special kind of dedication and practice, and typically a mentor. Despite, or perhaps because of, the challenges, few things in life are as rewarding as these high levels of mastery. The true sign of the master is the individual who at some point feels the need to share what he or she knows with others.

Just like exploration, mastery knows no age boundary, but adulthood is the period in our lives when we are most likely to achieve complete mastery of our chosen interests (although in some areas—for example, certain sports, mathematics, and music—youth can be a real advantage). In order to achieve proficiency in something requires effort and usually a mentor who has also mastered the skill or topic. And since much of the learning we require in our complex, knowledge-based world represents the collective learning of countless generations of individuals, mastery of a subject requires time. The formal education sector as well as the workplace have historically been the places people think of as sites for developing learning mastery. Both are well designed for facilitating the kind of focused, long-term investment in learning that mastery demands. Historically, the free-choice learning sector has not been as well suited for facilitating mastery, but this, too, is changing as more and more free-choice learning organizations begin offering courses, programs, and tutorials. Although mastery is something that can and does occur anywhere, many if not most of the true masters in the world achieved their mastery within the free-choice sector. This is because mastery, perhaps even more than exploration, is about intrinsic motivation. Mastery is about the determination to achieve and learn, not because you are told to, but because you want to; and this, after all, is the essence of free-choice learning.

When, then, should free-choice learning occur? Across the entire life span, of course! Ah, but as we've just begun to see, rarely is anything related to learning that simple or straightforward. At each stage of the life cycle, there are learning needs and opportunities specific to that stage of life—needs and opportunities that free-choice learning is ideally suited to satisfy.

Part II
LEARNING OVER A LIFETIME

Learning at home (Photo by Oluwole and Monika McFoy)

CHAPTER 6
BEGINNING THE LEARNING JOURNEY: THE EARLY YEARS OF CHILDHOOD

Give me a child for the first seven years, and you may do what you want with him afterwards.

—Anonymous

Seven-month-old Joey sat in his high chair as his dad prepared lunch at the stove. Joey seemed fascinated by the spoon that his dad had placed on the high chair tray. He picked it up and examined it for a few moments and then put it in his mouth. He then began turning it and moving it from hand to hand. He hit the tray with it, enjoying the banging sound. And then, by accident, the spoon fell from his hand to the floor with an even louder clanging sound. Joey's dad picked it up and placed it back on the high chair for him, but it was only a moment before Joey's dad was doing so again. Joey repeated this activity a few more times until lunch was ready, and each time he looked down to see where the spoon fell, laughing in glee when it hit with its loud clang.

Those of us who have been around children have experienced a moment like this and often have tended to think about it from the perspective of the adult—trying to get lunch or dinner made and wondering why this child's behavior is so purposely annoying and frustrating. However, during this simple exploratory activity, Joey has actually begun to learn about cause and effect and temporal sequence in the real world, all important concepts that will shape much of his future thinking. Joey was also expressing his autonomy and his intrinsically motivated joy for experimenting and learning.

Humans are naturally inquisitive and curious animals, and from early in life make sense of their world through such observation and inquiry activities. Learning is an ancient, intrinsically pleasurable, and rewarding experience, a fact that is very evident when watching Joey play with his spoon with such enjoyment and glee. Children find innate joy in learning. They seem to learn some of humanity's most challenging tasks, such as walking, talking, getting along with others, assimilating the basic rules of their culture, as well as complicated ideas such as cause-and-effect, almost effortlessly. And, as perhaps best evidenced by the young (and young at heart), learning is a whole-body, emotionally rich experience. Children learn exuberantly, with their eyes and ears, their hands and feet, their mouth and nose, their "head" and "heart."

Born to Learn

Infancy and early childhood represent the beginning stage of the lifelong learning journey, and free-choice learning is a major vehicle by which this journey is undertaken. Under the best of circumstances, it is during early childhood that people develop the foundation for lifelong learning skills that will enable them to travel safely, joyfully, and competently throughout a lifetime of learning. Although many skills are mastered later in life, most critical abilities are laid down during this time. Three learning needs/opportunities emerge at this stage of life to which free-choice learning is well suited:

1. a need on the part of the child to explore, discover, and make sense of himself and his physical and social world;

2. a need for intellectual and social autonomy and ownership for his own learning; and

3. an opportunity early on for children to understand that learning is a lifelong process, something that all children *and* adults do, all their lives.

Importantly, adults significant to children (parents/guardians, other family members, neighbors and friends) can play a vital role in helping children fulfill these three learning needs/opportunities.

Given young children's innate curiosity, interest, and energy, learning during infancy and early childhood is as natural as breathing. The challenge for the adults in young children's lives is helping to support and foster learning as both a natural and joyful experience, so that children develop the habit and joy of learning their whole life through.

Exploration and Discovery

Susan Narayan's niece, Sarah, started to softly coo in her crib, the sign that she was waking up from an afternoon nap. Susan walked quietly into the room and sat in the rocking chair near the crib. Sarah was only a few months old and Susan had offered to stay with her for a few hours this afternoon while her mom, Sally, went and got a much-needed haircut. It was a real treat for Susan—she was self-employed and it was easy enough to rearrange her schedule. As she rocked gently in the rocking chair, she watched Sarah in her crib. Sarah was lying on her back, playing with her right foot, which was almost in her mouth. Susan sighed;

at age thirty-five she was an avid amateur ballet dancer and envied Sarah's flexibility. Having exhausted the curiosity factor of her foot, Sarah now directed her focus from her foot to her right hand and began looking at it intently. Susan watched in fascination as Sarah rolled over slightly and moving almost in slow motion, reached for a colorful crib toy attached to the side of the crib and after a few tries grasped it. Over the course of the next ten minutes she engaged in this activity repeatedly, each time reaching for the same crib toy and only beginning the process again once she had successfully grasped it.

To be a human, particularly a very young human, is to explore and learn about the world, even when the world appears to be nothing more than your own foot! Gone is the long-held notion of infants as empty slates, arriving in the world with no prior knowledge or experience. Every infant is born well prepared for their lifelong learning journey. So much so that every normal infant is capable of mastering many of life's most complex learning tasks in just a few short years. For instance, during infancy and early childhood a healthy child will master a number of skills including holding up her head, sitting up, crawling, walking, talking, and controlling her bowels.

Recent research suggests that infants at only a few hours of age already recognize human faces and show a marked preference for their mother's voice over another female's. Research has shown newborns to be amazingly perceptive. Even at the age of only a week or two, infants are able to discriminate colors, shapes, and sounds. In some cases, for example in the area of color discrimination, infants' abilities are amazingly refined and adult-like. In other areas, such as shape detection, infants do seem to start from the bottom of the learning curve, building up a reservoir of experience on which to base future learning. Providing the infant with choices of stimulating objects to look at, manipulate, and touch, interesting and varied sounds to listen to, and diverse foods to taste and explore will enrich his or her early learning experiences.

The mastery of fine motor skills from diffuse, gross motor movements is also an important component of an infant's developmental repertoire; in fact, it is almost impossible to separate physical development from intellectual development at this age. For instance, the ability to extend the hand and touch or grasp an object, as Susan observed Sarah doing, is called *visually guided reaching* by developmental psychologists and is a major advance in the infant's exploration and manipulation of her environment. Landmark studies with infants in institutionalized settings demonstrated that, deprived of visual stimulation or the opportunity to explore and act on the environment through their own movements, infants did not develop normally physically, emotionally, or intellectually. For all intents and purposes, infants are finely tuned exploring machines that even have built-in adaptive safeguards that ensure that they explore and learn about their world relatively safely. In the 1960s, two Cornell University psychologists demonstrated such safeguards, showing that by the time children were able to crawl, most infants had developed rudimentary depth perception, distinguishing deep from shallow surfaces. Infants behaved in ways that suggested they detected *and* avoided potentially dangerous drop-offs, what these psychologists called the visual cliff. Providing safe but curiosity-provoking environments for infants to explore is another way of encouraging and facilitating children's exploration and discovery of themselves and their world.

Between six and eight months of age, infants also develop a more sophisticated ability to perceive and interpret the world around them. These abilities to remember and learn orally and visually are key elements in the intellectual development of infants and toddlers. As infants become increasingly aware of their environment, the need for quality stimulation increases. Talking and reading to babies, singing and playing with them, and allowing them to investigate appropriate objects and toys are fundamental components of normal development. The family and other significant adults and children in a child's life at this stage are his or her first and foremost teachers. All children, including infants and toddlers, should be given the opportunity to discover an ever-expanding world, to see new places and meet new people.

So, clearly, infancy is a critical period in the intellectual, emotional, and physical growth of a person, continuously filled with a never-ending need to investigate the world orally, visually, aurally, and through smell and touch. Properly nourished—physically, intellectually, emotionally, and socially—infants grow into healthy children. By supporting this nourishment adults help infants construct a platform for learning in the early childhood years and beyond which will provide the foundation for all future learning.

One early morning a few years ago while attending a professional meeting in Minneapolis, Minnesota, we were walking from our hotel to the conference center along a busy city street. On the way we passed a very active construction site and were fascinated to watch a group of about fifteen young children, varying in age from two-year-olds in strollers to fairly sturdy three-year-olds, avidly watching the construction site and its busy workers. The children, with two adult chaperones, were from a local day care center, and boys and girls alike were observing carefully; those who could speak were asking questions, noticing all sorts of details and exceedingly curious about what was going on as cranes moved and lifted this and that. The younger children seemed no less fascinated as their heads moved back and forth, watching the busy workers, the crane, and the other heavy equipment moving around.

We were mesmerized as we observed what appeared to be a simple but profound free-choice learning experience for both the children and adults present. The young children's questions demonstrated the keen observational skills and inquisitiveness of the young child. What was fascinating was how pleasant the whole thing felt; people walked by and said hello, workers called out to the children and visa versa. It was very difficult to walk by that construction site and not break into a big smile. There was an energy and rightness about seeing these children of varying ages so animated and excited, enjoying their world. The children and adults were clearly taking advantage of a wonderful, unplanned free-choice learning moment and it felt good.

Upon reflection, we realized that what made this seem so right was that it *was* so right. These children were immersed in the rich physical and social world of a busy city street and construction site, exploring together, engaged in personally interesting inquiry and learning. They were experiencing and learning about the world around them, in the most appropriate learning setting of all, the world itself.

Toddlers and young children between the ages of two and six or seven are different creatures indeed, moving from dependent infants to increasingly independent children. As we suggested, during infancy children are focused on the development of physical and emotional stability, and the mastery of basic skills like walking and talking. Between the ages of two and five, the focus of young children's learning changes. The very young child has acquired much of the basic framework for understanding the world, but missing from that framework are all the details that we, as adults, take for granted. For example, a young child may understand that mommy and/or daddy go to work every day, but they have no idea why, where they go, or even what it means to "work." Young children truly are learning sponges, exploring, investigating, and constantly questioning, seeing the world in their own unique and typically concrete way. At this age, humans begin to move from a world that is entirely concrete to one that is more abstract—beginning to develop the ability to understand and use symbols—the symbols of language, number, and relationships. As they become increasingly independent, young children also develop a strong sense of self and a relationship with their rich physical and social world. Therefore, it should come as no surprise that the children we observed were so fascinated by the construction site—what a rich and novel physical and social environment for a young child to investigate!

Child psychologists interested in young children's intellectual development have investigated how young children first make sense of the world and construct their own memory structures. Findings suggest that children as young as three remember familiar daily experiences in terms of "scripts" or stories, organized representations of events in the world that provide a general description of what occurs and when it occurs in a given situation. An experience coded in script form provides the child with a basic organizing device for interpreting everyday experiences, such as going to nursery school or eating lunch. Scripts that are held in long-term memory can be used to predict what will happen in the future on similar occasions. With increasing age, as well as with repetitions of a particular kind of experience, children's scripts become more elaborate and complex, and ultimately more abstract.

There is also evidence that a young child's memory is remarkably adult-like. In a recent study of a four-and-a-half-year-old dinosaur enthusiast, his dinosaur knowledge was found to be remarkably similar to that of adults. This finding suggests that the basic organization of memory is similar throughout development, with age affecting the interrelatedness of knowledge rather than how the knowledge is constructed. Such studies are only still in their infancy, and much remains to be discovered about how young children learn.

As a consequence of this research, child development experts recommend that the focus of the early childhood years include exposure to a wide variety of experiences, experiences which hone a child's observational and inquiring skills. In addition, children should have ample opportunity to interact with people of all ages so that they learn how to collaborate and get along with others. Relevant and valuable learning experiences at this stage of life (which are often called *age-appropriate* in research and writings about early childhood), emphasize exploration and discovery; exploration and discovery help to reinforce and extend the learning foundations constructed *in utero* and in infancy. In the example above, young children were being exposed to a construction site, but virtually any situation in the young child's life can serve as a suitable foundation for future learning. Taking children to hardware, grocery, or fabric stores, and on other errands, or allowing children to help with home and work tasks—all are examples of rich free-choice learning experiences. The free-choice learning landscape of the young child is endless. There are things to explore at home, and at the homes of family and friends (what African and Native American legends describe as "the village"). There are museums, television, books, movies, and the great outdoors. Anyone who has ever been around children of this age knows what great joy young children derive from just being outside, experiencing the world. The simplest experience can become a wonderful learning opportunity. But not all early childhood learning experiences can or even should be orchestrated for the child. Children need time alone to learn also.

Autonomy and Ownership

As part of a project we were working on, we recently made a visit to a day care center and observed a four-year-old boy sitting in the corner all by himself (we later learned his name was Lu). Totally surrounding him were piles of wooden blocks and, completely oblivious to the chaos and cacophony around him, Lu was totally focused on building a block tower. Piece by piece he assembled his tower, and as we watched him for what must have been fifteen or twenty minutes, we were struck by what a significant learning experience this was for Lu. First, Lu seemed undaunted by failure. Time after time he built up his tower, only to have it all come tumbling down, at which point he started again.

Lu also learned a great deal about the variables that influence tower building. For example, over time, Lu made the base of his tower bigger and wider. Also over time, Lu seemed to discover that he would have more success if he used the larger blocks at the bottom and smaller blocks toward the top of his tower and, as a consequence, Lu was able to progressively make his tower taller and taller. We also could not help but notice the sheer joy that Lu seemed to have in his task. Despite his extreme concentration, Lu had a huge smile on his face while he worked and an aura of supreme satisfaction seemed to flow from his being, particularly as *his* tower attained greater heights.

Children need to have time to investigate their world on their own terms, for their own purposes, and in the process, achieve success and failure on their own. One critically important way children at this age accomplish this is through what is called "creative play." World-famous child development expert Bruno Bettelheim defined a young child's play as "activities characterized by freedom from all but personally imposed rules (which can be changed at will), by free-wheeling fantasy involvement and by the absence of any goals outside of the activity itself."

From the moment a child is born, play is an important learning activity in which they engage. Think back to Joey—his effort to interact with the spoon was an important form of infant play. But play becomes an art form as children move from infancy into early childhood—think of Lu with the blocks—all culminating in creative, imaginative play.

Generally between the ages of two and three, play moves from being totally an expression of energy (running, jumping, climbing, dropping spoons off high chairs) to an intentional activity within the sphere of the child's imagination. One first observes this kind of play when the child pretends to eat and drink or talk on the telephone. This type of pretend play comes through the imitation of things the child has done or seen people around him do. Interestingly, children imitate not only the action but the associated emotions present when they observed the activity. So, if your daughter observed a worker hammering a nail in anger, she will copy the movement *and* the associated anger.

The progression of play from movement to imaginative play is quite ritualized and can be seen in a young child's relationship to an object, such as a rocking chair. At first there is no concept of *chair*, just the joy of the rhythmic motion that the chair makes when acted upon. The idea of being a mommy or daddy and rocking a baby in the chair comes next. And finally, the rocking chair is incorporated into the five-year-old's elaborate story about the baby taking a trip with her mommy and daddy, who find a room with a magical rocking chair and rock the baby to stop her from crying in a strange place.

Creative play is also the way that children investigate their physical and social worlds—the world of space, time, and the cosmos, the world of nature, and the world of humans. Free-choice learning at this age is both joyful—watch a young child engage in a free-choice learning activity such as imaginative play, trying to solve a not-too-hard problem, or reading a favorite book aloud to a younger sibling—and useful as a building block of lifelong learning. There is also good evidence emerging from early childhood research that engaging children in creative sociodramatic play promotes cognitive, socio-emotional, and academic development in young children. As one child development expert stated, "There is nothing that human beings do, know, think, hope and fear that has not been attempted, experienced, practiced or at least anticipated in children's play."

Allowing children to engage in independent, unstructured creative play is one of the most important gifts an adult can give a child. Today's parents, consumed with fears about children's safety and anxious to provide their children all the "right" experiences and opportunities, can forget that sometimes the best thing they can do for their children is leave them alone. They forget that in their own childhood, often the best gift at the holidays was not the fancy motorized thingamajig, but the big empty box that everyone could climb into and make into a fort, or a car, or a rocket ship. Toys that allow for open-ended play, like blocks, Legos, and dolls, end up bringing more long-lasting and educational joy than the latest electronic toy or movie spin-off advertised on the cereal box or Saturday morning cartoon show. Give children the opportunity, as well as the tools to be autonomous, intrinsically motivated learners.

Learning is Everywhere

"I think the olives should be the capital cities and the mushrooms all the mountains," said eight-year-old Danny as he looked down at the pizza shell shaped like the United States sitting on the kitchen counter.

"But I don't like mushrooms," whimpered Lara, his little four-year-old sister.

"Then you don't need to eat them," soothed Lynn, "but they will make very fine mountains!"

Although unstructured creative play is a building block of lifelong free-choice learning, there is a place for more structured learning as well. This scenario describes an example of a popular free-choice learning activity we engaged in with our children on many a weekend as they were growing up. About twenty years ago, while at the Smithsonian Institution, John initiated an educational effort called the Smithsonian Family Learning Project. A major goal of this project was to develop science-oriented activities that families could do at home. All of the activities were designed to be both fun and educational. A key feature of all these free-choice learning experiences was that they were intended to take place during typical family activities such as eating, doing laundry, taking care of pets, and traveling in the family car. Perhaps one of the most inspired activities to emerge from this project was *Pizza Geography*, an activity developed by John, Jamie Harms, and Laurie Greenberg, which converted the most popular food in America—pizza—into an educational tool. As long as families are going to eat pizza anyway, why not design an activity that encourages the family to make a pizza in the shape of a state, country, or continent and learn something in the process? The basics of the activity involve making pizza dough from scratch (which in itself is novel for most families these days) and then forming the dough into the shape of a map; say, for example, a map of the United States. Once the pizza is molded into the right shape (usually requiring the use of a map and lots of discussion among family members, each an important aspect of free-choice learning), the toppings such as pepperoni, olives, onions, and peppers can be used to create the geographical and geological features of the place. By the end of the experience, you have enjoyed not only a great homemade pizza, but learned something about the geography of some place in the world. In our family, it became a tradition to do *Pizza Geography* any time we had a guest over for dinner, creating a pizza specific to the region of the country or world our guest came from. Over the years, we used this device to help our children learn about dozens of different states and foreign countries. Our guests enjoyed it also. They got to eat a good meal—and a typical American meal if they were from out of the country—and were the center of attention during the family activity, since the guest was the *de facto* geography expert about their corner of the world, with instant credibility and status—a win-win situation for everyone. *Pizza Geography* was just the beginning of such free-choice learning in our family.

We also felt that it was important in our increasingly global world to immerse our children in other cultures early on, encouraging them to learn other languages and to enjoy the foods, music, and customs of other countries. Young children have a natural affinity for learning foreign languages, but also a natural antipathy toward "strange" foods and customs. Our goal was to try to reinforce and support the positive natural tendencies and subvert the negative ones. So when our children were young we developed another fun, structured free-choice family learning activity—international nights on weekends. We would choose a foreign country to focus on and would research the language, food, music, culture, and clothing of that country. When we could, we would all dress up, prepare a meal, try to learn a few words, and listen to the music; we even drew flags of the countries we were exploring. We not only learned together in a fun way, we also got to eat much more exciting food than most people with young children generally do. We are convinced that these experiences are why our children, now young adults, have much greater fondness for travel and international food than their peers. However, not everyone has to invent their own activities; fortunately, we live in a world where there are myriad structured free-choice learning opportunities for young children available to any parent or guardian willing to avail themselves of them.

One such resource is museums. Museums, broadly defined, include science centers, art galleries, zoos, and botanical gardens. They afford visitors rich opportunities for free-choice learning since, for the most part, visitors can choose where to go, what to attend to, and what to learn. One of the greatest resources for free-choice learning for the very young child is children's museums. Children's museums give children, particularly young children, an unrivaled opportunity to navigate through a world made to their specifications, in which they have the opportunity to choose what, when, and how to learn. Perhaps most important, these settings place the young child in a position to be much more in control of their own exploration and learning. For better or worse, children live in an adult-centered world. When they enter a magical world where this is not the case, it is a truly enervating experience.

It is clear as you enter a children's museum that you have entered the world of the child, as you notice the scale of the furnishings and exhibitions. Children are running, climbing, and sitting everywhere, and everything seems built to their dimensions, a world designed to accommodate the small of frame, the small of hand. Watching children enter the space, particularly for the first time, you are struck by the expressions that come over their faces when they realize that this place is built for them. This whole amazing place, just for them! This feeling creeps into the children's very being, the sense of ownership and empowerment that comes from being in a place which is exclusively designed for them, unlike anywhere else in their world. Once, as we entered a children's museum's "grocery store," a little girl looked at us and said, "I want to check these out," pointing to the groceries in her miniature cart. It took a second to realize, but we had entered her imaginary world and we were expected to play a role also. She was in charge; it was her world we were entering, not the other way around. So, of course, we walked behind the register and checked her out!

Children in children's museums get to choose which hat to try on, which rope to pull on, which blocks to play with, and what roles to select in the child-sized stores. And as our interaction with the grocery shopper suggests, children take these roles very seriously. Children love to dress up, love to role-play and pretend, love to build, climb, and explore. Children's museums provide opportunities for children not only to choose between all these sensory and intellectual treats, but also to decide to which aspects they will attend. They have permission to start what they want and stop when they want. In the "real" world, other people are always telling them what to do and when to do it. In the children's museum world, they are in charge, as our shopper clearly demonstrated. What an amazing experience! Imagine being five years old and for this brief moment being in charge of your parents. It is a truly memorable and thrilling experience. Perhaps it is one of the reasons that there is one other thing that immediately strikes you upon entering a typical children's museum—the ever-present feeling of childlike glee that hangs in the air.

Children's museums, as well as zoos, science centers, and other similar free-choice learning settings, are also places where adults have permission to cast aside inhibitions and play. What a wonderful thing for children to see their parents down on their hands and knees playing with ropes and pulleys, trying on funny hats and capes, joyfully pointing and gawking at animals. These are ways in which parents can model for their children that learning is not just something for the young; the joy of learning is a gift for all ages.

Although we emphasize free-choice learning experiences at this age, we do not mean to suggest that there are no basic skills important for young children to learn. We do recommend, however, that early childhood educators resist the current movement toward emphasizing the acquisition of academic skills such as learning letters and numbers and instead maintain the more traditional emphasis on the acquisition of experience and basic lifelong learning skills, such as observing, measuring, inquiring, problem solving, and communicating. These lifelong learning skills can be emphasized as young children are immersed in appropriate physical and social free-choice learning environments. Properly grounded in these "process" skills of life, children will easily pick up the basic academic skills of literacy and numeracy later in childhood. Unfortunately, many children are deprived of these basic lifelong learning skills, a handicap from which many never recover. It is important to remember that if we do not use this stage of life to provide young children with opportunities to explore and investigate their world, to experience new and interesting environments, they may never have the opportunity again. Likewise, when will they have the time for creative, alone-time play, or rich family learning experiences? Only by modeling for young children that learning is an integral part of all life and is something that is truly fun and satisfying, will they learn to know and understand this. For what is important at this stage of life is to help children acquire the lifelong learning skills that will enable them to find the right learning path for them, so they will always know how to satisfy and fulfill their learning needs throughout their lives.

Learning at a Girls At the Center workshop (Photo by The Franklin Institute Science Museum and Girls At the Center)

CHAPTER 7
THE EAGER TRAVELERS: OLDER CHILDREN

Your children are not your children, They are the sons and daughters of Life's longing for itself . . . You may give them your love but not your thoughts, For they have their own thoughts.

—Khalil Gibran, *The Prophet*

Rawanda Collins, an eleven-year-old girl from Dayton, Ohio, woke up early Saturday morning, too excited to sleep. She and her grandmother and cousin, were once again going to participate in a *Girls at the Center (G.A.C.)* program at the Museum of Discovery, their local science museum. The *G.A.C.* project, a collaborative effort between the Franklin Institute Science Museum in Philadelphia and the Girls Scouts of the U.S.A., provides science experiences for girls and an adult partner (a parent, guardian, or other significant adult) in economically disadvantaged communities across the country. Participants attend a series of Discovery Days at their local museum or science center, which include a hands-on workshop and related activities on a particular topic such as electricity or water. In addition, there is a full day of other fun activities, such as attending an IMAX film (if there is a theatre at the museum) or having free time to go anywhere in the museum the pair chooses. At the culminating event, a Family ScienceFest, girls and their adult partners share their science experiences with other friends and family members.

Rawanda had started going to *G.A.C.* the previous fall and had attended three *G.A.C.* Discovery Days with her grandmother and her cousin, Tashika, over the past year. They enjoyed doing the fun science activities together and the chance to explore the museum together on their own. Of course, it was also great to meet the other girls. Before starting *G.A.C.* Rawanda and her grandmother had never been to the science museum where it was held, although her cousin had visited once a few years earlier with her school class. Before she started participating, Rawanda had only a marginal interest in science, preferring to spend her free time playing basketball and being outside. However, she had heard from a friend at school that *G.A.C.* was fun, which is why she had been willing to go the first time.

The *G.A.C.* events were held from 9 A.M. to 1 P.M. on Saturdays, which was hard for her grandmother, because she worked the Friday night shift and usually did not get any sleep before bringing the girls to the events. But Rawanda's grandmother kept bringing them. She had never seen Rawanda and Tashika so excited about science before and they seemed to be learning a lot, so she wanted to support that learning. An adult portion of the program had emphasized that children's free time is an important time for learning and that girls are often not encouraged enough in science, thus later lacking the necessary preparation to pursue science careers if they choose. These factors especially made Rawanda's grandmother eager for the girls to attend. And truth be known, she enjoyed the program herself; it was fun to do the science activities together and especially to spend quality time with her grandchildren—and she was also learning things about science she had never known before.

Rawanda, Tashika, and their families are only a few of the hundreds of thousands of girls, boys, and their families who have participated in structured free-choice learning opportunities such as *G.A.C.*; the *G.A.C.* project alone has served several thousand girls since its inception in 1996. In addition to these types of programs, millions of school-aged children in virtually every community in America annually participate in organized sports programs, arts and crafts, and dance and drama classes, as well as summer camps, computer camps, and a huge assortment of other extracurricular activities. When well designed and executed, these programs provide in-depth exposure to the new activities and interests of older children and help them further develop and refine their lifelong learning skills in real world contexts. The best of these programs also help children and adults learn together in increasingly meaningful ways, about their world and about one another, enabling older children to begin their transition from childhood to adulthood.

Inquiring Minds, Developing Minds

Older children are at the next stage of their lifelong learning journey, and free-choice learning becomes a tool to satisfy the following learning needs/opportunities that arise at this age. In particular, older children need:

1. to develop and practice lifelong learning skills in real world contexts;

2. to engage in more in-depth study of topics or areas of interest than schooling experiences generally offer;

3. to learn and interact with family and other significant adults in increasingly meaningful ways, modeling adult thinking and social problem solving including acceptance, self-confidence, self-monitoring, and team play.

Once again, adults significant to older children (parents/guardians, other family members, neighbors, and friends) can play a vital role in helping older children explore these three learning dimensions.

Older children, between the ages of seven and twelve years, are at a critical stage in their development. They are increasingly independent and developing an ability to move from the concrete to more adult-like abstract reasoning. In school they are learning more involved mathematics and science and beginning to grasp some of the complexities of topics like politics, geography, and societal issues. Using the new brain-imaging tools of PET scan and MRI, scientists have discovered that the brain actually changes over time, confirming that not all parts of the brain mature and become useful at the same time. These findings confirm the developmental sequences described by psychologists such as Jean Piaget and others. The brain matures from back to front, with the parts of the brain most involved with concrete imagery developing first, while the part of the brain most involved with higher and more abstract reasoning developing later. Developing last of all, around the time of puberty and adolescence, is the part of the brain that regulates higher level problem solving and moral reasoning. Developmentally this means that older children begin to live in two worlds: the world of the child and the world of the adult. Although children at this age may seem less inquisitive and spontaneous than their younger counterparts, they are very earnest and eager learners.

Developing & Using Learning Skills in Real World Contexts

Older children have a real need to begin to master the tools of the adult world. They love to learn—wanting to know how things work, how to make things happen, how to create new and different things in the world. As suggested, they first understand the immediately observable aspects of their world, such as physical appearance and overt behavior. Later, for some not until adolescence, they grasp less obvious, abstract processes such as intentions, motivations, and time. In general, thinking becomes more organized and integrated with age, as older children gather more and more concepts about their world.

Allowing older children to explore and learn within real-world contexts is essential to their healthy intellectual, emotional, and social development. Schooling at this age is designed to provide children with the basic knowledge and skills they need to function successfully throughout their lives, and given the nature of schools, this learning and skill building generally occurs in the very out-of-context classroom. The world of free-choice learning affords children opportunities to practice and use these skills by immersing them in real world contexts in which they need to learn new skills, as well as to apply what they are learning in school in rich interdisciplinary ways.

Good parents and classroom teachers have intuitively understood this for a long time, often immersing children of this age in involved project-based activities that require them to practice and use the skills they are developing in personally meaningful ways. Projects can vary greatly depending on the interests and preferred learning styles of the child, but we'll mention a couple that were effective for us over the years. For example, there was the third grade science fair project focused on the behavior of the family cat, in which our son chose random times to observe the cat and investigate her behavior (generated by choosing times written on slips of paper out of a hat). In the course of working on this project, he practiced and used the science process skills of observation, inquiry, problem solving, and communication and also learned a great deal about the cat which allowed him to be a much better pet owner. Another example occurred while building a new home when our two sons were young. We wanted them to be able to see what the house would look like when it was built, but all we had was a set of blueprints. At the ages of seven and eight years, being able to envision a finished, three-dimensional house from a set of two-dimensional plans would have been very difficult (moving from a two-dimensional drawing to a three-dimensional house is even challenging for most adults). So, with some assistance from the children, we used the blueprints to construct a three-dimensional model of the home out of cardboard. Not only did this exercise prove helpful to the children, but in the course of translating the two-dimensional plans for the home into a three-dimensional model, we discovered that one aspect of the design needed to be significantly modified. We used the model to communicate this problem to the builder and ended up saving considerable time and money—very real world indeed!

Free-choice learning experiences such as these can go far beyond being just "enrichment" experiences. In and of themselves, these experiences provide children with some very fundamental and important educational lessons. A good example of this is provided by the *G.A.C.* program described earlier in this chapter. The Institute for Learning Innovation, a nonprofit learning research and development organization that we direct in Annapolis, Maryland, recently completed a five-year longitudinal study of 324 *G.A.C.* participants to investigate just what kinds of impact the program had on participating girls and their families. A major strategy of the program was to immerse girls and accompanying adults in the activities of doing science—observing, classifying, experimenting, and hypothesizing. During core science workshops, girls and their partners were encouraged to pursue the questions that interested them, within the context of the scenario provided, designed to specifically relate to real life. Participants were encouraged to see how a theme connects to their own lives by recalling previous experiences they had that might relate to the problem they were trying to solve.

Results suggested that the following outcomes resulted from this approach:

- the program stressed girls' ownership of their discoveries, and the creativity and diversity in problem solving required to make discoveries in science;

- the program encouraged and facilitated the importance of using the processes of science—wondering, asking questions, experimenting, and discovering—rather than getting the "right answer";

- the program modeled ways to design experiments to explore personally meaningful questions;

- as a result of participating in G.A.C., girls had a broader and enriched conceptual understanding of science and a stronger grasp of how it related to other parts of their lives.

Other free-choice learning projects that we have been involved with have had similarly impressive results. For example, two projects at the Smithsonian Institution's National Museum of American History, *OurStory* and *The Story in History*, demonstrated how a free-choice learning program can directly influence children's literacy habits. A major goal of these two programs was to improve children's attitudes toward reading in their free time, particularly history-related nonfiction books. The project evaluation demonstrated that even months after the program, the children who participated were not only reading more and different kinds of books than they had before the program, but they remembered what they had read, and looked forward to reading nonfiction and fiction books in their free time.

Free-choice learning experiences that allow older children to practice and use lifelong learning skills can be structured events like *G.A.C.*, but they can also be more spontaneous and unstructured. However, whether spontaneous or organized, these experiences play an important role at this stage of life. Today childhood in America is not as unstructured as it once was, but children still do find time for unstructured play and exploration, such as poking sticks in ant-hills, drawing pictures alone in their rooms, reading books rather than watching sitcoms, surfing the Internet in search of "cool stuff," and generally investigating their world. What makes all of these experiences meaningful is that they all occur within an appropriate context.

One extreme example of how free-choice learning can result in real world learning is what an East Indian business person and researcher in New Delhi, India, calls "the hole in the wall experiment." He took a PC connected to a high-speed data connection and imbedded it in a concrete wall next to his company's headquarters. The wall separates his Indian software and education company's grounds from a garbage-strewn slum. He simply left the computer on, connected to the Internet, and allowed any passerby to play with it. He monitored activity using a remote computer and video camera mounted on a nearby tree. What he discovered was remarkable: The most avid users of the machine were ghetto kids, about six to twelve years old, most of whom had only the most rudimentary education and little knowledge of English. Yet within days, the kids had taught themselves to draw on the computer and browse the Net. The physicist has since installed a computer in a rural neighborhood with similar results. He is convinced that 500 million Indian children could achieve basic computer literacy over the next five years if the government put 100,000 Net-connected PCs in the community and let children just use them.

Engaging in In-Depth Study of Topics or Areas of Interest

Often free-choice learning explorations and projects lead nowhere, but sometimes such solitary or group explorations lead to the most profound of discoveries—personal interests and motivation, the bedrock of free-choice learning specifically and lifelong learning in general. One of the benefits of these types of learning experiences is that they provide children opportunities to pursue interests and hobbies in greater depth than schools typically allow, opportunities to begin to "try on" what may become lifelong vocations and avocations. For example, in the case of the two American history projects described above, a few families were planning family trips and vacations to places they had read about in their nonfiction history books, in order to pursue their newly found free-choice learning interests further.

Additional results from the *G.A.C.* study also supported the role that free-choice learning plays in fostering and supporting new and existing interests. The program provided valuable and much-needed opportunities for girls and adults to engage in enjoyable science inquiry and discovery experiences, free-choice learning opportunities in which not all participating families traditionally engaged.[1] Participants responded very favorably; girls very much like Rawanda and Tashika loved the events, especially "all the experiments and stuff, because you get to experiment and brainstorm and try out all your own ideas!"

Findings suggested that participating girls found these free-choice learning experiences personally meaningful. Similar to results from other studies, many of the girls distinguished what they called "*G.A.C.* science" from "school science," commenting how they used to think science was boring and hard, especially science at school. These same girls loved *G.A.C.* science, perceiving it as "fun because you get to build and create things and you don't have to memorize lots of stuff that does not really make sense [to you personally]."

Findings also suggested that participating in *G.A.C.* not only improved girls' self-reported interest in and attitudes toward science, but also was beginning to influence their perceptions of "scientists," as well as influencing their ability to recognize connections between science and everyday life. In fact, as a result of participating in *G.A.C.*, many girls were actually beginning to think of themselves as scientists! As one ten-year-old girl in Minneapolis said: "[I feel like a scientist] when I get to try things out with my own hands, like touching the cow's heart, and doing experiments like trying to clean up polluted water with different kinds of tools." Girls' self-confidence and perceived confidence in science also improved to the point that after participating in more than one *G.A.C.*

event, the number of girls contemplating science-related careers rose from 13 to 53 percent. After participating in *G.A.C.*, girls indicated that they wanted to be a doctor or an engineer or a biologist, rather than a teacher, the most common response provided before. These are the kinds of outcomes most science educators would agree any quality science education program should facilitate, whether in or outside of school.

In-depth exploration can happen at home, too. Over the years, we developed another fun and enjoyable way to encourage our children's interests, which also had the added benefit of providing opportunities for us to spend quality time alone with each child, a big challenge when you have three children. We had an arrangement with each of our children that, once a month, each of them would be able to have a "special day/afternoon." This was an opportunity for them to pick any activity or topic they wanted to explore, and one of us would spend time with them facilitating that exploration. Over the years, special days included visits to zoos and museums, painting pictures and doing craft projects, making dolls, and just "hanging out" together and playing games. For that afternoon, that child was "special" and had the opportunity to control the learning agenda. For that afternoon, we parents had the opportunity to individually, and personally, share a "special" learning experience with one of our children.

Interacting with Adults in Meaningful Ways

Over time, as older children become more intellectually sophisticated in their thinking and understanding, they also begin to revise their conceptions of the causes of behavior, moving from simple, one-sided, egotistical explanations such as "I got blamed for trouble because my father hates me," to complex interacting relationships that take into account multiple variables such as, "I got blamed for the trouble because I was caught starting a fight with my younger brother three times last week, which meant my father felt that no matter what might have actually happened this time, I probably was somehow to blame for the current trouble." This increased ability to understand the complexity of human behavior, to see someone else's perspective, makes this an ideal time to build the life-long learning skills of acceptance, self-confidence, self-monitoring, and team play. And once again free-choice learning has a role to play in building these skills.

Adults can help to support older children's efforts to monitor their own learning and behavior, by helping them to develop formal and free-choice learning goals (both in school and out of school), and revisiting those periodically is a great way to encourage self-confidence and self-monitoring.

No better context exists for learning about acceptance and team play than the family. For example, at about age ten or eleven, our son became interested in the issue of apartheid after reading Mark Mathabane's book *Kaffir Boy* in school. To help support this interest, we checked out the movie *Power of One*— a wonderful story that presents this difficult issue from the perspective of a child living in South Africa, a child who happened to be the same age as our son at the time. We watched the movie together as a family and then, over the next several weeks, proceeded to have rich conversations on the topic of racism and apartheid. Our effort to support his thinking in this area through free-choice learning was a great way to discuss acceptance and class issues, and to compare and contrast the race situation in the United States with South Africa. It also resulted in the family sharing some wonderful African music together—still our favorite musical genre to listen to when we gather.

Adults can also encourage the development of acceptance and collaborative learning skills in children through engaging in out-of-home free-choice learning experiences with them. Returning to the *G.A.C.* example, another set of outcomes that resulted from this program was a heightened awareness on the part of the adult and girl partner about each other and their learning needs. After participating in *G.A.C.*, partners were more likely to:

- recognize the importance of building on each other's existing knowledge and experience;

- appreciate that people bring different levels of knowledge and styles of learning to a situation; and,

- support and value each other's differences and understand the value of bringing different perspectives to a scientific investigation.

Clearly, free-choice learning programs like this are positively influencing children's learning, but what is equally exciting about these efforts is that adults are learning in these programs also, as well as the family unit as a whole. In the case of *G.A.C.*, the program broadened adults' understanding of the importance of girls' learning about science and also boosted adults' confidence, inspiring their creativity and initiative as they helped their child partner explore science. In the case of the *OurStory* and *The Story in History* programs, adults were learning that their children interested in history and that museums and libraries were rich resources for doing so on your own, in your free time. And in all cases, by working to involve the whole family in free-choice learning, the programs were modeling the benefits of lifelong learning.

Modeling, also called *social learning* or *observational learning*, is learning through observation and imitation. Modeling is another common and powerful way that people engage in free-choice learning, and the most common way that people learn (or in some cases do not learn) principles of acceptance and team play, particularly in childhood. Modeling has been studied in both animals and humans, and the data supports the fact that role models are powerful mechanisms for affecting learning and behavior. Much of what we learn, including many of our most fundamental and individually characteristic patterns of behavior—such as how we talk, walk, and raise our children, what foods we eat, what we value in entertainment and lifestyle, even our political views and affiliations—are *nonverbally* learned. Much of this modeling takes place during childhood by observing our parents, siblings, close relatives, and friends.

An extensive line of laboratory investigations by behavioral psychologist Albert Bandura and his associates in the 1960s demonstrated that modeling is the basis for a wide variety of children's learned behaviors, such as aggression, affiliation, and sex stereotyping. Bandura recognized that from an early age, children acquire many of their responses simply by watching and listening to others around them, without direct rewards and punishments or without being explicitly "instructed." An important way to promote lifelong learning in our society is to ensure that we not only talk about learning with our children, but demonstrate it as well.

Projects like *G.A.C., OurStory,* and *The Story in History* represent examples of creative approaches to modeling free-choice learning, but they are only three of several such projects around the country that we are familiar with, all led by free-choice learning organizations such as museums, zoos, libraries, youth organizations, and public television stations. Many of these are funded by the Informal Science Education division of the National Science Foundation, the Institute for Museum and Library Services, National Institutes for Health, and hundreds of private foundations around the country, all committed to providing meaningful free-choice learning opportunities for school-aged children. These organizations are playing major leadership roles in their communities, working with other community-based organizations like Boys and Girls Clubs, YWCAs, scouts and faith-based organizations, to provide high-quality free-choice learning experiences for children and their families. These efforts are fostering and modeling learning in many communities, particularly poor ones, resulting in significant positive impacts on individual children, families, and communities.

Creating learning situations in which children and parents can jointly share the joy of learning is an increasingly important goal of many free-choice learning institutions, and an increasingly important goal of many parents/guardians. Some adults feel so strongly about the need to provide mutually reinforcing learning situations for their children and themselves that they are willing to set aside other personal goals and devote the bulk of their day to "schooling" their children at home. And in an increasing number of cases, those who home-school their children are obliterating the boundaries between schooling and free-choice learning.

Home Schooling & Free-Choice Learning

Twelve-year-old Jessie crammed one last shirt into her suitcase, sitting on it to squeeze it shut. She was very excited. Tomorrow she was leaving to head to the capital for a week to participate in an "honorary capital page" program for children at the state legislature, including tours of the legislature, meeting with representatives, and participating in discussions about the legislative process. Ever since the recent presidential election and state legislative session, she had been fascinated by politics, inspired by many family discussions, learning about current events, and writing to legislators about issues that concerned her—all as a part of her home-schooling activities. Jessie and her eight-year-old brother, Sam, live in Beaverton, Oregon, with their mother, Judith Landis, a lawyer who works out of their home, and their father, Steve Landis, a software developer. The family has been home schooling for three years, although they find the "home-schooling" label an inaccurate and misleading descriptor of their approach to education, since they are most often neither "at home" nor doing "schooling." They are, in fact, practicing free-choice learning.

Each year millions of families choose to educate their children at home and in the community, and this number continues to increase each year. Although some choose to do so for religious reasons, increasingly a number of families are choosing to educate their children at home for more philosophical reasons that relate to supporting the fundamentals of free-choice learning or to dealing with children who have unique learning styles not supported well in large classrooms. In most cases these families are successfully "teaching" their children and enjoying the experience as well.

Although home schooling is not for everyone, Judith and Steve have found that they enjoy it and that they are learning as much as their children are. One of the first lessons their children taught them was the distinction between *teaching* and *learning* and the roles these play in the educational process. *Teaching* suggested that they had wisdom to impart, and that the imparting of this wisdom would result in learning. While Steve and Judith still believe they have some wisdom to share with their children, they have discovered that the pearls of wisdom that they volunteer are not always eagerly received by their children, and are rarely integrated into their day-to-day perceptions. On the other hand, the discoveries that their children make and the answers to the questions that they ask during their own exploration immediately become part of their model of the world around them. Therefore, Judith and Steve have redefined their role from that of "teachers" to that of "learning facilitators." They guide and facilitate their children's own exploration, rather than dictating it.

With the exception of some math materials, they use no packaged curriculum—Judith and Steve have found that their children learn best by doing and exploring, so they seek out learning opportunities, rather than textbooks. Think back to Jessie—her political activities, including writing letters to legislators, reading about current events, and participating in the capital page program were all active ways for her to learn about the political process that she had become interested in. Many of these activities were initiated by her and facilitated by her parents. Another time, the Landis family attended a presentation arranged by another home-schooling family, featuring a woman who survived the Holocaust, wrote a book about it, and now speaks to children about her experiences. This presentation led to more family reading and discussions about the Holocaust, the causes, other countries' responses, and other "ethnic cleansing" situations. Judith and Steve feel that the Holocaust has far more meaning for their children than it ever did for them since they only read about it in a history textbook.

In their opinion, one of the many benefits of home schooling is that each family can choose the approach that works best for the child and the family, and this approach can be adjusted as the child's and family's learning needs change. They have tried a wide range of home-schooling approaches: structured "classroom-like" teaching at home; unit studies where they explored a particular topic from all angles; co-op studies with several other families; and child-initiated learning. They currently use an eclectic approach with some structure, some group projects, and a lot of child-initiated learning.

The Landises are also firm believers in giving children time alone to imagine, create, ponder, and integrate all that they are learning into their own frameworks. Even getting bored has its advantages—it usually spurs the child to find something interesting to explore or to participate in one of their parents' activities. They feel that their approach to their children's education has given them valuable time with their children, the opportunity to build deeper relationships with one another, and the chance to help each child develop their unique gifts according to their own developmental timetables. It also seems that they are helping to provide their children with the skills and interest to support a lifetime of continued learning.

They use community resources a great deal, such as the capital page program that Katie is participating in next week. Jessie and Sam also volunteer several hours a week at a local library. In the course of their work there, they have learned, practiced, and applied many important basic skills. They now know how to use the Dewey decimal system, how to alphabetize and retrieve books, how to easily find books of their own choosing through the computer catalog, and how to use the computer to reserve books and check their circulation records. They have learned how to work with and take directions from a superior and how to show up on time to do work that is expected of them responsibly, in spite of distractions. All of these are important lifelong learning skills. Interestingly, Judith and Steve have found that as a consequence of their work in the library, they do not have to set required reading goals or provide reading lists for Jessie and Sam, either. Now their children find books that interest them in the course of working in the library and they are self-motivated to explore a wide variety of fiction and nonfiction works on their own.

The Taylor-Blodget family is another successful home-schooling family living in Austin, Texas, who make every effort to include free-choice learning strategies in their activities. Beth Taylor, an emergency room physician, and William Blodget, a software developer, have one son, Brent, age twelve. Like the Landis family, we learned about the Taylor-Blodget family through a special program on National Public Radio. The Taylor-Blodgets say they find it very difficult to generalize a "how to" for home schooling, feeling that there are as many different ways to home school as there are home schooling families. In fact, a friend once asked if she could come over and watch them "do" home schooling. They laughed and suggested that she move in with the family for a few days! For their family, home schooling is more of a lifestyle than an activity. They do the same sorts of things that families with school kids do to enrich their children's lives, they just have more time and flexibility to do it. They make lots of trips to libraries, bookstores, and museums, and attend both home schooling and general community activities.

They are frequently asked what kind of curriculum they use. When their son was elementary school age, they used to say that they had a "game-based" curriculum. He played a lot of computer, board, card, dice, and word games which required math, reading, or vocabulary to play. Monopoly and the Carmen San Diego computer games are good examples. There was also a lot of good probability theory in family poker games.

At the beginning of sixth grade, they discovered mathematics competitions. Now they say they have a "contest-based" curriculum, at least for math. The best contests are those that require creative problem solving and draw from a broad gamut of mathematics, rather than just memorizing mental arithmetic tricks. MathCounts for middle schoolers, and the AMC exams leading to the International Mathematics Olympiad for high schoolers, are good examples.

Textbooks are one thing they do not use in their learning program. They own a few that they use for reference, but generally they look for other media, making extensive use of audio and video materials, recording programs from PBS, The Learning Channel, and The History Channel. They have also bought, rented, or checked out from the library a lot of educational videos and books-on-tape.

In addition to books, videos, contests, and educational TV, they take extensive advantage of the expertise of others. They have hired a graduate student in mathematics who meets with Alex as a mentor, to discuss the type of mathematics that professional mathematicians engage in. They also have a phonics tutor and a chess tutor. They have participated in learning groups organized by other home-schooling families interested in studying geography, rocketry, deductive reasoning, chess, etc. They also take advantage of commercial summer camps and Saturday or after-school programs. This provides some group activities and exposure to things like juggling, computer programming, robotics, diving, and fencing. As they remarked: "There are more [free-choice learning] opportunities out there than we could possibly take advantage of!"

Hopefully, these rich examples have painted a picture in broad strokes of what free-choice learning for the older child can and should look and feel like. Clearly, free-choice learning represents an exceedingly important dimension of this stage of learning. Through both structured and unstructured activities, older children begin to develop lifelong learning skills and capabilities and have opportunities to practice and use lifelong learning skills in context. By learning along with their parents, children learn important lessons about collaboration and acceptance, and the notion that you are never too old to learn is reinforced and modeled. As older children make the important transition from childhood to adulthood, experiences inside and outside of school are essential to their healthy maturation and development. Childhood is not the end, though, but rather just the beginning of a lifelong learning journey. Let's explore the next stage—adolescence.

Note

1. Because of the nature of these programs, science exploration and discovery were the outcomes; however, we have observed similar results in art- and history-related programs.

Learning Tae Kwon Do (Photo by Gregory M. Dierking)

CHAPTER 8
A JOURNEY IN SEARCH OF
A PURPOSE: ADOLESCENTS

Your children were not born to complete your life, They were born to complete their own.
>   —William Martin, *The Parent's Tao Te Ching: A New Interpretation*

Oh, Dad, please, please, PLEASE. I just HAVE to do this!! I will learn so much more French if I really just travel around. The program will be great, but when I travel around after is when I'll really become fluent and learn about the culture. That's what Ms. Sims (Ivy's French teacher) said—she really mastered her French when she moved over there and worked as a waitress."

"Yes, Ivy, you've told us that story before, but she was also twenty-two and a graduate student. You are only sixteen and we won't feel comfortable knowing that you are traveling around France and Europe unsupervised," her dad, Dave Roberts, responded.

"But, I'll be with Laura so we can watch out for one another." Dave did not have the heart to tell her that her traveling with Laura was no comfort at all and that even if Laura had been as mature and responsible as Ivy, that would not have sufficed. But he also knew that Ivy was right. This competitive learning abroad program that she had worked very hard to get into, combined with a chance to further explore and apply the things that she had learned in an extended trip afterwards, did make sense. Perhaps the same approach that he and his wife Susan had used to encourage her to achieve the goal of participating in the learning abroad program would work on resolving this situation also.

Dave still remembered the day that Ivy, then fifteen years old, had brought home the information about the program that her French teacher had shared with her—a semester-long immersive program in French in Paris. It was a dream come true for Ivy who, like her mother, at an early age had demonstrated great aptitude for learning foreign languages. By the age of twelve, Ivy could speak Spanish and French fairly well, though her real love was anything French—French movies, French food, and French clothes.

Although the program sounded wonderful it was very expensive and the family was already a bit financially strapped, having recently put two older children through college. However, Dave and Susan talked and felt that they could afford most of what it would cost for Ivy to participate in the program. They had presented Ivy with a proposition: earn one third of the tuition herself by the time she needed to confirm her participation, about eight months from now, and they would contribute the rest.

At first, Ivy was less than thrilled. "Everybody else's parents are paying for it," she said, "and where will I ever come up with twelve hundred dollars in that short of a time?" However, after a few days it was clear to Ivy that these were the terms and even her most persuasive skills were not going to change that. Since she really wanted to participate in this program, perhaps more than anything she had ever wanted to do in her short life thus far, she got psyched and began to develop a game plan. She composed a letter to all of the people that she had ever babysat for or done odd jobs for, explaining that she was trying to go to France and would they help her do so by hiring her. She also put a flyer in people's mailboxes and posted it at the grocery store and other places around the neighborhood, as well as her dad and mom's offices. Her mom, dad, and English teacher helped by reading what she had written in the flyer and making editorial suggestions, and her dad, a wonderful artist, had even appropriately illustrated the flyer with a furling French flag, which she colored in to make it eye-catching.

In eight months Ivy had the money she needed to apply to the program, joyfully was accepted, and had filled out the paperwork for a passport. It probably had not hurt that she could write such a strong essay suggesting why participating in this program was important to her. The fact that she had worked so hard and had earned a third of the money she needed was strong evidence of her interest, commitment, and willingness to give the program her all. Happily for Ivy, she was also going to be able to extend the trip. Again the parents had placed the ball in Ivy's and Laura's court—they could extend their trip for three weeks if they could arrange a supervised situation that was acceptable to each set of parents; they also needed to cover the additional costs. With some help from friends and family, and to the wonder of both sets of parents, they figured it out by utilizing interactive chat lines on the Internet. Dave and Susan were delighted, and truth be known, a little teary as well. Although they had hoped that Ivy would rise to the challenge, they had not expected her to do so quite as well as she had. However, when Ivy wanted to do something she could be a very determined young lady and she had proven herself again.

Fourteen-year-old Aaron sat on the edge of his bed, alternately staring at his computer and the book sitting next to him; both computer and book were devoted to the game *Dungeons and Dragons*. He had been studying how to deal most strategically with this one particular scenario for two hours, and as he paused, realized that he was very hungry. But he continued; next week he would be traveling to Baltimore to compete in a *Dungeons and Dragons* state tournament and he needed to be prepared. Aaron's father tapped lightly on the door, bringing a sandwich that Aaron gratefully gobbled down. "How's it going?" his dad asked, but Aaron was too engrossed to do much more than grunt. Aaron's dad, Arturo, stared blankly at the screen, then the book, then the screen again, totally perplexed by what he saw. Finally he shrugged, unable to make heads or tails out of the complex maze and instructions that his son pored over. Although he lingered briefly, the total absence of a response from Aaron prompted him to make a hasty retreat. "Try not to stay up too late," he offered lamely as he closed the door behind him.

Lives in Transition

Ah, the teenage years! We have all been there and some of us have experienced a teenager in our home firsthand and can relate to these vignettes. Adolescents are driven to explore and experiment and will do so regardless of adult support. However, probably more than at any other time in their learning journey, adolescents need positive adult support and understanding as they investigate the boundaries of life and convention. With such support the drive to explore and experiment can be constructively channeled into efforts that are positive, life-enriching, and meaningful.

The adolescent years are among the most interesting and challenging years of a person's life. During these years, all kinds of adult-like capabilities, largely absent in children, are developed:

- The intellectual ability to deal with possibilities, hypotheses, and abstractions.

- Strong social relationships that can progress from friendship as playmates to relationships of intimacy and understanding.

- A growing ability to assume responsibility for one's own actions and a willingness to do so.

- A concern for social and political issues.

In addition, adolescents possess a series of very non-adult-like traits, including:

- A lack of a strong sense of self, and hence a need to fit into "a group."

- The tendency to be extremely awkward physically, emotionally, and socially, with a heightened sense of self-consciousness.

- The ability and need to assert their independence from parents (although parents and family are still a significant influence, there is a natural developmental desire to withdraw from and reject this influence).

At this stage, three important learning needs/opportunities manifest themselves:

1. A desire to explore and experiment with efforts to be increasingly independent and responsible.

2. A need to begin to master skills and interests, to make initial decisions about the kind of life they hope to pursue and build, and, in the process, to develop a sense of self.

3. A need for supportive mentors, particularly peers and adults other than parents, who can provide guidance and supervision as adolescents practice and experiment with lifelong learning skills.

Independence and Responsibility

Interestingly, in the vignettes above some parents might wonder whether it was wise to give Ivy so much responsibility or might complain about the hours that Aaron spent in his room, engrossed in a game like *Dungeons and Dragons*. But in both cases, the parents wisely understood the need that adolescents have to immerse themselves in areas of personal interest and by doing so to assume increasing ownership and responsibility for their own learning. At the same time, they also understood, valued, and respected that adolescents are beginning to master some skills and interests and are making initial decisions about the kind of life they hope to pursue and build for themselves—in other words, they are developing a sense of self.

As suggested above, Aaron's father was actually grateful that Aaron had found something that he cared about and was willing to focus on and master in his free time. He told us that he always knew that Aaron was going to be an interesting and probably quite successful adult—the challenge was how to help him get through school and adolescence! Aaron had always been a difficult child, exceedingly bright but fiercely independent and not an exemplary student at school. He had been slow to read, in fact, slow to do many of the things expected of him in school, with the exception of mathematics, which he adored and in which he excelled. For the most part he had always hated school, particularly now that he was in high school. He rarely read in his free time or did much schoolwork and instead spent hours hanging out with friends, usually watching television or movies. But when he discovered *Dungeons and Dragons* a few years ago, many of those habits changed. He would spend hours poring over books related to the topic, became fascinated with the world of politics, and communicated with fellow Dungeys around the world on the Internet. He had even been trying to learn some French so that he could communicate with a young French woman he had met on-line, herself an avid *Dungeons and Dragons* aficionado. Come to think of it, his father realized he and Aaron had engaged in some pretty interesting conversations about the game and its relevance to world politics and intrigue. Although his passion for *Dungeons and Dragons* had not made him a better student at school, it had alleviated his father's fears that the boy was not able to focus on a goal and do whatever it takes to excel. After all, he was competing in the *Dungeons and Dragons* state tournament next week!

By contrast, Ivy had always been a good student, but her parents wisely knew that it would take more than school to be a productive, fulfilled, and satisfied adult. They knew that the travel abroad program, in concert with some time to travel around afterward with her friend Laura, would allow Ivy to explore new avenues, and to focus more in depth on her interest in things French. She might even be able to investigate some career options and see how her interests in French could become her life's work. They also realized that this experience would give her ample opportunities to gain some new skills in adult communication, while providing a real world context in which to practice other skills she already had. In order to get into the program, she needed to write letters, make contacts, and use e-mail internationally. In the program she would travel in other countries, and communicate without the support of her family or a program. Dave and his wife appreciated that developmentally, adolescents need to see and experience the world, get a taste for how real people live their lives, and have some choice and control in what they get to do and how they go about doing it, while still having the gentle guidance and facilitation of a knowledgeable adult. After all, only through these kinds of exploratory experiences can an adolescent like Ivy intelligently decide how to invest her educational time and capital in the future and continue along the lifelong learning journey as a self-directed adult. Besides, Ivy had proven herself, meeting the challenge of earning money and making the travel abroad opportunity happen by a major commitment of her own. What a girl like Ivy needed, more than anything, was an arena for practicing and implementing her developing skills, abilities, and curiosities.

Free-choice learning experiences are often among the few places in our society where an adolescent can use his or her intellectual, physical, and social skills to full capacity without being judged poorly for doing so. Often at this age, adolescents find schooling useless for anything but socializing with their peers, and parents only useful in terms of providing food, shelter, and money. However, free-choice learning activities such as sports, special interest clubs, and the arts can provide rewarding and acceptable outlets for adolescents' interests and abilities, as can free-choice "work" experiences such as summer jobs or work study experiences.

For example, throughout high school and even after, our daughter's boyfriend, Matt Wilson, has worked for his former football coach helping him do carpentry. Matt has no aspirations of becoming a carpenter, but working with "Coach" has taught Matt to be responsible and to be depended upon. Matt has also learned some very practical skills that will serve him well throughout his life, no matter what he ultimately chooses to do professionally. He can now build a garage or a house, he knows how to repair a roof, and he knows how to design and landscape a garden. As Matt said, "Doing it first-hand showed me things that no book could ever have provided me. These are skills I can use for the rest of my life."

Few experiences are more exciting and more important for adolescents than internships and work-related experiences. These experiences provide real-life opportunities for adolescents to prove what they can do while learning what it means to be an adult. There is new evidence that if work is a greater part of a teen's life, they remain much more engaged in learning in general, and that these experiences can also keep them in school. A recent report, "School-to-Work: Making a Difference in Education," suggests that high school internships appear to reduce dropout rates and increase the likelihood of college enrollment. However, the true benefits of internships and work experiences are not that they keep teens in school, or even increase college enrollment, but that they provide adolescents with a sense of purpose, a measure of success and evidence that they can be competent people, doing real things in the real world. These are all vital ingredients in becoming an independent and responsible adult, and they are the kinds of outcomes that free-choice learning experiences seem particularly well-suited to supporting.

Free-choice learning experiences allow adolescents to immerse themselves in meaningful activity, where they can test their skills and abilities against others like themselves. It is a situation in which they feel they can be fairly judged. In short, free-choice learning experiences such as internships, club activities, and sports allow adolescents to ease into the adult world, to begin to make that important transition from childhood to adulthood.

Mastering Skills and Interests and Developing a Sense of Self

As we initially discussed in the last chapter, appropriate free-choice learning experiences can support the pursuit of personal interests while developing self-confidence and physical and social skills. During adolescence, free-choice learning experiences become even more valuable as the adolescent begins to master skills and interests, to make initial decisions about the kind of life they hope to pursue and build, and in the process, to develop a sense of self.

Kate took a deep breath like her teacher "Master Lee" had taught her and she had practiced so many times. Tae Kwon Do is a Korean martial art, now recognized in the Olympics. Master Lee, her *Sah-bum-neem* (Korean for "master") nodded toward Kate. It was her turn to be on the mat. Kate Darling moved swiftly across the mat to face her opponent. She was thirteen and tiny for her age, but Master Lee had been impressed with her strength, agility, and toughness from the moment she had walked into his school four years before. Most of the time she competed against herself, but since this was a tournament she was "competing" against a student from another Tae Kwon Do school in her hometown of St. Petersburg, Florida.

Over time Master Lee had also observed two other useful traits in Kate—she was persistent and she was patient. At each practice she would arrive a bit early and warm up appropriately, and, despite being the smallest in the class, would work diligently for the entire hour, seemingly never tiring, trying routines over and over again until she got them right. Her peers tended to initially underestimate her abilities because of her size, but over time she had gained their respect and, in some cases, their envy.

She moved through the first few levels of belts easily. Master Lee seemed well aware of her potential. He guided her with special attention to both the physical and mental aspects of Tae Kwan Do. Master Lee taught Kate how to relax and breathe and psychologically overcome her opponents. Once, when talking to her father after a practice, Master Lee let him know that Kate was developing very well and learning very quickly. Gregory, her dad, shared with Master Lee how much Kate liked to share the philosophy ideas he gave her at home. So one evening Master Lee asked her to stay briefly after class. She was only eleven at that point and waited nervously while the last of her classmates were picked up by their parents. He had never asked her to stay late like this and it worried her. However, he merely quietly removed a small leather book from his pocket, filled with Tae Kwon Do philosophy. Kate was thrilled and put the book in a special place in her room, reading a few passages each night before she went to sleep.

The hard work was beginning to pay off. Just recently, Master Lee had placed her in an intermediate class, primarily composed of adults. Master Lee was always extremely patient with all his students, though very strict about the requirements. Kate was now ranked first in the city for her age level as a result of tournaments and had a good chance of being ranked at the county level if she performed well at this tournament.

Kate could tell as she now faced her opponent, a much taller but skinnier girl, that this girl had already underestimated her skill. During the first two years of competition this had really frustrated Kate horribly. She was sick of always being the shortest and consequently the weakest! She had never been much of an athlete; in fact, as a child she had been quite awkward. However, by participating in Tae Kwon Do she had discovered an area of interest and physical toughness that she did not even know she had. Her master had helped her to see that her size and manner were tremendous advantages, physically and mentally. She was able to move swiftly and quietly, and she often achieved mental superiority very quickly because opponents tended to too quickly underestimate her skill. Focusing on Tae Kwon Do skills was teaching her discipline, persistence, and respect, and allowing her strengths and proclivities to be optimized. These were important attributes for home and school, attributes that would also serve her well throughout her lifetime. Over the past four years, under the careful and skilled guidance of Master Lee, Kate had been learning how to use these attributes to her advantage, as she worked to master the form.

Kate went on to win the match. Her search for mastery in Tae Kwon Do, though, has really only just begun. Kate is one of those fortunate few who has the potential to become a true master at a demanding sport. However, mastery, even for someone with the mental and physical skills of Kate, does not just happen. Mastery in Tae Kwon Do requires a lifetime of dedication and practice. In fact, it is highly unlikely that Kate will end up becoming a true Tae Kwon Do master—the percentage of students who actually pursue martial arts to the point of real mastery is quite small. However, it is likely that Tae Kwon Do will remain important to Kate and that she will continue to engage in it at some level throughout her adult life.

As originally postulated by the psychoanalyst Erik Erikson, it is generally agreed today that the primary task of the adolescent years is the development of a sense of personal identity. In Erikson's view, the teenager's task is to bring together all of the various and sometimes conflicting facets of their being into a working whole that at once provides continuity with the past and provides focus and direction for the future. According to the educator David Elkind, "This sense of personal identity includes various roles (son or daughter, student, athlete, musician, artist, and so on), various traits and abilities (quiet, outgoing, timid, generous, high strung), as well as the teenager's personal tableau of likes and dislikes, political and social attitudes, religious orientation, and much more."

Adolescence is the period in life in which many, if not most, people acquire the deep interests and master the skills that persist throughout their lives. For example, this is when the truly talented and dedicated athletes are separated from the many who are only of average talent and dedication and when most future artists and performers emerge and begin to truly hone their skills. This is also the age when most future scientists, engineers, historians, mechanics, carpenters, and politicians discover that they possess an aptitude and passion for their chosen fields. Some go on to become professionals; others just become avid amateurs.

Still other adolescents invest long hours in mastering a sport, art form, skill, or subject, only to abandon it later. This, too, is okay. The time invested in mastering a form is never wasted. Even if Kate never practices Tae Kwon Do as an adult, she will have immeasurably gained by her experiences during adolescence. She will have learned what it takes to become accomplished at something, the dedication and self-discipline required for mastery, and this alone will have been well worth the effort. Adolescence, more than any other period of our lives, is a time of alienation, self-doubt, and solitude, a time in our lives when we feel misunderstood and misjudged by everyone. Involvement in free-choice learning experiences, particularly ones that give youth opportunities for successful mastery of challenging skills, is often the single most rewarding and satisfying experience of these years. Testimonials abound of successful professionals who, reflecting back on their careers, attribute their current success to the opportunity to explore and master something of significance during their adolescent years. Adolescence and free-choice learning are natural partners. Free-choice learning is fundamental to the development of a sense of self, essential to the development of a whole, fully functioning adult, and this is often not done alone.

Supportive Mentors

For many adolescents, the only places where they can safely and comfortably explore the adult world, with supportive, effective facilitators present to optimize the circumstances, are free-choice learning experiences. In contrast to the compulsory and sometimes authoritarian worlds of school and home, free-choice learning experiences afford an opportunity to self-select an area of personal interest and competence in which to excel. Much like Ivy, Aaron, Matt, and Kate, if given the opportunity and appropriate support, adolescents can display amazing self-confidence, leadership, and competence when in the appropriate context.

As the testimonials we alluded to earlier show, however, successful professionals also frequently attribute their current success to the guidance of an adult mentor during the critical adolescent years. Free-choice learning experiences provide one of the few opportunities for youth to interact with adults on their own terms, affording adolescents an opportunity to display competence and achieve success, self-confidence, and leadership skills. At this age, despite the effort to push parents away, there is a strong desire to affiliate and connect to other adults as role models and mentors.

Looking back at each of these vignettes, one appreciates that rarely was this free-choice learning done alone. In fact, more often than not, it was facilitated by an effective adult mentor or mentors. Ivy had considerable help from her mom, dad, French teacher, and English teacher to reach her goal. She grew up in the process, learning what it meant to be an adult and to take full responsibility for her life. However, she was aided in this maturation by a supportive educational infrastructure which included her school, friends and family, and myriad parts of the free-choice learning sector. Her mentors helped her to attain the lifelong learning skill of knowing how to tap into the vast reservoir of learning resources, both at home and abroad. Because of this a rich world of opportunity and meaningful learning experiences await her both now and in the future.

Matt also appreciated the mentorship of "Coach." Our conversations with Matt revealed another important set of lessons that he learned from him, ones that Matt probably does not fully appreciate yet. By working all these years with his coach, who by all accounts is a very skilled craftsman, Matt has learned the importance of careful planning and a commitment to excellence and quality. This, too, is knowledge that Matt will be able to use for the rest of his life, both inside and outside the realm of home improvement.

In the case of Kate, there was also very active mentorship. From the outset, Master Lee had helped her to appreciate the strengths she brought to Tae Kwon Do—strength, agility, toughness, persistence, and patience—and encouraged her to use them to her advantage. As she moved through the first few levels of belts easily, Master Lee, sensing her great potential, began to guide her with special attention, training her mentally, sharing wise words from the poets and philosophers, teaching her how to relax and breathe and psychologically how to overcome her opponents, even giving her a book filled with Tae Kwon Do philosophy. He helped her to see that her size and manner were tremendous advantages, physically and mentally, and over the past four years, under the careful and skilled guidance of her master, Kate learned how to use these attributes to her advantage, as she worked to master the form.

Then, there is the case of Aaron. Aaron, too, had mentors, but his mentors were not adults. At this age, it is not only adults who serve as mentors. Although Aaron's dad was exceedingly supportive his *Dungeons and Dragons* activities, Aaron received support for his learning primarily through peers. For many of the needs and explorations of adolescence, peers represent the mentors of choice. Having the right friends is more than a cliché at this age.

Clearly, free-choice learning represents an exceedingly important dimension of learning for the adolescent. Through increasingly self-structured activities, adolescents begin to independently practice and use lifelong learning skills and capabilities, with more and more opportunities to practice and use these skills in the real world. However, adolescence is not the end of the learning process—there is a whole lifetime of learning ahead, and at the next stage young adults are no longer practicing their lifelong learning skills—they are using them daily.

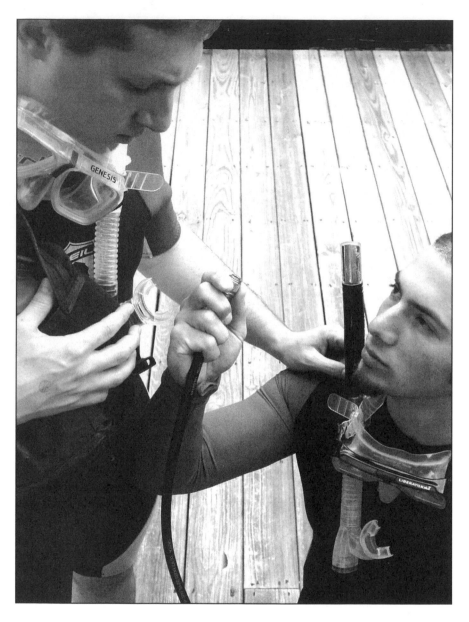

Learning how to dive (Photo by John H. Falk)

CHAPTER 9

NEW ROADS, NEW ADVENTURES: YOUNG ADULTS

I wanted only to try to live in accord with the promptings which came from my true self. Why was that so very difficult?

—Hermann Hesse, *Demian*

K eith had always fancied himself a good athlete. After all, he had been on his high school football team and played intramural sports throughout college. So when a friend suggested that he try mountain biking as a hobby he assumed it would be just like normal bicycle riding, only down a mountain trail—no sweat! But his first effort had been a near disaster. Careening down a hill strewn with boulders and branches, he hit a root and flew head over heels over the top of his bike. He landed in a heap, stuck between a tree and a huge rock outcrop. It was a minor miracle that he didn't do any serious damage to himself. He gingerly dragged his battered body back down the mountain, careful to avoid the hurtling cyclists who kept whizzing past him.

In the months that followed, Keith learned what it took to successfully ride mountain bikes. He discovered the benefits of proper gear and bicycles, and how to maintain both. He learned techniques that allowed him to safely navigate the mountain, which of course in mountain biking is a relative term. And as he started to compete in races, he learned strategies and techniques that allowed him to be competitive. He also discovered that he needed more than strategies and techniques to stay competitive, he needed to train religiously. It was only after more than a year of riding and practicing, in as much of his spare time as he could manage, that Keith began to feel truly competent as a mountain biker.

Free at Last

As the adolescent matures into the young adult, a whole world of learning awaits them—they are no longer just practicing lifelong learning skills, they are living and using them daily. For many young Americans, this is the first time they will live on their own, filling their own refrigerator and paying their own bills. If lucky, these years are filled with both ample discretionary income and substantial leisure time in which to spend that income. At the age of twenty to twenty-five, most young adults can look forward to another sixty or more years of life; in fact, most of their life still lies ahead. And, for perhaps the first time in their lives, these young adults find themselves faced with the decision of how to fill their discretionary time—often a lot of it. For the moment, these fortunate young adults are freed from most of the obligations and responsibilities that plagued them earlier in life such as parental rules and schoolwork. And for a while anyway, they are also free from the types of obligations and responsibilities that will plague them later in adulthood, including children, demanding careers, mortgages, and eventually, aging parents.

For other young adults, the demands of adult life are greater, sooner. Faced with limited financial options, for reasons of birth or circumstance, life for the less economically fortunate can be very demanding. However, for both the affluent and not-so-affluent young adult, free-choice learning represents an important way to build identity, spread one's wings, and generally revel in the freedom of the age. At the same time it provides young adults a way to improve themselves, in some cases allowing them to escape the realities of America's economic and social order. At this stage of life, free-choice learning satisfies two major learning needs that present themselves:

1. Increased opportunities to fill discretionary time, build identity, and begin establishing intimate relationships.

2. A desire to improve oneself, either personally or professionally.

Fast forward ten years, and the young adult's life has changed again. No longer as care-free and unburdened, the thirty-something adult is beginning to experience the overwhelming realities of adult life—maintaining long-lasting relationships, raising children, building careers, and the accompanying financial burdens that often result from these realities. Learning, free-choice learning in particular, becomes a mechanism for dealing with many of the pressures and realities of life, something to look forward to in one's increasingly scarce leisure time, a way to satisfy the other overwhelming learning need at this stage of young adulthood:

3. A desire to relax, connect with family and friends, and find meaning in the midst of the pressures of daily life.

Free-Time/New Experiences

Life at twenty-two is great! What shall I do this evening? What shall I do this weekend? What shall I do with my life? Young adults invest considerable mental and physical energy in deciding how to best take advantage of their newfound freedom. Partying, watching the tube, hanging with friends? Yes, and a surprisingly large number of young adults are also currently choosing to spend their time learning.

Jason had always wanted to travel, to see the world, but there were always things that constrained him—school, parents, and just those internal hesitations and doubts that got in the way. Now, only a week after graduating from Rutgers University, Jason was boarding a plane for South America. He wasn't really sure how long he would be gone, or even exactly where he was heading—though his ticket had him arriving in Lima, Peru. He had told his parents that he would be gone for at least a month or two, but he really did not know. He felt that he was on the cusp of a great adventure and he was very, very excited.

As has been common for hundreds of years, many young adults take time off from education or work to wander the globe and learn about the world. Where once it was considered obligatory for every cultured young man and woman to visit "The Continent," today more exotic lands beckon. It is not that Europe is not a popular destination, clearly it is, but equally popular today are Asia, Australia and the South Pacific, Africa, and South America. In fact, given the ease and limited cost of air travel, no place seems too distant. Few experiences are more educational than experiencing first-hand different people, places, and cultures. Few educational experiences more fully embody the spirit of free-choice learning—learning what you want and need, when you want it, and with whom you choose.

Back on the home front, tens of thousands of young adults are taking classes at community colleges or from community organizations like the YWCA. Enrollment in evening and weekend courses is at an all-time high for this age group. Today's young adults are also far more health and fitness-conscious than any previous generation; consequently gyms and fitness centers are full of young adults working out on evenings and weekends. Also popular among Gen-Xers are extreme sports of all types including mountain climbing, snowboarding, whitewater kayaking, and participating in triathlons. These sports not only require nerve and stamina, they require considerable training and practice. Recall Keith, the friend of one of our sons who tried mountain biking.

Whether learning to ride a mountain bike like Keith or traveling like Jason, young adults are finding it satisfying to engage in free-choice learning. It is an exhilarating period, filled with a seemingly endless string of new opportunities and personal challenges. In a society that artificially extends childhood well into the early twenties, young adulthood for many is the first time in their lives when they live away from home, earn a living, and take full responsibility for their own actions. It is also the period in which many young adults learn to live with another person or persons outside of their immediate family. Young adulthood is the period in their lives when most people first experience true intimacy, establishing relationships designed to be long-lasting.

It is also the time in our lives when most of us finally make the break from our parents, a time of building the personal identity we began creating during adolescence. For building identity is not accomplished merely by the rebellion of adolescence; it is not just a matter of deciding, once and for all, who we are and what we are going to do with ourselves. The search for personal identity is a task that we find ourselves trying to accomplish continuously throughout our lives, a process begun in adolescence but further developed during early adulthood. Carl Jung called this process "individuation"; Abraham Maslow called it "self-actualization." Unlike adolescence, it is the stage in development in which we have achieved the self-confidence and ego-strength, the confidence and self-assurance to really take on the world. Young adults are capable of trying new things, some of which they'll fail at, in a way that would have been devastating only a few short years before. During their twenties, adults eagerly begin new jobs, new social relationships, new interests, and find new things to learn. It is a vibrant and exciting time in life, full of new opportunity and new lessons.

Most of the lessons learned during these years involve skills and abilities not taught in any classroom. It is only in the real world, in truly free-choice learning circumstances, that most of us really learn how to cope with life—how to buy groceries, how to get a job and hang onto it, how to balance a household budget, and how to forge meaningful and hopefully lasting personal relationships. While immersed in this stage of life, time seems forever on our side, optimism abounds, and the world appears to be miraculously designed for people just like us. Despite the euphoria of the time, it is also a period when many young adults are seeking to improve themselves.

Improving Oneself Personally and/or Professionally

Lori had always enjoyed cooking, but for most of her young life had grabbed something quick, having grown up in the world of fast food, microwaves, and convenience. She had worked to put herself through undergraduate and graduate school in accounting and most of the time found it easier not to bother cooking, preferring to eat something quick. But at twenty-five she realized that she now had the time, and the desire, to invest some effort in making good healthy food at home. After all, she was a successful accountant working for a growing firm and, with the exception of tax time, actually had a life. So she did some investigating and discovered that there was an Asian cooking class at the local community college, and she enrolled. She loved it; her teacher was a very interesting Japanese-American woman who not only knew how to cook well, but also understood the Eastern aesthetic about food and was eager to share that approach and philosophy toward food as well. Lori always felt that she left class a little more centered and serene. This free-choice learning experience served as an important anchor in her life—providing both self-improvement and relaxation at the same time.

Not every young adult in America participates equally in the "American Dream." Not all get to enjoy a carefree life of freedom and exploration like Lori. But even for those living in more difficult circumstances, free-choice learning can open up opportunities and foster new perspectives. Particularly for those individuals who have experienced rough times in their lives, free-choice learning represents a way out and provides a view of what a better, more fulfilling life can look like. Through free-choice learning, young adults who have been losers in the formal education system, many now in prisons and in drug rehabilitation programs, can all find new opportunities. There are numerous examples of special programs, all featuring free-choice learning, that demonstrate just how powerful a tool it can be. Here is just one such example.

Two years ago we met Estelle Rogers, a woman who lives in western Massachusetts, where she directs a home for young mothers and abused women. Although the women in her program range in age from fifteen to twenty-five, most are in their late teens and early twenties. The vast majority of the women in her home are high school drop-outs, so one of the important programs offered by her small not-for-profit organization is the opportunity to earn a General Education Degree (GED). Not being a professional educator, she assumed that the standard GED curriculum would be just what was required. Although the program seemed designed with the best of intentions, Estelle realized a few years ago—right before meeting us, in fact—that the program was just not working. The women enrolled seemed unmotivated to learn and were dropping out of the program, even though they were highly motivated to improve their lot in life.

Then Estelle attended an area workshop where Lynn was speaking, describing the elements of free-choice learning and the implications these elements have for the design of education programs. Estelle had a revelation! The GED program she was using was designed to recreate a standard high school situation, complete with traditional lesson plans, homework, and tests. Unfortunately, this was exactly the kind of situation that most of the women in her program had already failed in, at least once. She realized that teaching these young women as if they were in a traditional school classroom, where the content was out of context and the lessons were presented as if all of the learners were identical clones, was a waste of everyone's time. The women were not progressing, and worst of all, the program was all about getting the GED, not about how the women would use the GED to improve their futures. She realized in its current one-size-fits-all design, it was not really helping the women to develop personal learning goals and action plans for accomplishing these goals.

Estelle returned to her community, eager to incorporate some of the free-choice learning principles into the GED program she was offering. When we talked to her later, Estelle enthusiastically described what had happened when she did so. She was able to transform her traditional GED program into a unique one, with tailor-made personal learning programs for each individual participating. Each woman took the lead in negotiating her own curriculum, a curriculum based upon her own personal interests and future goals. According to Estelle, this free-choice approach was working wonders, allowing previously daunted learners to accomplish their immediate goal of fulfilling the GED requirements, while also creating a personalized course of study that helped each woman work toward her own unique future goals.

It stands to reason that choice and control over learning make a difference for these learners, who in most cases, are exactly the individuals who have gone through life with the fewest choices and least control over their lives. This is the first time for many of these women, as well as other people in similar programs we know of, when they have actually felt fully in control of their lives. Providing opportunities to experience meaningful freedom in learning not only results in short-term learning success, it models how to live the rest of one's life as well.

Relaxing, Connecting, and Finding Meaning

Feeling in control is great, but by the age of thirty to thirty-nine, many adults aren't quite sure who is in control. Are they in control, or are the events around them in control? By the age of thirty most Americans are settled into a comfortable routine. Most have found a significant other, have a steady job, live in a permanent residence, and typically have started a family. Not so very long ago, a thirty-year-old was approaching the end of his or her expected life. Not so today—the bulk of an individual's life extends far beyond the age of thirty. But sitting in the middle of your thirties, it's sometimes hard to see anything but the middle—endlessly stretching out to infinity. An infinity of workdays, mortgage payments, soccer games, ballet lessons, business functions, school functions, church functions, function functions. Each day filled with much the same needs and responsibilities as the day before. Even in this seeming morass of sameness, opportunities for free-choice learning exist, and often flourish. For most, this stage of life is about building a career and/or caring for and raising a family. These are anything but carefree years. Arguably, these can be the most stressful years of an individual's life, in large part because of the myriad problems, issues, and decisions that need to be made daily. Free time will never be in shorter supply. The demands of job and family eat at discretionary time from both ends, leaving the individual feeling pressed and stressed. However, it is in coping with the demands of these day-to-day tasks that free-choice learning emerges as important.

It is through free-choice learning that today's young adults strive to keep themselves one step ahead of a rapidly changing workplace. Although employers may offer on-the-job training, keeping current and marketable demands skills and abilities most employers cannot or will not provide. Individuals are taking courses in Spanish, investment, and advanced computer-aided design; or just as often downloading materials from the Internet and teaching themselves. For others, this period of life is not about preparing for a different career, but insuring that one's current career is as successful as it can possibly be. Many thirty-year-olds spend long hours at work, building credibility and establishing their careers. Americans spend more hours working than any other first world country, and a huge chunk of the hours logged by young adults are invested in improving their skills and advancing their knowledge. Although job related, much of the learning going on is discretionary rather than obligatory, more for personal satisfaction than professional necessity.

Not all free-choice learning time, though, is invested in work. It is also through free-choice learning that many adults, isolated from the social supports of earlier years, seek and find information on relationships and child-rearing practices. Through books, courses at hospitals and Ys, and through word-of-mouth from friends and family, young adults strive to learn the intricacies of maintaining long-term relationships, preparing formula, developing schedules, and most importantly, providing a healthy and sustaining learning environment for themselves and their children.

In terms of parenting, whole new genres of stores, with whole sections on age-appropriate toys, books, and how-to books for parents, have developed that cater to the needs of young parents. There are materials designed for newborns, two-month-olds, six-month-olds, twelve-month-olds, and toddlers; each age with different challenges, each age requiring new knowledge and understanding on the part of the parent.

Children themselves offer new opportunities for learning, many unavailable since childhood. Children become the "ticket" for going to zoos, aquariums, and museums. They are excuses for going to the circus, learning magic tricks, and how to make rice crispy squares. As described in previous chapters, our own children prompted an exploration of the foods, customs, and dress of different countries. Our children were also what prompted us to hang out at Civil War battlefields and make a weekly visit to the public library. All of these child-driven experiences have great benefits for children, but they also have numerous spin-off benefits for the parents as well. As long as you're at the library, you might as well pick up a book for yourself. As long as you're bothering to explore dinosaurs with your child, you might as well learn something about them too, and as long as you're doing an art project with your child, it is fun to splash around and explore the paints yourself. Children represent a wonderful vehicle for facilitating lifelong learning, for parents as well as for the children themselves.

But thirty-year-olds don't need children to engage in fun, enjoyable free-choice learning experiences. One of the more interesting phenomena of recent years has been the exponential growth in the popularity of reenactments. There are reenactments of Old West pioneer experiences, of Revolutionary War soldiers, and the biggest by far are reenactments of American Civil War battles and life. On a recent summer afternoon, eight to ten thousand reenactors from all over the country spent three days restaging the First Battle of Manassas/Bull Run near Leesburg, Virginia. This was the 140th anniversary of the first major battle of the Civil War. Northern and Southern troops, all decked out in period woolen suits and sporting period muskets, lined up against each other. Teams of horses pulling caissons and period cannons were directed to opposing hills; the cannons detached, loaded, and aimed. Then, probably not unlike that day in 1861, all hell broke loose. The sounds of cannon and muskets were deafening; smoke totally filled the air. And the thousands of spectators, again not unlike that day 140 years earlier, gasped.

One of the reenactors that day was Thomas Holley. Weekdays, 36-year-old Thomas is a contractor working in Columbia, Maryland. Most weekends, spring through fall, he is a Captain in the Union Army, a member of the Patapsco Guards, a group of Howard County (Maryland)-area reenactors who are modeled on the real-life Union army unit that guarded the area's key railroad bridges and terminals during the war. During the Manassas/Bull Run reenactment, Thomas joined a larger Union regiment. There amidst the melee of screaming men, he charged down the slope toward the waiting Confederate lines. Thomas explained to us that he enjoys reenacting because it gives him a hands-on understanding of what life was like during this period of history. Always fascinated by the events of the Civil War, reenacting provides a richness of detail and facts that he could never get just by reading books or visiting museums. Some reenactors, in fact, focus on communicating their knowledge to others. Encampments of reenactors have become regular features at most Civil War battlefields, and battlefield visitors are invited to wander into camp and chat with the men and women there to learn more about the war and the people who fought in it. This, according to Thomas, is what really makes the experience worthwhile: "These days I really live for the opportunity to share my experiences with others, particularly children. To see the look of awe and wonder on their faces as my fellow troops and I describe how we live and the hardships we face in order to save the nation. That is wonderful beyond description."

For most young adults, the escape from the day-to-day is more ephemeral. Once a year, getting away, spending time away from children, job, and home. Many young adults look forward to these opportunities to be, in the words of one couple we met, "a real adult, all by ourselves." On a recent diving trip to Little Cayman Island, we met a couple in their thirties who try to take a diving trip by themselves at least once a year. Over the course of the week we were there, we spent several days diving together during the day and chatting with them in the evening. Their two young children were safely ensconced with the grandparents for the week, while Bill and Maggie Mangone were enjoying learning about the underwater world, the above-ground life of Little Cayman, and the lives of the residents and visitors to this small, lovely Caribbean island. Bill by profession is an insurance adjuster and Maggie a teacher, but for this week, they were both just divers. Both had been diving for years but in recent years diving had developed into a real passion. Both Bill and Maggie would conclude every dive by pouring over their field guides and writing in their dive logs, noting all the different species of fish, coral, and invertebrates they had seen.

Although still novices at the sea life identification game, they clearly enjoyed the effort. We felt a great affinity for them, as we also took great delight in trying to identify sea creatures we saw while diving. We spent many hours talking together about what we had seen on our dives, comparing notes, and looking at our collective store of field guides. On one particularly memorable dive, all four of us saw a very large sea turtle swimming near the top of the reef. Once back on the surface, we quickly agreed that it had been a hawksbill turtle. What then ensued was a lengthy discussion about sea turtle biology and conservation. It turned out that Bill was quite knowledgeable about the subject, having volunteered in a sea turtle conservation effort a few years back. This effort was what amounted to a sea turtle "emergency strike force." As soon as a new brood of sea turtles hatched out, a whole group of volunteers would descend on the beach and help keep predators, including humans, from picking off the defenseless baby turtles. The goal was to increase the number of young turtles that survived that first vulnerable stage in their life, and in the process dramatically bolster their chances of survival. The conversation spilled off the boat, into the bar, and didn't conclude until late that evening when everyone finally turned in for the night.

As a consequence of a week's fabulous diving and numerous engaging conversations with Bill and Maggie and several other interesting people we met that week, we left Little Cayman physically, spiritually, and intellectually enriched. We suspect that Bill and Maggie returned home equally charged up and ready to once again immerse themselves in their normal routine of work and family. Despite the challenges that life in our thirties presents, free-choice learning experiences, like diving and reenactments, provide many, if not most, young adults with a valuable and desperately needed release from the stresses and strains of daily life. Though it is sometimes hard to see from the vantage point of one's mid-thirties, life does change as one ages, and not always for the worse, as our society likes to portray.

Learning about birds (Photo by Leslie Kim, Stanford Alumni Association)

CHAPTER 10

WALKING THE CREST, AVOIDING THE RUTS: MIDDLE AGE ADULTS

The adult with a capacity for true maturity is one who has grown out of childhood without losing childhood's best traits... Ideally these are incorporated into a new pattern of development dominated by adult stability, wisdom, knowledge, sensitivity to other people, responsibility, strength and purpose.
—Joseph Stone and Joseph Church, *Adulthood*

Wiley was a real uncle—in fact, he liked the family so much that he married into it not once but twice!" Janette excitedly told her mother after visiting the cemetery to investigate a long-time question about the family. Wiley H. Bates was the founder of Bates High School, the first black high school in Annapolis. The family had always called him "Uncle Wiley" and a lively debate had broken out over whether he was really a relative. Janette had just discovered that he was buried with his two wives, two great aunts in her maternal line, making him clearly a relative, twice blessed. In 1998 Janette Hill was living in Pasadena, Maryland, recovering from intestinal cancer, after leading a successful career as a contracts manager. She had time on her hands during the long recovery period and her doctors encouraged her to do things she liked that would relieve stress. She decided to work on her family genealogy, spurred on by the question that had plagued the family for years—was Wiley Bates a relative or a dear friend who had earned the title "uncle"?

After solving this mystery, Janette's curiosity about her family history was piqued and a friend suggested she go to the state archives to look at the census records of family members. From these simple beginnings Janette began her own journey of lifelong learning, a journey that has led to a very personal understanding of her own heritage and the development of skills as a respected and dedicated historian.

Crossroads

As we turn forty, many of us think back wistfully to the carefree days of our twenties. Middle age is a challenging time for many—it is certainly no cliché to talk about the mid-life crisis. Between the ages of forty and fifty, plus or minus a few years on both ends, people find themselves at one of two points. They are either satisfied, comfortable with job and home life, but questioning how to extend and deepen the meaning of these experiences, or very dissatisfied and uncomfortable with job and/or home and eager to explore alternatives. Either way, the key to avoiding malaise is the realization that there is still a need in one's life to explore, learn, and grow. And to a great extent, the opportunities for this kind of exploration, learning, and growth exist through the vehicle of free-choice learning. For whether in "crisis" mode or not, the middle-aged adult comes to appreciate that maturation is not a goal, but a process; middle age not a destination, but just another stop along the learning journey of life.

Arguably, like the thirties, these can be among the most stressful years of an individual's life, in large part because of the number and complexity of problems, issues, and decisions that are faced daily. Free time is often in short supply. The demands of job, children, and aging parents leave the individual feeling stressed, with little or no free time. However, this is also a life stage when many people find that free-choice learning provides exactly the comfort and release they need.

The middle-age years can be remarkable years for learning, both in solitude and with friends or family. After the exploration of the twenties and the busyness of the thirties, it is at this stage that many adults choose a hobby to focus on, often alone. As children get older and become capable of higher levels of learning, the opportunities for spending quality family time with children and spouses or partners at museums, zoos, aquariums, and historic sites expand, as do opportunities for meaningful co-investigations into science, history, or the arts.

And at this age, necessity is often a source of learning. For example, it is during this period of life that most people find themselves dealing with the aging of their own parents and appreciating their own mortality. These realities can lead to learning about assisted living options, Alzheimer's disease, and cataracts, as well as learning about investing and financial planning. These are also times that can lead to discovering previously unknown facts about one's family relationships and history.

In addition to fulfilling one's curiosity in a weekend event or attempting to solve an immediate life challenge, the middle years are also notable as the time when many adults have the patience and commitment necessary for truly mastering a topic. The middle-aged years are also the time when many individuals find the patience and commitment necessary to become a mentor for others wanting to learn what they know. Few things in life are as rewarding as completing the learning cycle and supporting the learning needs of another. Thus, free-choice learning at this stage is a mechanism for fulfilling three learning needs:

1. a desire, and increasingly the time, to pursue hobbies and continue learning in personally meaningful ways;

2. a desire to achieve mastery; and

3. a desire to become a mentor and share what one knows with others.

Continuing Learning

While on a business trip recently in Los Angeles, we met a Canadian couple, Jessica and Christopher Aldrich, who run their own successful business making personalized pop-up greeting cards. They, too, were in Los Angeles on a business trip. Although they were attending a trade show, they found time to visit the Natural History Museum of Los Angeles County and the California Science Center in order to indulge their personal interests in dinosaurs and geology. Jessica commented: "We travel quite a bit and whenever we are in a new place we try to visit the museums and other attractions there to learn something about the place. Neither of us enjoyed school much and thought for many years that we were just not the intellectual type, but as we have matured and are not having to work as hard on the day-to-day activities of our business we find ourselves turning more and more to learning. It is satisfying and rewarding and something we enjoy doing together."

Indeed, despite the stresses and strains of the middle adult years, learning can and does for most provide a much-needed tonic from the hectic pace of life. Free-choice learning takes many guises and many people achieve immeasurable satisfaction in doing so. However, whether reexamining your professional life, expanding your personal horizons, or dealing with the needs of aging parents, the availability of learning resources today seems boundless. Take our friend Janette described earlier in the chapter. When she wanted to investigate her family genealogy she was able to tap into the resources of the state archives; there were also pamphlets provided by the local, state, and federal government, magazines, and even Web sites specifically designed to assist individuals in their research. If she was looking for assistance, she could have taken a genealogy course at her local community college or from the local historical society. Libraries and bookstores have shelves full of books promising to help with this, or for that matter any other conceivable life-expanding effort. And in the age of the Internet, access to vast quantities of information, including the names and addresses of virtually anyone in the world, are but a few keystrokes away.

The mechanisms for self-expression are almost as numerous as there are selves. Sometimes the effort is individual and solitary, like the man who carves water fowl all by himself down in his basement every weekend, or the woman who does needlepoint in front of the television every night. Increasingly, though, others facilitate our efforts at self-expression. As we have suggested throughout this book, a vast array of organizations are even beginning to cater to such learning interests and needs, appreciating the growing number of adults eager and willing to engage in free-choice learning.

Adults at this stage have developed a very different perspective on life than childhood learners, a perspective that influences what, how, where, when, and why they choose to learn. Recognizing this, noted adult educator Malcolm Knowles coined the term "andragogy" to describe the art and science of teaching adults, in contrast with the term "pedagogy," which refers to the art and science of teaching children. Interestingly, Knowles noted at the time that in many people's minds (including creators of dictionaries), pedagogy is defined as the art and science of teaching, and even in books on adult education, one can find references to "the pedagogy of adult education" without any concern for the contradiction in terms. In Knowles' estimation, "the main reason why adult education has not achieved the impact on our civilization of which it is capable is that most teachers of adults have only known how to teach adults as if they were children."

Knowles' principles for adult learning, which have been added to and refined by him and others since the 1970s include:

1. Adults *want* and *need* to learn.

2. For adult learning to be meaningful, learners need to have a major role in defining their own learning goals, based on individual needs, interests, and values, at their own pace and in their own way.

3. Adults require learning environments/situations in which their own knowledge and experience is valued and utilized—one-way transmission of information by an "expert" or "teacher" is of less value than a two-way dialogue, in which adults can share and actively use their own knowledge and experience.

As a society we have made some progress in this arena. Demonstrating the importance of adult learning, the Fifth International Conference on Adult Education was held in 1997 in Hamburg under the auspices of UNESCO. Ten themes were identified at the meeting reflecting the broad and complex spectrum of adult learning. Participants suggested that learning at this stage provides an essential opportunity for learners to participate in all cultural institutions, mass media, and new technologies to establish effective interactive communication and build understanding and cooperation between peoples and cultures. They called for a "new vision of adult learning which is both holistic, embracing all aspects of life, and cross-sectoral, to include all areas of cultural, social and economic activity." A couple of years later, in honor of the fiftieth anniversary of UNESCO, the United Nations inaugurated a worldwide learning initiative aimed at people over the age of fifty years.

In some cases people invest significant chunks of their time and resources to master new skills and knowledge in appropriate social, cultural, and physical contexts. In fact we would add a fourth principle to Knowles' adult learning principles: Adults are less interested in sitting in a classroom to learn, and seem to intuitively understand that meaningful learning takes place in appropriate social, cultural, and physical contexts. For example, we recently read about a couple, not farmers but urban organic gardeners, who actually journeyed to northern Portugal through an organization called Willing Workers on Organic Farms (WWOOF) in order to learn more about their gardening passion. In exchange for free room and board and some new knowledge about organic farming, they agreed to work six hours a day, five days a week! As the husband commented upon leaving for the trip, "My wife and I have long had a vague dream of one day moving to the country to grow our own food. We know farming is hard work. We are about to discover just how hard."

Over the course of the week they pulled brambles, built steps, weeded vegetable beds, tended goats, cleaned out goat pens, scythed a field, sowed seeds (oat and lupine), dug trenches, and processed food. Certainly, to master the techniques they would need to stay much longer than a week, but in the course of the week they did further develop their skills in gardening and farming. They left Portugal with a richer feeling for what it is like to live off the land, entwined in the lives of animals, plants, and a community of people devoted to the land and its bounty.

And this past spring, Lynn, accompanied by her mother, spent two weeks on an educational tour of Southern France, sponsored by a wonderful French store in Frederick, Maryland. Visiting artists' studios, chateaus, and of course sampling the local food and wine, a group of a dozen eager "learners" toured, shopped, and explored their way through Provence. Led by two knowledgeable and fluent guides who provided running commentary and translation during the trip, all came away feeling refreshed and enriched. It was a wonderful opportunity to learn about another culture and also provided a rich way for Lynn and her mother to interact and learn together as adults.

Take, for example, our Annapolis friend quoted at the top of this chapter. Her effort to become knowledgeable about her family's heritage, although originally prompted by a doctor's order to find something to relieve stress, was primarily driven by an internal desire to understand her genealogy. Janette had the luxury of recuperation time on her hands, but even those adults with busy and challenging lives and little free time have discovered that their own personal needs and potential are worth nurturing. Thus, it is not surprising to discover that many, if not most, adults strive to carve out some small piece of their life for personal growth and development; a process that almost always includes free-choice learning.

And the middle years of adulthood often bring us to major crossroads. Here, too, free-choice learning can play a major role since it is often deeply personal with a strong spiritual component. For example, a couple we know in Virginia, the Foxes, recently described their motivation for participating in a weekly church class:

> Humans have a great desire for understanding why things happen in their lives and in the world, how things came to be, and what lies ahead in the future. As Christians, we seek that understanding as well, and find it through classes at our church. By studying the Bible alone, or within groups, we gain new perspectives. Leadership by those more mature in their study present new and different insights. Through reading on our own and personal contemplation we develop a greater personal understanding. We gain a clearer insight and, by interacting with others, find a shared and collective meaning as we discuss God's plan of salvation for the world. Just as we change and go through phases of our lives mentally and physically, so we also grow and mature spiritually. Frequently, we study sections of the Bible that we have explored many times before, but because we are at a different place in our individual life or within the life of our church community, the stories find new meaning and application.

We also recently met a Lakota Indian elder who teaches at a Native American college in the West. As a professor of Lakota Studies, he has a number of Caucasian students each year, primarily middle-aged women, interested in learning more about native traditions and philosophy. They often leave their homes and families to live on the reservation for the duration of the course, desiring to learn more about harmony, balance, and connectedness, all beliefs sacred to the Lakota people. Learning about the Lakota way of living provides great satisfaction for these students and they return to their twenty-first century city lives different—culturally and spiritually. However, taking a course on a reservation, even a long course, will not, in itself, make you harmonious, balanced, and connected. These things take more effort, and more time.

Achieving Personal Mastery

Maybe it's just a fantasy. Sometimes I see myself greeting guests on the sunny patio of a guesthouse on a hillside with grapevines everywhere. Or perhaps it's my son's complete fascination with the world of ancient Rome that has struck a chord in me. Or it could be a lifelong interest in learning foreign languages. But whatever the reason, I'm determined to learn Italian! I'm now in my third semester of college Italian at the local community college to learn the grammar, and I meet once a week with a native Italian-speaking tutor to practice speaking. It's slow going. To really learn to speak a language fluently, I think you have to hear it all the time. So although I can do fine in a written situation where I can methodically put a sentence or a paragraph together, speaking is a lot harder.

And understanding when a native speaker starts to rattle off a story to me, it is still quite daunting! But every once in a while, while sipping a cappuccino during my meeting with my tutor, Francesca, at a little Italian cafe in Annapolis, I realize that for a few precious moments, I haven't been translating what she's been saying to me word for word in my head. I have simply *understood* her and responded. Then I realize that I really have made progress and learned something. Who knows, maybe one day I *will* greet guests on my sunny Tuscan terrace on a hillside, glass of wine in hand, grapevines blossoming, living part of my life in Italian!

Free-choice learning for many middle age adults involves dabbling in a number of topics, but some people develop considerable skills and knowledge through their free-choice learning pursuits for no other reason than personal fulfillment and satisfaction. Our friend's effort to become fluent in Italian is not motivated by job or family necessity, but by an internal drive to speak Italian well. Despite its busyness, middle age is also a time in life when many people eke out time to seriously explore one or several topics of interest in depth, what we used to call hobbies. Hobbies include the more traditional manual arts like gardening, knitting, and woodworking, but also myriad others such as genealogy or homeopathic medicine, even the collection of vintage toasters. (At the Toaster Collectors Association convention held in Branson, Missouri, August 24–25, 2001, a rare 1929 Mattatuck model sold for $3,000. Toaster collectors suggest that it is a great way to learn about the history of electricity in homes.) A recent *Washington Post* article suggested that there are 100-plus listings in the D.C. metropolitan area for home-related craft classes. As a research psychologist suggested in that article: "Most of my time I spend very cerebrally—I think, I read, I write. So the past several years, I've really enjoyed doing things that relate to the creative side of me. I'm striving for more balance, rather than working all the time." Although some folks are satisfied with making their hobbies a superficial part of their lives, others stop at nothing short of complete dedication to their field and often develop considerable skills and knowledge through their free-choice learning pursuits.

In the middle years of life, achieving personal mastery is hard work. For example, unlike the nearly effortless process involved in an infant mastering her native language, developing mastery of a foreign language at fifty years of age requires years of hard work. Remember the phrase, "success is 5 percent inspiration and 95 percent perspiration!" Mastering something requires some basic skill, competency, and aptitude in an area, but on top of that, mastery involves lots of commitment, hard work, and diligence. Talk to any skilled dancer, musician, scholar, or seamstress, and what you will hear about are the years of dedication and practice required, in addition to the basic fundamental talent. For example, unlike his colleague Gene Kelly, who was a natural athletic dancer, Fred Astaire apparently spent years practicing and perfecting his dancing style. We also recently heard a story on National Public Radio about a world-renowned opera baritone who practiced every day for years because he lacked innate abilities and range. Although mastery requires dedication and practice, the rewards are among life's greatest. If people are fortunate, they will master one or two skills or domains of knowledge over the course of a lifetime.

In addition to a great deal of practice to develop competence and skills in the chosen discipline, personal mastery also requires spiritual growth and approaching one's life as a creative work—personal mastery becomes a discipline in and of itself. Personal mastery at this level has two components: (1) vision—the continual clarification of what is important and where the path is; and (2) reality—the clear sense of where one is now. The juxtaposition of vision (what one is striving for) and a clear picture of current reality (where one is, relative to where one wants to be) are the zone Peter Senge referred to as "creative tension." The essence of personal mastery involves learning how to generate and sustain creative tension in one's life.

"Learning" in this context does not mean acquiring more information, but expanding the ability to produce the results one desires. It is the ultimate lifelong generative learning apex. People with a high level of personal mastery share several characteristics. They have a special sense of purpose that lies behind their visions and goals. Their vision is a calling rather than a mere task. They also live in a continual state of learning. In a sense they never arrive at mastery—because personal mastery is not something that you possess. It is not a product, but a process and a lifelong discipline.

Personal mastery is also rarely a solitary task. Although at one level it is all about individual proficiency and excellence, it often involves a period of time under the guidance of a skilled facilitator. Our friend has a native Italian-speaking tutor with whom she practices her spoken Italian. The couple who went to northern Portugal did so in order to work side-be-side with organic farmers. Social psychologists, building on the Russian psychologist Vygotsky's ideas about the role social interaction plays in learning that we discussed in chapter 5, have extended his ideas to suggest that all learning occurs within a context they call a "community of learners" or "communities of practice." Throughout human history, the primary means of sharing knowledge in a community of practice has been by spending time in an apprenticeship situation with a master or masters engaged in real, ongoing activity. Such apprenticeships were once a common feature of all enterprise, whether it was child rearing, farming, hunting, or some type of trade. Today, we rarely think about apprenticeships in all learning situations, but they remain a remarkably effective way to transmit knowledge and are the primary mechanism by which a person can acquire knowledge and skills in an area.

Mentoring

Although initially spurred on by idle curiosity and the need to fill her time, Janette's odyssey into African-American history (the vignette described at the beginning of this chapter) became a goal unto itself. Once Janette was well again, she decided not to return to her previous high-stress job and instead decided to see if it would be possible to turn this passionate avocation into a satisfying and productive vocation. She now conducts research at the State Archives, working with local archaeologists and historians, creating plays, performances, and presentations about the African-American experience in Annapolis and elsewhere in Maryland. Today, Janette is considered one of the leading authorities on African-American history in Maryland, but she did not achieve this mastery all by herself.

Janette says she could not have achieved personal mastery without the aid and support of what she describes as her three "angels." The first angel was a retired state archivist. When Janette started showing up day after day at the state archives, it became clear that this was no longer someone trying to work on their personal genealogy, but someone who was on a personal quest to understand the African-American experience in Annapolis and Maryland. The archivists working at the state archives realized that Janette's needs had surpassed their expertise so they suggested she call a former state archivist. They were sure that this person could help Janette. After all, this retired archivist had been the person who had assisted Alex Haley in his research for *Roots*.

Janette's second angel was more unusual. Janette was befriended and mentored by a white man descended from slave owners, who for many years had been seeking the right person to pass along the information and artifacts he held about the African slaves on his family's plantation. Her third angel was a fellow African-American historian who took her under her wing and ultimately became her partner in her research efforts. These three individuals perceived Janette as committed and worthy enough to take under their wing and mentor. As she described it to us, "My interest and pursuit of knowledge in this area was much easier because of these three 'Angels.' They took an interest in my learning and helped me pursue it further. After beginning to 'work' with the three of them, other historians started contacting me also and I learned to ask [for information]. I sought out old families descended from slave owners who had maintained their family history and saved the information. Many had held onto these documents for many years but did not know how to share them because blacks often did not want the information shared by Europeans. I became 'The Hope' in order to share what they had saved." And in turn, Janette has become a mentor to others. In fact, rumor has it that she is starting to mentor her ten-year-old daughter to carry on the family tradition of keeping and making history.

In addition to their own learning, mature persons have a sincere desire to be productive and to pass their knowledge and sense of responsibility on to others. Teaching or mentoring provides an important outlet for this desire. We recently ran into a couple who offer nature photography workshops for amateur photographers. Avid amateur photographers themselves, they do not make their living as photographers, nor for that matter do they earn their primary living running workshops. However, they have found that they enjoy not only the teaching, but also the opportunity to share their knowledge of photography and nature with others. It is worth the effort to offer these free-choice learning workshops for a very nominal fee for the pure satisfaction of passing along their passion and skill in photography. They also told us that the mix of adults, young and old, who sign up for their workshops, running anywhere from a long weekend to a week, boggles the mind. There are professionals and blue collar workers, executives and secretaries—all united by a joint love of photography and nature. Over the years, their former and current students have formed an extended family, not only sharing cards and e-mails, but getting together for parties and the sharing of life events.

Although once a topic little studied, today mentoring is quite a hot topic, particularly within the business world. In the late 1970s a provocative article, "Much Ado about Mentors," appeared in the *Harvard Business Review*. The author reported that business executives who had mentors earned more money at an earlier age and were happier with their career progress. He also reported that mentoring was on the upswing. All of a sudden, mentoring became the new business solution, the panacea to all that ailed American business. Twenty years and considerable research later, mentoring is no longer considered the "magic bullet" for what ails business. However, few would argue with the assertion that significant benefits can accrue for both the mentor and the protégé. According to one recent article by Matelic, the benefits for the mentor include the opportunity to:

- guide and influence other people;

- develop a base of technical support, a valuable resource for completing routine projects and encouraging innovation and creative problem solving;

- gain a sense of satisfaction, confirmation, and rejuvenation, which can be essential to one's well-being and continued professional and personal growth.

However, as much as anything, being a mentor is part of the process of being a master. The final stage of the process of mastering an area of expertise is the desire to pass those skills and expertise along to the next potential master. This seems to be a hardwired trait in us, since this need, and the satisfaction it produces, occurs in all peoples and in all societies. Sharing one's knowledge with others is part of what it means to be human.

This sharing need not be part of a structured "mentorship." Much of the learning that adults engage in is fostered by informal conversations with friends, family, colleagues, even chance acquaintances. On another business trip, this time to Hawaii, we met a middle-aged man pursuing a career change. He was interested in establishing his own business and when he heard that we had established a successful not-for-profit organization, he eagerly engaged us in conversation, intent on gleaning everything he could about how to accomplish his dream. To date, he had done much of his research on the Internet and at the library, but now he was ready to start asking real questions, questions that were best answered by those who had already journeyed to where he thought he wanted to go.

This type of exploration can lead to wonderful results. Similar to the gentleman from Hawaii, we have a good friend in Frederick, Maryland, an artist and a former French teacher, who was also exploring a career change a few years ago. She wanted to combine her interests in France, traveling, art, and teaching, with a long-held desire to open a retail store. Like the man in Hawaii, she spent time on the Internet and at the library, and wrote away for free government brochures. Ultimately, she spent considerable time talking to successful boutique retailers. She attributes these informal conversations to being the ultimate catalyst that emboldened her, at the age of forty-five, to make the leap into becoming an entrepreneur. She found a site in a small shopping district in Frederick, Maryland, and established a retail store selling beautiful hand-crafted French items. In addition she offers educational trips to France; you may remember Lynn and her mother participated in one. Her store and the travel business have become a great success, and three years later, it shows no signs of slowing down.

The human learning cycle of exploration, guidance by a master, the development of mastery, followed by the new master helping to guide the exploration and skill-building of new individuals, has persisted for thousands if not millions of years, and will continue as long as there are perceived learning needs and wisdom to share. Personal learning and mastery are not something that you possess but, like maturation itself, a lifelong developmental process—a process that continues on into old age.

Learning on a study tour in Thailand (Photo by Kevin Lemons, Stanford Alumni Association)

CHAPTER 11

THE LEARNING JOURNEY COMES FULL CIRCLE: OLDER ADULTS

The increase in the life span and in the number of our senior citizens presents this Nation with increased opportunities. . . . It is not enough for a great nation merely to have added years to life—our objective must be to add new life to those years.

—John F. Kennedy, Special Address to Congress

Last February a good friend of ours, Mary Chapman, retired after a lifetime of hard work as a medical technologist. It has been exciting to watch her develop over the last year as she chooses, perhaps for the first time in her life, how to spend her time in satisfying and personally meaningful ways. For Mary was a mother and wife in the 1950s and 1960s, dedicated to her family. She successfully raised five children, the youngest quite single-handedly after her marriage ended in divorce. There was never quite enough money or time to live extravagantly, and it was not even clear to Mary when she retired at age sixty-eight whether she would be able to make ends meet during retirement.

So it has been a year of exploration and challenge. In a way that had not happened since adolescence, Mary was asking herself questions like, "What do I want to do with my life?" Unlike adolescence, though, she was also asking questions like, "How should I spend my leisure time? Do I need to get another job? Should I sell my home and move into a smaller place? What kinds of hobbies do I want to pursue?" All of these are questions that Mary has explored over the past year as she has assumed a whole new set of responsibilities. As a result, she has been trying new foods and eating in a style more to her preference than what she served her family for years. She even grinds her own coffee beans each day! A few years back her children bought her a computer so that she could keep in touch by e-mail, and her computer has now become a useful tool for her personal learning and exploration. She now purchases her airline tickets online when she goes to visit her grandchildren in Wisconsin and Maryland.

A highlight for her was participating in her first Elderhostel program in Maryland. A gift from one of her daughters to commemorate her retirement, it was a wonderful experience with many dimensions—social, personal, and physical. The group of twelve seniors and a facilitator visited the Naval Academy and historic houses, learned about colonial military history, architecture, lifestyles, and much more. They visited the historic eighteenth-century Carroll House, participated in a living history program, and heard a presentation at the Banneker-Douglas Museum about African-American history in Annapolis. Mary's group literally walked all over Annapolis. Mary now knows more about Annapolis's history specifically, and colonial history in general, than most of the residents of Annapolis, and certainly more than any of her friends or relatives. Here's what Mary herself had to say about this program:

> I had always disliked history, partly because Nan [Mary's mother] always told Lillie [Mary's sister] and me how much she hated it. Being raised on British and European history, it was *old* and *dry* and seemed to have no purpose to me. It was just a series of dates and events that I memorized rote fashion and promptly forgot as soon as I could, mostly because it went back thousands of years. It influenced my interest so much that I did not like historical novels or movies. However, after going to the Elderhostel program, maybe because the period was so much shorter, or the interesting way the information was presented, it seemed to have so much more cohesion. Before, history was kind of like a fairy story, but now I could see the places and saw how, and more importantly why, the events took place. I suppose enjoying math and science as I do, there has to be a logical system to everything, and somehow the Elderhostel program gave sense to the sequence of events.

The Elderhostel experience was so positive, Mary is eager to participate in another program. The wonderful thing about Elderhostel is that children can attend as well, as long as they are accompanied by a true senior citizen. So Mary and her daughter are planning an Elderhostel trip together, which will result in rich multigenerational learning as well as special quality time together.

Mary's explorations, though, are not limited to new foods and new ventures into colonial history. She needs to decide where she might work part-time in order to pick up a modest amount of additional income, for she has discovered that in fact, she can not live entirely on her pension. Although she spent years working as a medical technologist in hospitals, she is seriously considering another type of job. For years, she has been a master seamstress. For example, she made a senior prom dress for one of her granddaughters, wedding and bride dresses for three daughters, and in the past made all of her children's and her own clothes. One thought that has crossed her mind is to work in a fabric store, blending her avocation with a part-time vocation. She loves fabrics and notions, and this would be a wonderful way to get paid to do something she really enjoys and does well—another master passing along her passion and skills. Once she solves this problem, there are still questions about finance, real estate, and much more for her to explore and learn about! One thing is clear—her retirement has certainly not been boring.

The Senior Years

Yes, being sixty or seventy was old once! But as Mary's situation demonstrates, today, as life spans push beyond 100 years, sixty years is but the beginning of a new life stage, a stage that for many is filled with larger amounts of discretionary time, and for some, discretionary income to match. Even for those seniors not fortunate enough to have large incomes, opportunities are open to explore part-time jobs in new areas or to pursue less costly hobbies. Making the most of these years need not be a burden, and can be one of life's sweetest challenges. Few activities are more fulfilling and more accessible to the older adult than free-choice learning.

Times have changed for older adults, too. Current research is debunking many misconceptions and beginning to unravel, if not solve, some of the mysteries surrounding the aging process. There are a few things that gerontologists—researchers who study the aging process—do know, however. Aging is a universal process, does not follow a steady and uniform progression, and is exceedingly multidimensional, encompassing the mind, body, and emotions as well as relationships with family, friends, and the larger society. And the number of aging Americans is growing. By 2030 about 25 percent of the people in the United States will be over sixty-five.

These later years need no longer be spent consigned to the rocking chair. Today's older adults are better educated, healthier, and more active than any comparably aged people in human history; demographic reports suggest that Americans are living healthy and productive lives into their eighties and nineties. Conditions once thought to be synonymous with aging, such as heart disease or dementia, are now understood to be diseases rather than a normal part of aging, and potentially preventable through behavior and life-style changes. What this means is that with their careers and family obligations largely behind them, many older adults find themselves with unprecedented amounts of discretionary time and income. Consequently, older adults rival children in their ability to invest large chunks of their day in free-choice learning.

We are never too old to explore and learn new things, and as we age lifelong learning often blossoms. The elder years are not only a time for exploration, but they are also the time when we wish to bring closure to our lives, make peace with ourselves. For many also, making connections with others, particularly with young people, has proven to be a wonderful way to close the circle of life and to help bridge the gap between a life lived partially and a life lived fully. Old age is a time in life when we become eager to share what we know with others, including the wisdom derived just from having lived so many years. With so many life experiences under our belts, sharing those experiences becomes important and rewarding—for the one sharing and the one experiencing the sharing. Thus free-choice learning at this stage is a mechanism for fulfilling two learning needs:

1. A desire to explore new avenues.

2. A desire for closure in life, which for many means sharing what one has learned with others.

The New Explorers

"No, I'm afraid you've got the wrong person. I'm not going up there, thank you," sixty-year-old Bill tells Paul, a lean, muscular young man draped in ropes, belts, and assorted metal hooks. He stands in front of X-Rock, an intimidating seventy-foot cliff in Durango, Colorado. A few minutes later, much to Paul's and everyone else's amazement, Bill hooks his harness to the rope and heads up the rock, full of determination.

Bill is one of a dozen individuals attending a week-long Elderhostel program of hiking and camping in the Weminuche Wilderness. The group includes four couples and four singles, ranging in age from fifty-five to seventy-five. The program, called "Legendary Southwest Colorado: Geology, Mining, and History," is designed to examine the processes that shaped mining and railroad development in the Old West in general, and Colorado in particular. In addition to scaling mountains with Paul, the geologist, the program involved riding the Durango Silverton Narrow Gauge Railroad and following the Animas River through the rugged San Juan Mountains. They visited old mine shafts and mining ghost towns, walked down dusty trails, and downed a few brews at local watering holes. Over the course of a week, Bill and his intrepid crew learned from the Elderhostel faculty and each other about railroad builders, miners, and mining techniques during the state's boom and bust cycles. For example, one of the participants on this particular trip was a retired mining professor from Colorado State University, another was a railroad buff from Vermont. The dinnertime conversations proved fascinating. Each of the participants discovered that they had some knowledge they could contribute to the conversation. The participants also learned something about themselves—for example, Bill learned that he was capable of scaling a seventy-foot mountain face!

Aristotle is attributed with saying nearly 2,500 years ago, "Education is the best provision for old age." This was true in the fourth century B.C., and is certainly true today. In fact, the number of elderly learners has never been larger. Perhaps more than any other age group, the elderly are enjoying a renaissance in free-choice learning opportunities.

Two organizations, in particular, are taking full advantage of the free-choice learning interests of the "young" elderly. The American Association of Retired Persons (AARP) is the nation's leading not-for-profit organization for people age fifty and older. It serves the needs and interests of this group through information and education, advocacy, and community services, all provided by a network of local chapters and experienced volunteers throughout the country. The organization also offers members a wide range of special benefits and services, including *Modern Maturity* and *My Generation* magazines and a monthly Bulletin.

A visit to their Web site—this age category is one of the fastest growing segments in society to be taking advantage of the Internet—reveals many rich resources for free-choice learning, including information about computers and technology, pertinent legislative updates, leisure and fun, health and wellness, and more. There is also a discussion center, where it is possible to have on-line chats to share information about books, travel, history, and other topics with other senior learners. The Web site even includes a learning and growing section, focused on educational leisure and fun.

Elderhostel, Inc., the program that both Mary and Bill participated in, has a catchy slogan epitomizing their educational perspective—"Adventures in Lifelong Learning!" They have twenty-five years of experience providing high-quality, affordable, educational programs for adults fifty-five and older. These short-term educational programs are a fun way for people of this age to share new ideas, explore new places, and make new friends. Elderhostel accomplishes its mission by supporting a full set of educational programs, offered nationwide and abroad, through over 200 independent Institutes for Learning in Retirement across the United States, Canada, and Bermuda. Elderhostel works with colleges, universities, and community centers to sponsor outdoor, travel, and arts experiences for people ages fifty-five and up. Started in 1975, the organization has more than 2,000 international participating institutions. Last year more than 300,000 people attended programs in the United States, Canada, and seventy other countries. Some lived in dormitories, ate in college cafeterias, and got acquainted in common areas. Others congregated at dude ranches or rustic lodges, on houseboats, in tents—even in covered wagons.

These efforts are supported in part by the Elderhostel Institute Network, a voluntary association of the Learning in Retirement movement. This movement is opening up college and university campuses as well as a variety of free-choice learning facilities like zoos, historic houses, and museums across North America to the experiences and vitality of older adult learners under the banner of Institutes for Learning in Retirement. The Elderhostel Institute Network, in partnership with Institutes for Learning in Retirement, capitalizes on the strengths and opportunities derived from belonging to an association. The Network shares two goals with Institutes for Learning in Retirement on college, university, and free-choice learning campuses across North America: (1) to extend the lifelong learning concept to new people on new campuses in new communities; and (2) to strengthen and support the effectiveness of established programs. The

Network is the voice for the entire "Learning in Retirement" Movement and provides a unique set of specific services to Institutes for Learning in Retirement, including helping to start new programs and maintaining Elderhostel's mailing list of over 750,000 older, active learners.

Elderhostel staff feel strongly that the "Learning in Retirement" Movement is successful because older adults care about education and learning. They are intense, self-motivated learners, and they prefer to be free-choice learners, defining their own educational experiences and pursuing their own interests. The Movement fosters and capitalizes on these strengths, empowering older people to continue learning, to expand their horizons, and to enhance their personal development. It also ensures that older learners will be part of well-run learning environments full of diversity, insight, wisdom, and intellectual and cultural stimulation, and that they get to share in the joys of learning and friendship.

Although Bingo games are still common at many community centers catering to the elderly, these days the educational bus trip is even more common. Safely ensconced in a chartered bus, the intrepid elders travel near and far in search of educational experiences. Elders visit local museums and historic sites during the winter, in the fall they visit New England to see the autumn leaves, they travel to the South in the spring to see the azaleas and rhododendrons in bloom, and they travel to arboretums and botanical gardens to see summer garden shows. The old are on the move, but not all elder-oriented movement involves group activities.

More and more retired couples are buying campers and trailers and traversing the length and breadth of the continent. Retirees are also buying boats and cruising the inland waterways, and even going down to the Caribbean. Airlines like Southwest find that an increasing percentage of their customers are seniors, lured by cheap fares, eager to explore the country.

Much like other adults, seniors are also engaging in hobbies, attending one-day seminars and workshops or participating in a wide range of clubs. For example, we recently read about a ninety-four-year-old woman, who has participated in a book group at her local library for years. These days, she does not see or hear well, but a friend reads her the book and then drives her to the library. Everyone talks loudly so she can hear the conversation and participate. She was quoted as saying, "I don't hear very well, so I miss a lot of it, but I do like the dialogue."

However, not all ninety-year-olds are still actively attending educational programs. Learning never ends; right up to the last moments of life, we continue to learn. However, our present society does not make it easy to age and learn. It attempts to not only take away the right to die, but for many the right to live! Often the elderly are robbed of choices, the very thing for which they have spent a lifetime of struggle to acquire. Without meaningful choices, many older people are relegated to dehumanizing lives of isolation and helplessness. The elderly are our link to community memory and most possess not only a desire but, dare we say, a *need* to learn. Fortunately some exemplary programs are attempting to meet this need, particularly for those most marginalized and isolated—the frail elderly.

With funding from the Commerce Department's Technology Opportunity Program (TOP) at the National Telecommunications and Information Administration, the Cleveland Museum of Art has initiated a Distance Learning for Seniors program in art education for elderly adults unable to visit the museum for various reasons. Using a combination of archive video and broadcast interactive video, the program offers free-choice learning in the arts as well as opportunities to socialize. The museum is partnering with local organizations including the Public Broadcasting System affiliate WVIZ, an Internet service provider, and six to eight senior-care facilities and ten homebound individuals. These older adults are in socially isolated locations such as residential care facilities, rural areas, or are simply homebound. The goals of the program are simple but are proving highly successful. First, develop an art program to intellectually stimulate and facilitate social engagement among older adult learners, then develop a delivery medium for the program, and, finally, develop a replicable model that can be used by other cultural organizations seeking to reach a similar audience.

In a somewhat similar vein, though in a less high-tech manner, a good friend of ours has for more than twenty years run a successful nonprofit organization, Museum One, which offers art education programs for seniors in the D.C. and New Jersey area, as well as training to facilitators who work with older adults around the country. Her organization offers slide sets and curriculum materials that can be used to deliver a high-quality art program to seniors in residential care facilities, adult day care programs, community centers, and assisted living sites. These programs are of high quality and allow seniors, many of whom are close to the end of their lives, to have some pleasurable moments enjoying the exploration of human creativity and productivity.

Learning, and Sharing, to the End

Right up to a month before she died, John's mother, Edith, continued to volunteer at the local hospital. She worked in the pediatric ward and said that the time she spent talking with children and parents was the highlight of her week. She was not trained medically, and she modestly would say that she provided no real "vital" service. However, she felt, and who could disagree, that the human connection, the personal care she provided helped the children get better, sooner. Although she had worked nearly all her life, she felt that it was important to give something back to her community. In particular, she said she found it satisfying to share what wisdom and knowledge she had gained in her life with others. No doubt the children and parents, as well as the other hospital staff, benefited by Edith's volunteer efforts. But at some very basic level, the true beneficiary was Edith. She was able to maintain a connection with others, share her love of life, and leave this life feeling that she used her time well.

A similar example we know of involves a collaboration between two institutions, a school and a convalescent home, rather than one individual. It is not uncommon these days for schools and convalescent homes to exist in close proximity, but usually that is the only thing they have in common. In Tempe, Arizona, an elementary school and adjacent convalescent home have decided to capitalize on their shared real estate. Each week, fifth and sixth grade students visit the home and receive instruction in a whole range of crafts, from whittling to quilting to needlepoint. The children are being taught all the handicrafts that are slowly being lost as skilled craftsmen age. It is a wonderful sight to see young children huddle near their adopted grandparent, as the elders demonstrate their skills. By all accounts, both children and seniors eagerly await these weekly visits. As we suggested in the previous chapter, mentoring and sharing wisdom from young to old is an important dimension of free-choice learning, a critical way in which all of us become knowledgeable, but in this case it is not just the children who are learning. As one older woman in the program stated, "Well, I know they are supposed to be learning from me, but I can't begin to describe how much I've learned from them about what's going on in the world today. Those little children are my window to the world."

The experiences of Edith and the elders at the Arizona convalescent home are by no means unusual examples. As we age, most of us feel the need to bring our life to some sense of closure, a need to feel the time we spent on this earth was worthwhile. Some find this a time for spiritual pursuits, some for personal reflection, but most find sharing with others, whether grandchildren, children or nonrelatives, particularly fulfilling. The desire for learning up until the very last days of our life, once a rarity among our older citizens, will become increasingly common. It is already common among the better-educated seniors in our population, and the aging Baby Boomers are the most educated and learning-oriented generation in history (unless you count their offspring). The next forty years will be the years of "Gray Learning Power"!

Regardless of one's formal education, though, the final chapter of our lives should be as much a time for learning as any other time. Our maturity is forever developing and can only be defined by the degree and quality of its presence throughout our lives. There is never an end to the need or desire to acquire knowledge. It is a concept of both being and becoming. The real challenge to all of us is to be true to each stage of our life. Although there are true limitations imposed by the biological and physiological deterioration that occur as we age, there are no limits to our desire to feel, share, and learn. The elderly, like every person at every stage in life, can and should find solace in the hope and joy that lifelong learning brings. Years of living bring the potential for great emotional and intellectual dignity. The minimum we should ask from our society, then, is the opportunity to develop, and share, that dignity each and every single day of our lives. We are never too old to think, to listen, to smile, to learn. So saying, we all can learn from 104-year-old Rosina Tucker, a Civil Rights activist who, during a recent interview, was asked, "What was it like in your day?" She responded, "My day? *This* is my day!"

Part III
TRANSFORMING EDUCATION IN AMERICA

Reenactment of Bill of Rights debate, Colonial Williamsburg (Photo by Colonial Williamsburg Foundation)

CHAPTER 12
THE FREE-CHOICE LEARNER'S
BILL OF RIGHTS

It is time . . . that we did not leave off our education when we begin to be men and women. It is time that villages were universities, and their elder inhabitants the fellows of universities, with leisure . . . to pursue liberal studies the rest of their lives.

—Henry David Thoreau, *Walden*

To change in structure, appearance, or character. That is the definition of transformation. By that definition, America has already begun its transformation into a Learning Society. As we have tried to demonstrate through numerous stories, Americans young and old are already vitally involved in learning every day of their lives. America's vast network of free-choice learning resources has facilitated a quantum change in the structure, appearance, and character of learning in America. Never before in human history have so many learning resources been available to so many people, and never before have so many people been involved in learning new ideas, skills, and behaviors every single day. However, even the most optimistic among us would have to admit that there's still plenty of room for additional "transformation."

Although lifelong learning is alive and well, facilitated primarily by the remarkable learning opportunities the free-choice learning sector makes possible, we certainly do not believe that every American equally benefits from the free-choice learning community as currently configured, or that the quality of education Americans derive from their free-choice learning experiences is currently optimal. Even though America is well on the road to becoming a Learning Society, aided immeasurably by the free-choice learning sector, it is far from becoming a fully actualized Learning Society, and the free-choice learning sector is far from achieving its full potential or fully meeting its educational responsibilities.

As we gathered the many examples of free-choice learning throughout this book, we also implicitly created a framework for thinking about what optimal community support for free-choice learning might look like. In this chapter, we will make this framework explicit, a framework of five key principles, which derives from the why, where, when, and how of free-choice learning. Collectively, these five principles constitute a Free-Choice Learner's Bill of Rights, which applies to all learners, regardless of age, gender, abilities, ethnic background, or economic situation—a set of principles upon which all quality free-choice learning can and should be built.

Free-Choice Learner's Bill of Rights

In order to satisfy his or her individual free-choice learning needs, each person should have:

1. access to the learning resources of all parts of the community;

2. a breadth and depth of educational opportunity available to them sufficient to satisfy personal curiosity, a need to know, and to ensure a full and satisfying life;

3. opportunities to learn in supportive and educationally reinforcing social and cultural environments;

4. the opportunities to learn in supportive and educationally reinforcing physical environments;

5. access to age-appropriate exploration and mastery learning opportunities at every developmental stage of life.

Much as the promise of freedom in America requires the upholding of the Constitution's Bill of Rights, fulfilling the promise of free-choice learning in America requires upholding the ideals represented by the Free-Choice Learner's Bill of Rights. The responsibility for upholding these ideals rests with each individual, organization, community, and ultimately, the entire country. This Bill of Rights has two very important functions. First, the five rights are tools for guiding the development and optimization of the free-choice learning sector. Second, it represents a vision for free-choice learning in America that can be used as a measuring stick to gauge progress toward a more optimal state. Let's begin by exploring the implications of each of these five "rights" and the guidance they provide for practice.

Access to the Learning Resources of All Parts of the Community

Learning is not something that can, or should, be restricted to one small part of the community. In fact, the beauty of free-choice learning is that it is about learning any time, anywhere. When an entire community's resources are made available for learning, the traditional restrictions of time and space become less problematic. Learning can and should happen throughout the day, on weekdays and weekends, throughout the year, indoors and outdoors. All people, regardless of race, ethnicity, religion, gender, age, or physical or mental ability should be engaged in learning. When you begin with the assumption that all the world and all its human inhabitants represent learning resources, the opportunities for learning become infinite. A fully actualized free-choice learning sector would assure access to all of these resources.

Space and Time

It has often been said that the only real limitation to human potential is human imagination. So it is with free-choice learning. The boundaries of our free-choice learning opportunities are often arbitrary and maddeningly based upon historically valid, but currently invalid, assumptions. Limitless access to resources requires opening up our minds to new possibilities and the needs of new and extended audiences.

For many who run or utilize the traditional media of free-choice learning, there appear to be significant logistical barriers preventing wider access. However, as suggested above, the problem of access is primarily limited by our imaginations. If you assume the boundary of a museum is defined by its four walls, then security and hours of operation are limits to access. And the boundaries of a television special can be defined by the constraints of program scheduling, which limits viewer access. And certainly the boundaries of a community organization's class offerings can be defined by the availability of instructors and limited marketing dollars. However, if you begin with the assumption that learning knows no boundaries, certainly not institutional boundaries, then these traditional limits emerge as less real. By thinking creatively about resources, by forming coalitions and collaborations, free-choice learning organizations have the ability to extend what they can offer the public in time and space.

For example, throughout the country, more and more free-choice learning institutions are exploring ways to extend the scope and range of their services. One of the more successful of these is the effort by Public Television Stations to continuously offer their viewers access to additional materials and resources. Historically, these efforts centered around companion books. Virtually every major PBS special is accompanied by a book providing similar but often somewhat elaborated material. Of late, PBS has been relying on the Internet as its vehicle of choice for extending the time and space of its presentations. It is now almost impossible to watch a PBS show that does not refer the viewer to their Web site in order to access more information, references, or links to other resources. In some cases, the content of the Web site is merely a reiteration of the content of the show, but increasingly PBS Web sites provide a wealth of new and additional information, the kind of detailed treatment of content totally impossible to provide within the context of a television show. Hence, the Internet is allowing PBS to extend its educational reach not just in time and space, but also in content.

The Internet has been viewed by many as *the* answer to opening up access, since individuals can log on any time of day and night, from virtually anywhere on the globe. And unlike the airwaves or the real world, virtual space is functionally limitless. Unfortunately, to date, the potential for providing significantly greater public access via the Internet has exceeded the reality of greater access. Despite the Internet's potential for almost infinitely extending institutional walls, success has been limited by poor to nonexistent knowledge about not only who uses the Internet and why, but for what reasons and to what result. Like any new medium, it will take time to understand how to most effectively utilize the Internet as a learning tool. Once this is accomplished, the Internet will no doubt prove to be much, though certainly not all, that it has been hyped to be. The same is also true of other emerging technologies such as interactive video, broadband television, and technologies that will appear in the coming years that none of us can even imagine at the moment.

Equal Access

A survey of the free-choice offerings in any community, or for that matter even within any single free-choice institution, reveals not hundreds but thousands of opportunities and experiences designed for a wide range of users. And as we have stated numerous times, these offerings are not shrinking, but growing at an exponential rate. Unfortunately, many if not most of the rapidly proliferating free-choice learning experiences available to the public come at a cost, a cost that significantly limits accessibility geographically, economically, and often intellectually. Particularly penalized are historically underserved populations such as recent immigrants, the long-term poor, the very young, the very old, those limited by physical or mental disabilities, and those living in areas with poor transportation or learning infrastructure. Many of the most educationally oriented free-choice learning institutions, including museums, public television and radio, specialty magazines, and even to a degree newspapers and books, have variously been accused of being elitist, a label that is often unintentionally warranted. This propensity to cater primarily to the affluent, mobile, and well educated is clearly short-sighted, since it trades short-term expediency for the long-term security that building a broad, diverse constituency would afford. It also runs counter to the long-term needs of a broadly educated public.

Although many free-choice learning providers have made considerable strides in recent years to become more accessible, proactively reaching out to underserved communities, much remains to be accomplished in this arena. As for-profit free-choice learning providers compete against traditional nonprofits for the time and dollars of an increasingly educationally oriented public, the best intentions of many will fall victim to economic necessity and expediency. It is likely that significant public subsidies will be necessary to completely insure equal accessibility to all parts of the free-choice sector. This is not only a nicety, but a necessity. If we, as a nation, are to achieve our lifelong learning goals, as well as social and economic promise, no one can be left behind due to their economic, mental, chronological, or physical limitations. Financial support would make it possible to serve the needs of those currently excluded.

However, access to free-choice learning resources is only partially limited by finances. For many, access is limited less by money than by know-how. This implies a lack of knowledge of how and why to use the resource rather than a lack of physical access. For example, there is increasing evidence that the much-discussed "digital divide," though in part a hardware problem, more often is a software knowledge deficit. It is not that the poor lack access to computers; more commonly they do not have the skills and expertise to use them with any facility. In addition, they also often lack an appreciation for how computer use could make their lives better. In other cases, restrictions are caused by more direct or indirect discrimination against individuals due to race, religion, ethnicity, age, gender, sexual persuasion, or physical disabilities. Just as these forms of discrimination have no place in a free society, neither do they have a place in a learning society.

Fortunately, there are myriad examples of how individuals, institutions, communities, and national funding agencies have attempted to reverse these trends. One particularly interesting project, supported by the Lila-Wallace Readers Digest Fund under their Museum Accessibility Initiative, was an effort by the Virginia Museum of Fine Arts (VMFA) in Richmond to increase the number of African-American visitors to their museum. Richmond has a large African-American community, which historically eschewed visiting the museum. The reasons for not visiting were many, including, at worst, racism and, at best, benign neglect. The situation was compounded by the fact that the museum was located in an area of town historically unwelcoming to blacks. For all these reasons, African Americans were significantly underrepresented at the museum. Despite the fact that more than half of the residents of Richmond and surrounding communities were African American, prior to the start of the project African Americans represented only 7 percent of the museum's visitors.

The major focus of the Lila-Wallace project was to expand the overall audience of the Virginia Museum of Fine Arts, in particular to attract new individuals to the museum and expand its existing base of African-American visitors. The primary vehicle for this effort was the *Spirit of the Motherland* project, a reconceptualization and reinstallation of the VMFA's extensive African art collection, a series of associated programs, and a gallery guide designed specifically for families.

The initiative involved not just a new exhibition, but a variety of marketing strategies and program initiatives designed to appeal to a larger percentage of African Americans in the community than traditionally had visited the museum. A major thrust of the marketing was to promote the museum as a great place to spend quality time with children and to insure that advertisements included photos of families of color interacting with the exhibitions. These advertisements were placed on the sides of buses and distributed as flyers through African-American churches and businesses, such as barber shops and beauty parlors. Information about the exhibition and associated programs were also advertised on African-American radio and television stations. During the Opening Day celebration, schoolchildren, who had learned African dancing and drumming from an African master visiting schools for several weeks before the opening, gave a performance. The museum was packed that day. Many in the audience were the families of the schoolchildren who came to proudly watch their children perform, many of whom had never set foot inside the museum before.

The museum was successful in increasing African-American attendance during the course of the *Spirit of the Motherland* exhibition and associated programs; in fact, attendance for all visitors increased. There was also evidence to suggest that the Virginia Museum of Fine Arts had the potential for a long-term increase in African-American visitation. However, it has only been because of the continued commitment to this effort by the institution that these short-term gains have been sustained. Changing historical use patterns is a long-term and arguably never-ending process, one that must be started but can never be stopped. The key to long-term success is twofold: (1) a commitment to tapping into people's personal history; and (2) creating personal connections with the institution that are not ephemeral, but long-lasting. These two ingredients are also fundamental to facilitating all learning.

Access to the Learning Resources of All Parts of the Community

We have touched on just a couple of the important considerations for designing quality free-choice learning experiences that use all parts of the community. Summarizing these, and adding a few others, we suggest that free-choice educators consider the following:

- Extend the time and space of offerings by building coalitions and utilizing new technologies.

- Whatever media is at the core of your organization's educational efforts, find ways to involve additional media—if you're a broadcast company, also utilize print and virtual communication; if you're a library, use exhibitions and film; if you're a museum, use radio and theater. The more ways you communicate, the more likely you will be to get your message across; the more you collaborate the broader will be your impact.

- Invest in research and development on how to effectively utilize new educational technologies. The only given is that what works in one medium will not necessarily work in a new medium. The key is to complement messages, not duplicate them.

- Explore creative ways to build and extend audiences to include those historically excluded by age, gender, and economics, cultural, physical, or mental disability.

- Develop collaborations with social service organizations that have considerable experience working with disadvantaged communities.

- Provide training programs that help traditionally underserved communities learn how to use the free-choice learning resources in their community; access to free-choice learning is only partially limited by money and physical proximity.

- Involve the communities you hope to serve in the development of educational offerings. Create free-choice learning experiences *with* them, rather than *for* them.

- Changing historical use patterns takes time and commitment; history will not be changed overnight, so appreciate when initiating these efforts that it is a long-term commitment.

- Building successful relationships with new audiences involves understanding their special needs and interests, hopes and aspirations.

Breadth and Depth of Educational Opportunity to Satisfy Personal Curiosity, a Need to Know, and to Ensure a Full and Satisfying Life

The free-choice learning sector is, and always has been, a bastion of educational diversity, in content, delivery, and the depth of experiences provided learners. Every community in America offers a range of free-choice learning options, whether through broadcast or print media, museums, community-based organizations, or increasingly on-line. Although collectively it is assumed that all these offerings ensure there is something for everyone, how often do we make the effort to truly determine whether the needs of the many, rather than merely the few, are satisfied? How do we judge the interests and motivations of the diverse public and how do we attempt to satisfy each person's learning needs?

User Motivation and Interest

People enter free-choice learning situations with a wide range of motivations and expectations, prior expectations and motivations that can and do affect learning. Even a young child brings years of experience to such learning situations. This means that by the time an individual begins a free-choice learning experience, to a large degree the nature and quality of the learning that will result has already been predetermined by the prior experience of the learner. But free-choice educators need not passively try to respond to these realities. Instead, the challenge is to connect with and build upon the experience by actively seeking to frame and shape appropriate learner expectations and motivations that can enhance potential learning.

Successful learning experiences, be they exhibitions, programs, or performances, provide "hooks" or entry points, enabling learners to relate their previous experience, prior knowledge, interests, and beliefs to the new experience. Because learners, either consciously or unconsciously, are seeking ways to connect the particular exhibition, program, or Web site to who they are, what they need, and/or what they are curious about, they need to "see themselves" within the free-choice learning experience. At a basic level, every learner is seeking to be enriched or transformed, so to be successful, the learner at some level has to understand why this particular experience is relevant to them, and if they attend to it or participate in it, how the experience and information contained within it will meet their learning needs. Of course, the challenge is that each person's Personal Context, his or her store of knowledge, interests, and beliefs, is different.

Creating a learning experience for a single individual, someone you know fairly well like a friend or family member, is relatively easy. Since there is only one person to design for, the content and presentation can be customized for that individual. However, if the learning experience you are trying to create needs to serve hundreds, perhaps even millions, of other people, it is not so straightforward. How do you design a learning experience for a mass market, which simultaneously accommodates the unique prior experiences and interests of a large group of potential users?

The simple answer is that you cannot design an exhibition, television program, course, Web site, or any other free-choice learning experience that equally accommodates the specific beliefs, interests, and knowledge of millions of people. Remarkably, though, it is possible to come close; the key ingredients are making an effort to connect the learning experience being designed to what people already know and are interested in, and then building opportunities for choice and control into the design of the experience. The exhibition *What About AIDS?*, developed in the early 1990s by a consortium of science museums, illustrates this idea well.

At the time, the vast majority of Americans had not only heard about HIV/AIDS, but were also deeply concerned about and interested in the topic. Although opinions differed widely on a number of HIV/AIDS-related issues—for example, who should take responsibility for prevention and treatment, whether it was ethical to widely distribute condoms to teenagers or distribute clean needles to IV drug-users—many, if not most, Americans still felt a strong need to know more about the subject. Thus, although potentially controversial, at the time of its development it was clear that an exhibition on this topic was going to be widely perceived by the public as interesting and timely. Through front-end evaluation, a process of talking to people at the beginning of an educational development process to assess what they know about or are interested in knowing about a topic, it was also determined that most Americans possessed a high degree of awareness about the HIV/AIDS epidemic and reasonable knowledge of basic "facts" related to HIV/AIDS. However, most Americans lacked detailed knowledge of the science underlying HIV/AIDS, for example, the nature of viruses and the workings of the human immune system, and most were totally unaware of the various permutations of prevention strategies. This information suggested that at least for this brief period, most people shared a common interest, a common level of awareness, and, in general, a common range of understanding about HIV/AIDS, though they did not share a common set of beliefs. Thus, a single exhibition that connected what was familiar and known about the topic to some of the new information exhibit developers hoped to convey had a reasonable chance of meeting the needs and interests of this diverse public. Interestingly, several years later, public interest, awareness, and knowledge has shifted considerably in the area of HIV/AIDS; consequently, although still a good one, this same exhibition would probably not be as effective since it no longer starts where most visitors are "at."

Using this information, it was possible to devise a strategy for how to present the topic of HIV/AIDS in an exhibition that would connect to the interests and prior understanding of the vast majority of the public likely to encounter the exhibition, yet also accommodate unique differences among individuals. The exhibition team could be comfortable in knowing that in the early 1990s there was a rare confluence of *general* interest, awareness, and knowledge afforded by the subject, but also needed to be aware that, although the public shared a general interest, awareness, and knowledge about HIV/AIDS, they did not share a *specific* interest, awareness, and knowledge about the topic. In other words, although two individuals may have been generally interested in HIV/AIDS and had roughly comparable awareness and knowledge, individual A, who was married, monogamous, and sixty-seven years old might primarily have been interested in learning about how the epidemic might influence the health care system and the economy, while individual B, who was nineteen years old and single, might have been primarily concerned with her chances of getting HIV/AIDS over the next few years. The *What About AIDS?* exhibition would not have been successful if it had been designed in a linear fashion, with a single entry and exit point.

A major element in the success of this exhibition was the incorporation of choice into the exhibition. Visitors could select from several general topics, and then could also select from a multitude of specific topics within each section. There were also choices for different learning modalities—for example, one could read, watch video, manipulate hands-on interactives, use computer programs, and/or listen to audiotapes. A visitor also could choose between a variety of different approaches to the presentation of information—for example, text containing facts and concepts, epidemiological charts and graphs, or tapes and photographs detailing firsthand accounts of individuals with HIV/AIDS. As a consequence, a wide range of visitors, each with their own diverse set of specific interests and knowledge, could select how and what they chose to learn about the topic. Unlike many museum exhibitions, the What About AIDS? exhibition afforded very personal experiences. A family group could enter the exhibition, split up, and each member utilize a separate part of the exhibition, occasionally coming together to share notes and suggest parts of the exhibition for others to see. In large part because of the subject matter, but also by design, this exhibition not only permitted but encouraged individual and small group exploration.

The developers appreciated that visitors were entering and exiting the exhibition with different learning agendas and purposes, and strived to accommodate these differences. The result was an exhibition that permitted, in fact encouraged, visitors to bring their own understandings and interests to the experience, an experience that yielded a wide diversity of equally appropriate learning outcomes.

When designing free-choice learning experiences, this should be the norm, rather than the exception. Unlike compulsory education where it is assumed that everyone will attend to a single lesson, with a single purpose in mind resulting in only a few predetermined outcomes, free-choice learning cannot make these same assumptions. Learning outcomes are always diverse in a free-choice context, because what people attend to, and why, varies so much and, thus, what they learn also varies. Quality free-choice learning experiences should always be designed in ways that support multiple motivations, interests, skills, and knowledge levels.

Finding Resources

Making great educational experiences available to the public is not sufficient; the public needs to know about them. A major problem of the free-choice learning sector is not a lack of options, but a lack of knowledge on the part of the public about the options available to them and which ones would best meet their needs. How does one identify and navigate among the free-choice learning resources available? What support is provided to individuals by organizations or by the community to help with this navigation? Take one resource, the Internet, which is notorious for making it difficult to access and navigate the many learning choices it opens up. As a colleague recently suggested, finding information on the Internet is like trying to drink out of a fire hydrant. The problem is not the availability of resources, but filtering what is available sufficiently to be useful.

Perhaps the best example we are aware of for meeting this challenge comes not from the United States, but from Britain. In September 2000 the British Department for Culture, Media and Sport (DCMS) created a new body with the working name of Culture Online (www.culture.online), a national effort to utilize the Internet as a tool for facilitating free-choice learning. Online's goal is to use digital technologies to widen access to the resources of the arts and cultural sector, for the purposes of learning and enjoyment both at school and throughout a person's lifetime.

Culture Online was designed to make a significant change in the public's ability to access information on arts and culture, as well as participate in arts and cultural activities. From the start, the idea was to create a highly participatory program that "enabled individuals and communities to use the technologies to pursue their own interests, create their own cultural resources, and interact with others. It should draw its materials from museums, galleries, libraries, heritage sites, archives of written, broadcast, and film materials, the performing arts and the new digital arts."

This is a rather bold and forward-thinking move on the part of the English government which grew out of an appreciation that the widespread problem of limited public use of arts and cultural resources, was not a shortage of resources, but a lack of knowledge of the resources available to them. In particular, the DCMS concluded that:

- A wide selection of free-choice learning opportunities exist in the community, representing an array of both popular and niche subject matters.

- This selection reflects a diversity of medium formats, e.g., video, courses, exhibitions, and print.

- This selection reflects a diversity of learning levels and depth of information, e.g., introductory, intermediate, and advanced.

- Tools are desperately needed to help learners navigate the choices and opportunities available to them.

- Learners need to be treated and respected as unique individuals rather than as all identical.

At this writing, the Web site has just been launched and includes some pilot materials. The DCMS is now conducting a full-scale economic appraisal of the project, refining the Web site, and exploring a range of possible strategies for bringing this ambitious project to full fruition. Regardless of its ultimate success, few could argue with the importance of the effort and vision behind its development. Let's hope a similar effort is soon initiated in the United States.

Recommendations for Maximizing the Unique, Personal Nature of Free-Choice Learning

We suggest that educators consider the following factors when designing free-choice learning experiences that meet the needs of unique learners:

- Reach out to the public, starting the free-choice learning experience before people arrive!

- Use marketing to build positive and realistic motivations for a free-choice learning experience and to provide meaningful connections with the institution or activity.

- Work to insure that what is to be learned clearly relates to the needs and interests of the learner. From the beginning it should be made clear that participating in the learning experience will enhance the learner's sense of self-worth, self-awareness, and self-respect.

- Design experiences that allow people to personalize the information presented; this will encourage ownership of information and insure that learners make the learning experience their own.

- Acknowledge that different learners prefer different types of learning strategies/styles and offer learners clear choices.

- Provide a variety of entry and exit points ("hooks") so that the free-choice learner can pick the point that best meets their personal needs at the time and that acknowledges the varying reasons people desire knowledge.

- Attempt to layer the complexity of the experience so that learners can self-select the complexity and depth of information they need and desire at the time.

- Always set as your goal to reinforce prior understandings and, occasionally, to help reshape understandings, attitudes, and behaviors.

- Work to affect *both* short-term and long-term changes in understanding, attitudes, and behaviors.

- Make experiences enjoyable and entertaining; fun and learning are not mutually exclusive. Enjoyment is not only possible, but essential to the creation of quality free-choice learning experiences.

- Insure that learners have the tools to find out about the programs and experiences that meet their needs and interests.

Opportunities to Learn in Supportive and Educationally Reinforcing Social and Cultural Environments

The free-choice learning sector suffers from a set of systemic problems that prevent it from functioning to its fullest capacity. First, many, if not most, types of organizations that currently comprise the heart of the free-choice learning sector began life as something other than educational organizations. For example, print media—newspapers and magazines—were created to present the news. Much of the broadcast media started out as an entertainment vehicle. Museums were established primarily as institutions for the collection, study, and preservation of natural, cultural, and artistic objects, and most youth organizations were founded for social service purposes. The fact that all of these entities now find themselves very involved in educational activities runs counter to their history and culture. Many do not fully appreciate, totally accept, or really understand how to exercise their educational functions effectively. Preparation for entry into broadcast journalism, museum curatorship, or the running of a community-based organization rarely involves training in education, psychology, or learning. How are these individuals supposed to know about current theory and practice in learning? Few resources currently exist that would enable a free-choice learning professional to learn about learning theory, particularly learning theory specific to the needs and requirements of free-choice learning. The result is that much of what passes as educational practice in the free-choice learning sector is based on outmoded or often poorly thought out foundations that are not supported by research or exemplary practice. For example, take theories of the sociocultural dimensions of learning and their importance in facilitating learning. An analysis of a random sampling of television programs, community-organization programming for adults or youth, museum exhibitions, and performances is likely to reveal a lack of understanding of just how best to maximize the social and cultural aspects of free-choice learning. Opportunities for learners to interact within social groups is often tolerated rather than designed for. Mediation by instructors, guides, or announcers is likely to be rigidly didactic and condescending. These are serious but fixable flaws.

Within Group Social Interaction

How can free-choice learning organizations better facilitate learning experiences that capitalize upon the sociocultural nature of learning? Interactions between family members and peers normally play a critical role in personalizing and facilitating free-choice learning. In fact, there are many situations—for example, when families learn together—when these interactions serve as the primary vehicle through which learning occurs. Recognizing this, a number of community-based organizations have worked in recent years to support family learning through sociocultural means. Among the most active have been public libraries.

Libraries for years served as resources for family learning. But in recent years it has become apparent that many families, in particular single-parent families strapped for time, disadvantaged families handicapped by economic and educational opportunity, and even affluent middle-class families deprived of relevant models, have yearned for more structured support for family learning. In hundreds of communities across America, libraries have set up programs that help parents know how to learn along with their children. Libraries provide reading lists and tutorials on how and when to read to and with children, and generally provide parents with support across a wide range of educational experiences.

Programs such as these, specifically designed to meet the needs of families, are only part of the solution. The total solution comes in designing experiences and opportunities for learners in such a way that they encourage and facilitate group learning. Even such seemingly solitary experiences as watching television or surfing the Internet turn out to be often done as part of a social group. We believe that there are ways to insure that any learning experience is "group-supportive." Guidance comes from one of our colleagues, Minda Borun, who, along with her colleagues working in the Philadelphia-Camden (New Jersey) area, developed a set of family-friendly principles for exhibitions. We have adapted their findings into five principles important to consider when designing free-choice learning experiences that support sociocultural interaction:

1. Experiences should be designed so that more than one person can participate at a time. It means that there needs to be opportunities for two, three, or even five people to all be able to see, touch, and, as appropriate, feel the experience simultaneously.

2. Since so many free-choice learning experiences involve different-aged learners, it is also important to design experiences so that people of varying ages can participate. In other words, both adults and children need to be able to engage in the experience and be able to understand what's going on.

3. It is also important that free-choice learning experiences be designed so that all participants, regardless of age or prior experience, are able to derive satisfaction from participating in the experience. This means that there should be multiple outcomes possible, and that the experience itself is rich enough, varied and complex enough to foster group discussion.

4. The experience should support different learning styles and levels of knowledge. Not everyone learns in the same way, so it is important to create experiences that allow different learners to intellectually access an experience in different ways.

5. Finally, and this is true of any learning experience but particularly important for designing educational experiences that facilitate group learning, the experience should provide links to the learners' prior knowledge and experience. This implies knowing something about the group who will actually be using the experience. At the end of the day, designing educational experiences with the end users clearly in mind is the key to any successful educational effort.

Guides and Mentors

Individuals outside the immediate social group of the learners also influence visitor learning and none so profoundly as teachers, guides, or facilitators. Theater represents one particularly powerful, and often underappreciated, way to facilitate learning. Everyone loves a performance! There are good reasons for this. Listening to someone tell a story is one of the oldest, and still one of the most powerful, ways in which humans learn. An excellent example of the power and potential of theater to educate was a theater program called *Heroes Just Like You: Careers in Science and Technology*, created by Dale Jones, at the time Director of Interpretation for the Baltimore City Life Museums. This program was originally developed in response to the Greater Baltimore Committee's challenge to Baltimore cultural institutions to support efforts that encouraged children to consider careers in the life sciences. Although it was not immediately clear what a history museum could do to meet this challenge, Jones felt that a theater performance might be an unusual but powerful way to meet this challenge. Since many children between the ages of twelve and fifteen start making life decisions that profoundly affect their future careers, it was decided that this was the age group that should be targeted. Since 80 percent of the Baltimore City students were African American, Jones also decided to focus specifically on that target audience.

Jones ended up creating a history-oriented theater piece that explored the employment of African Americans in three time periods—the 1890s, 1940s, and 1990s—and examined the point in people's lives when they made decisions that affected their careers' "turning points." Being good historians, the staff of the City Life Museum began by collecting data. They interviewed scientists and technicians who had overcome some obstacle to reach their career goals, such as racial or gender discrimination, poverty, drug dependency, or lack of parental support. They found that people did indeed have "turning points," not necessarily a discrete event, but more of a long-term change that usually involved changing peer groups and friends and seeking out education. They also interviewed both black and white women who were secretaries in the 1940s and conducted research about employment of African Americans in the 1890s. In addition, Jones researched contemporary sociological and psychological studies of peer group pressure among African-American youth.

The result was a play, infused with local African-American history, that attempted to help children understand that there can be turning points in people's lives and to realize and experience through theater the negative effects of peer group pressure. The play also attempted, without disparaging other types of work, to encourage children to consider the potential intellectual excitement, passion, and financial rewards of careers in science and technology.

Using his extensive theater experience, Jones knew the value of audience interaction with staff members, but he did not want to incorporate it in such way that it disrupted the dramatic flow of the piece. He also realized that order to use audience interaction successfully, you could not present a play then expect children to have a worthwhile discussion about it unless they had been "prepped" for it. To get them to talk at the end, you needed to give them opportunities to talk in the beginning. Thus was born the idea of an "Our Town" narrator who would talk to the audience before the play and establish a rapport that he could build on throughout the show. Also, since the narrator would play several characters during the play, the audience would experience the immediacy of the performance and the fascination of watching the transformation as the actor became the narrator again. It was also important to the audience that the dramatic structure of a scene not be broken.

The production was an overwhelming success. The performers were wonderful—young, "cool" African Americans who developed tremendous rapport with the children. Audiences included students on school field trips and family groups visiting on weekends. In all cases, the performers showed obvious interest and concern for the educational well-being of the hundreds of young adolescents with whom they interacted. Not only did the middle and early high school-aged African-American audiences enjoy the performance, but evaluation revealed a statistically significant change in attitudes about science. In fact, changes occurred among both black and white children, both males and females. In short, the *Heroes Just Like You* museum theater piece provided an immediate and powerful vehicle for presenting the history of Baltimore, as well as communicating important present-day information about careers and values.

There are two important take-away messages from this example. The first is that even a traditionally passive medium like theater can be made more interactive. Audiences can be actively engaged and challenged to become participants, not merely spectators. Second, success was achieved by creating learning facilitators rather than "teachers." The actors were guides, not pedants. The actors possessed knowledge and experience that allowed them to provide information and to "instruct," but they were always respectful of the knowledge and experience of their young audience. This is a delicate balance, but one essential to maintain for successful free-choice learning. Research into the social nature of learning, and particularly how adults and other "guides" facilitate learning, is currently a very active area of psychological research. Additional findings in the coming years promise to shed light on how to get increasingly better at this critical element of education.

Recommendations for Facilitating the Sociocultural Dimension of Learning

We have touched on just a few of the important considerations for designing quality educational experiences. Summarizing these, and adding a few others, we suggest that free-choice educators consider the following:

- At the most basic level, quality learning experiences and programs should accommodate the need for more than one person to share the experience socially and physically.

- Reward and foster social interaction rather than penalize and inhibit it.

- Invest in people; there are few more successful devices for facilitating learning than a quality human facilitator. Good facilitators require training, not just in the content, but most importantly in the art of communication; good communication starts with good listening!

- Create opportunities for group dialogue that extend beyond the temporal limits of the initial experience. Connect the experience to other media, such as Web sites, television programs, and museums.

- Create situations where motivated novices can work alongside knowledgeable mentors in an atmosphere of collaboration and shared goals.

- Utilize stories, songs, poems, dance, and/or music that help string together information for the learner in a profoundly human context.

- Be sensitive to the cultural specificity of language, gesture, and narrative and avoid the use of linguistic idioms and culturally specific humor when developing educational programs.

- Finally, recognize and build upon the diverse norms and values of many cultures.

Opportunities to Learn in Supportive and Educationally Reinforcing Physical Environments

Learning is not all in our heads but rather is a dialogue, a coming together of internal and external reality. As we have described in considerable detail in this book, successful learning experiences involve effective design and appropriate physical contexts. When designed carefully and thoughtfully, places like zoos, aquariums, arboreta, national parks, art galleries, historical parks, and homes are the quintessential "appropriate" physical settings for learning. Consequently, they have unprecedented opportunities to facilitate long-term, meaningful learning. Immersing the learner within a context that enables him to literally see how things are connected, to understand visually, aurally, and even through smell touch what something looks and feels like, is a tremendous learning tool.

child to actually see what people looked like, how they lived, and even how they might have talked in the past, is to open up a window to history that no amount of text in a book can ever duplicate. For an individual to not only see how a wing is shaped, but to be able to put on wings and stand in a wind tunnel and feel lift, is an unparalleled learning opportunity. Free-choice learning experiences provide learners with access to reality—simply, dramatically, and more than anything, authentically.

Not only does physical setting create a context in which learning can occur, but physical settings also have the potential to create a desire to learn. In the right setting, real or imagined, the learner is surrounded by the sights, sounds, and textures that foster curiosity and encourage intellectual exploration. So motivated, learning proceeds effortlessly and intrinsically; there is no need to force, prompt, or bribe. Regardless of the medium, the best free-choice learning occurs naturally in such physically rich and appropriate settings.

The essence of free-choice learning is that it enables individuals to experience real things, and under the best of circumstances, within real, meaningfully designed physical contexts. The keys to facilitating these experiences include using advance organizers, orientation, and well-designed educational experiences.

Advance Organizers and Orientation

The vast majority of national parks and historical monuments provide visitors with some sort of map or orientation sheet that describes the general floor plan and lays out the content of the site. The vast majority of these efforts fall far short of the ideal, primarily because maps are difficult for many visitors to use and the orientation to what is available, in both content and experience, are not well integrated into the experience itself. However, recently a number of places have explored efforts at making orientation a serious and central part of the visitor experience. In our opinion, one of the most successful efforts in this regard is the orientation experience at the Cahokia Mounds State Historic Park, a historic site located just across the Mississippi River from St. Louis, Missouri.

The Historic Park is the site of the largest prehistoric Native American city north of Mexico. Covering 16 square kilometers (6 square miles), it may have been inhabited by as many as 50,000 people of the Mississippian culture between A.D. 1050 and 1250. In addition to developing a complex agricultural system, the inhabitants moved more than 1.4 million cubic meters (50 million cubic feet) of earth to create their ceremonial mounds. Visitors to this modest-sized historic park first visit a small visitor center/museum, where they are strongly encouraged to begin their experience by watching a short introductory film, presented in a comfortable but fairly typical auditorium. The film is a well-produced description of the mysteries surrounding the Indian groups that built large mounds up and down the Mississippi Valley some 1000 years ago, discussing what is known, and not known, about these peoples—their customs, life es, and, of course, possible reasons for building mounds. However, the magic of the orientation is not so much the film but the ending—at the conclusion, the narrator invites the audience to visit the museum's recreation of a Cahokia Indian village. As the film ends, the screen turns from opaque to translucent, and through the screen visitors can see the activity and sounds of an ancient Indian village. For that magical moment, as the screen rises and visitors are invited to walk under the screen and into the village, it seems as if that ancient Indian village has actually come alive again, filled with appropriate sights, sounds, and activities.

In actual fact, the sounds of Indians at work and play are piped in and the movement of people within the village is a powerful illusion created by the movement of other visitors exploring the recreated village—the theater is actually in the middle of the space! However, the net effect is a compelling orientation and invitation to the village and a series of hands-on exhibits displayed around the perimeter of the village, helping the visitor feel truly ready to meaningfully begin exploring the visitor center and historic park. As visitors continue to explore the visitor center, examining artifacts, learning about the people and the archaeology being conducted on the site, they can still see and hear the sights and sounds of the village which provide an appropriate context for the entire experience. Leaving the visitor center, visitors then can take the short walk to the mound. Despite at present looking like not much more than a large hump of earth, having seen the film, visitors can imagine what it must have looked like a thousand years earlier when it was filled with temples and human activity. This is what successful advance organizers and orientation are supposed to accomplish. They are not just a nicety; extensive research shows that appropriate advance organizers and useful orientation significantly enhance learning.

Design

We believe strongly that the immediacy of experiencing real things, set in well-designed, appropriate contexts, facilitates optimal learning, enriching and extending meaning. This is one of the reasons that eco- and cultural tourism have become so popular. A photograph of Machu Pichu is stunning, but actually standing high atop an Andean mountain inside Machu Pichu (altitude 9,060 feet) literally and figuratively takes your breath away. Running your hand along perfectly hewn stone walls, peering out at endless expanses of virtually inaccessible valleys and unscalable mountains, provides a depth of understanding and awe that no photograph could ever capture. These are memories that will truly endure for a lifetime.

However, not everyone chooses or can afford to visit a place as remote as Machu Pichu; most of us have to settle for something a little closer to home. Today, there is a way to reconcile the value of the immediate with the realities limited time and funds. These contexts can be created in film and televi and they can be simulated at museums, zoos, aquariums, and theme Although the experience of diving in the Caribbean, surrounded by br colored fish and corals, is fabulous, so too is walking through a modern aquarium equally surrounded by brilliantly colored fish and corals. Although the thrill of visiting the Serengeti Plain and seeing vast herds of gazelles and wildebeest is a once in a lifetime experience, so too is a drive through Disney's Animal Kingdom or the San Diego Zoo's African Savanna. Today all of us have the opportunity to learn about rain forests while exploring a simulated rain forest at our local natural history museum, about American history by watching and talking with costumed characters at a historic site, or about nineteenth-century art while strolling through a recreated artist salon at our local art museum. Although not totally the "real thing," these simulations are close enough to the real thing to support and facilitate meaningful learning.

Recommendations for Facilitating the Physical Dimension of Learning

We suggest that educators consider the following physical context factors when designing effective free-choice learning experiences:

- Strive to frame the learner's experiences within real, richly described or appointed, relevant, and appropriately complex environments. Successful educational developers appreciate that effort invested in placing learners in appropriate settings is a waste of neither time nor money, but essential to the learning process.

- The best learning environments help the learner navigate from one experience to the next, in the absence of overt directions or instructions. In other words, within an appropriate learning context, the setting itself helps to direct and motivate learning.

- Educational experiences should have clear goals and appropriate rules and these should be made explicit for the learner. In other words, the learner should always know what is expected of him or her and how well he or she is doing. This implies providing visitors with appropriate advance organizers and building into all experiences continual, unambiguous feedback that lets the learner know how well they are understanding the intended information, perspective, or skill.

- Experiences should be designed so that they have appropriate levels of challenge; the opportunities for action and thought should always balance with the skills and knowledge of the learner.

- The most compelling learning experiences are all-encompassing with all of an individual's sensory channels engaged in the experience, reducing competing information without reducing complexity. Such all-encompassing experiences provide a sharper focus and a more memorable experience. This is why multi-channel/multi-modal learning— learning through all the senses—works.

- In the same way that learning experiences can be enhanced by creative use of the physical context, they can also be affected by poor ambiance. It is critical that learners feel that they are in clean, comfortable, and safe environments when engaged in free-choice learning.

Access to Age-Appropriate Exploration and Mastery Learning Opportunities at Every Developmental Stage of Life

Most communities have a selection of free-choice learning opportunities available for school-aged children but fewer have a similar array of free-choice learning experiences appropriate for seniors or preschool-aged children. Fewer still have programs for teens and young adults. Every age group should have equal access to free-choice learning opportunities, and all of these opportunities need to be designed age-appropriately. As the demand for free-choice learning increases, so too will the demand for targeted experiences aimed at specific age groups.

The free-choice learning sector also needs to figure out better ways to offer a range of educational experiences for learners, experiences that afford both exploration and mastery. Some media and some organizations are better suited to offer exploratory activities and some are better suited to facilitating mastery. Rather than being perceived as a handicap, this should be an advantage. Currently the free-choice learning sector as a whole has failed to appreciate that it is collectively part of a much larger community, an assemblage of interacting and intersecting organizations, an integral part of the educational infrastructure. The consequences of this failure to see the constituent components as part of a larger whole, has resulted in fragmented efforts and a failure to form strategic alliances and collaborations with others parts of the learning community. These kinds of strategic collaborations are now beginning to occur, but they are sporadic, and generally piecemeal. Consequently, most free-choice learning experiences are rarely designed in ways that directly relate to or reinforce the public's experiences in other parts of the educational infrastructure, free-choice or otherwise, and rarely are they designed to thoughtfully and systematically span the lifetime.

Age-Appropriate Experiences

A number of organizations have been trying in recent years to meet the appropriate needs of a vast, diverse, and multi-aged public. A large asse of museums, science centers, public television stations, and libraries have been trying to create varied programming and opportunities. So too have community-based organizations, perhaps none more diligently than the YWCA. The YWCA, although retaining its focus on girls and women, has rapidly evolved into an organization that sees itself as a basic support organization for the community.

Local Ys offer classes for preschool-aged children ranging in topic from tumbling to science, courses and tutoring for school-aged children, and special courses for adolescents in topics as varied as babysitting, first aid, and leadership. They offer courses for young mothers and infants, a wide range of adult courses on virtually any topic imaginable, and many now offer programs specifically for seniors including courses on childrearing issues for grandparents, aging, and maintaining health and fitness. Most YWCAs have training programs for women interested in getting back into the workforce covering topics such as resume writing, interviewing skills and computer literacy, counseling, and even sometimes placement services as well. They offer courses for the body, the spirit, and the mind, providing continuing support and learning across the entire lifespan, opportunities geared to the ever-changing needs of girls and women.

Strategic Collaborations

It is essential that free-choice learning institutions think about their educational offerings as existing not in a vacuum but within a larger arena of learning. Sometimes television shows, Web sites, exhibitions, books, and programs are developed as if no other medium, at no other place or time, has ever presented this information before or will ever present it again. If this were true, it is unlikely that anyone would partake in the programming. It is because the topics presented by free-choice learning institutions relate to events outside the institution that the public shows an interest in the first place. They flock to an exhibition of Vincent Van Gogh's work because they are acutely interested in his art. It works the other way, also; the success of the film *Titanic* heightened public interest in the events surrounding the sinking of the *Titanic* and that period in history, resulting in a number of books, television programs, and exhibitions on the topic. To ignore these realities, or even worse to disdain them as trappings of popular culture, is to severely limit the learning opportunities afforded by the free-choice sector. Learning is a continuous process that begins before the individual engages in a free-choice learning experience and continues long after. Successful free-learning experiences facilitate connections between prior and subsequent experiences, encouraging utilization of other learning resources within the community.

This approach is particularly important when it comes to communicating ific messages, for instance trying to change public attitudes and knowledge health or environmental issues. These complex issues present sufficient ges; unilateral, one-shot efforts are almost guaranteed to fail. For example, a large number of leaders in environmental organizations as diverse as the Sierra Club and the American Zoo and Aquarium Association, have recently determined that one single, overarching issue should take precedence above all others, the issue of declining biodiversity; it turns out to be a challenging message to communicate to the public. A wide range of studies, some of them conducted by our Institute, have found that few in the public are familiar with this term or understand its deeper scientific meaning. One organization, the World Wildlife Fund (WWF), is particularly noteworthy for its broad-based, multipronged approach to communicating the importance of biodiversity to the public.

The WWF has attempted to communicate the importance of preserving biodiversity through a wide range of efforts focused on a variety of public audiences. They have sponsored advertising initiatives, public events, school programs, teacher training efforts, news stories on television and radio and in newspapers, newsletters, adult lecture series, fund-raising promotions, film series, Web sites, and most recently a traveling exhibition. All of these efforts have approached the problem from a slightly different angle, appropriate to the medium of communication selected, but all have focused on the single core concern that a decline in the number and diversity of life forms threatens all life on earth.

At the same time, WWF has worked to form coalitions nationally and internationally with concerned organizations that share the WWF's commitment to preserving wildlife. Partners have included The Nature Conservancy, World Resources Institute, Sierra Club, American Zoo and Aquarium Association, U.S. Fish and Wildlife Service, TRAFFIC North America, Disney's Animal Kingdom, National Geographic Society, and a score of corporations. By partnering with a wide range of governmental and nongovernmental, nonprofit and for-profit organizations, WWF has helped to broker relationships with both large and small organizations, all in a broad-scale effort to change public awareness and understanding of issues related to biodiversity. Given its size and stature, it is likely that WWF working alone could have made a dent in the public's understanding and awareness of biodiversity issues. However, by working in collaboration with hundreds of like-minded organizations, it stands an even better chance of accomplishing its goals.

Recommendations for Facilitating Age-Appropriate and Extended Free-Choice Learning

We suggest that educators consider the following issues and concerns when designing free-choice learning experiences:

- Different-aged learners have different needs; make sure that experiences are designed with learners of a specific age in mind.

- The greatest current need is for free-choice learning experiences that meet the learning requirements of very young children, teens, and seniors.

- Some resources are better for some aged learners than others. This is not a problem as long as, across an entire institution—or better yet, community—every aged learner has access to ample learning resources. No institution should think of itself as an educational "island."

- Attempt to make learning experiences boundless; in other words, the experience should start from the learner's innate interests and experiences and enable him/her to continue, or extend the learning beyond the temporal and physical confines of a single experience. Consequently every experience should provide the learner with concrete references to past experiences and suggestions for future experiences that he or she can have which will extend and expand upon the learning experience.

- Members of the free-choice learning sector should form broad-scale coalitions to collectively invest in and encourage efforts that support free-choice learning in the community as a whole. United, the free-choice learning sector can be the most powerful and important learning sector in America; divided it will be much, much less.

Assessing Free-Choice Learning Experiences

As stated at the beginning of this chapter, the Free-Choice Learning Bill of Rights can be used both as a guide to better practice and as a measure to gauge success, an essential process ensuring the success of free-choice learning in America. Quality education requires quality assessment. However, if as a society we have found it challenging to define quality education, that's nothing compared to our problems understanding, designing, and actualizing a quality assessment program. Most of us grew up in a system where the focus and purpose of assessment was significantly perverted. For all intents and purposes, in most communities we possess absolutely no measures of the quality of education, even at the pre-college level where assessment through repeated standardized testing is rampant. Twenty-five years of assessment-focused education in schools leaves us still ignorant for the most part about how good or bad our schools are, how good or bad the teachers are, and how good or bad most children are as learners.

The entire premise on which traditional educational testing rests is inherently flawed and inappropriate for the world of free-choice learning, emphasizing the judgment of learners and institutions, rather than supporting people in their learning and institutions in their facilitating roles. Although standardized test scores have high reliability (consistently they measure the same thing), they often have no validity (what they measure is not meaningful learning) and they tend not to predict success in later learning much at all. This is why the president of the University of California recently advocated eliminating the use of standardized tests such as the SAT I as a requirement for college admission. Assessment, in the form of measuring and documenting meaningful learning and assisting learners in attaining their learning goals, is poorly executed to non-existent in virtually all parts of the education system, including the free-choice learning sector.

The entire purpose of assessment should be to provide useful and continuous feedback to learners and the individuals and institutions intent on supporting learning, helping them to accomplish the learning goals to which they individually and collectively aspire. Devising a comprehensive approach to assessing free-choice learning is a daunting task. Most of us have not spent much time thinking about assessment, an area long viewed as arcane and difficult by even professional educators. Fortunately, at least we think so, we have collectively spent nearly fifty years thinking about assessment, working as professional free-choice learning educators, researchers, and evaluators. We believe the key to meaningful assessment in the free-choice learning sector hinges on two principles—*continuous, ongoing assessment* and *feedback*.

Continuous, Ongoing Assessment

Most of us grew up in a system in which assessment was the test at the end of the unit, marking period, or course, and the assessment was the letter grade or promotion dispensed by the teacher or supervisor telling us whether we were excellent or failing. We had little or no input into the process, a system that seemed devised to separate those who were deemed worthy from those who were unworthy. The worthy were advanced, while the unworthy were held back. Consequently, and not surprisingly, most of us share a deep and abiding distrust and fear of assessment.

But there is no rule that says that assessment needs to be judgmental, and there is definitely no rule that says that assessment should only occur at the end of some time period. The best way to implement assessment is to conceptualize it as a strategy for helping learners to learn. In short, we advocate an approach to assessment that is consistent with the spirit and essence of free-choice learning, one that facilitates intrinsic motivation, rewards initiative and improvement and encourages personal responsibility. To be effective, it needs to start much sooner than it currently does—at the very beginning of the learning proc[e]. Assessment is crucial at the first stages of learning, helping to identify the m[ake] up of learners, including their prior knowledge, experience, interests, and providing insights into the best "hooks" to connect to learners' person[al inter]ests, prior knowledge, and experience.

However, ongoing assessment does not end here, but continues throughout the development process as feedback loops are built into the design of educational experiences, ensuring that they are truly meeting learning needs and goals and providing opportunities for modification and refinement, if necessary. Assessment continues through the implementation of the learning experience, providing designers and facilitators with feedback on what is working and not working, and why. In this way, future efforts can continue to be improved and future learners are better served.

The assessor, either a teacher, facilitator, or evaluator, serves as the helmsman on the ship, facilitating the navigation. The helmsman is not necessarily the person who determines the course, nor is he the person who judges whether it is a successful journey or not. He is the member of the crew who helps provide feedback to the ship. The helmsman is no more important than the cook who feeds the crew or the mechanic who keeps the engines functioning. Although a critical member of the crew that helps make the voyage possible, he is just one of many critical crew members. Ideally in some cases, the helmsman is the learner himself. In this case he does guide the ship and even directs the course, while always adjusting should prevailing currents disrupt his course or should different goals or opportunities seem more appropriate or timely at the moment.

In this way, assessment is not the end goal of education, but a crucial part of the learning process itself. And although positive assessment is not the goal of learning, positive feedback, should and must be. For the system to work, all components—the learner, the facilitator, and the organization—must receive a never-ending stream of feedback so that all parties know how well they are doing and how to do what they are doing better. In this model, assessment is not something to fear, but rather something to look forward to.

Feedback

Continuous feedback is the key to meaningful assessment. Telling someone they failed, or even succeeded, on an exam without telling them how and in what ways does not facilitate learning. Nor does telling an organization at the end of a program, exhibition, or theater presentation that they failed, or for that matter succeeded, without telling them how and in what ways. And only telling someone that they have failed or excelled without understanding how all parties in the process—learner and facilitator, apprentice and guide, child and parent, individual and institution—contributed to that failure or excellence, does not facilitate learning. All this type of assessment does is create dependent, impaired earners.

The best way to implement quality assessment is to conceptualize it as a tegy for helping learners to learn and institutions achieve their learning goals. if helping learners is the goal, then ongoing, continuous feedback is the elpful approach. Facilitating meaningful learning requires a system that continuous, nonjudgmental feedback, feedback that serves the needs of all participants in the process—the learner as well as the facilitator, the individual as well as the institution. We must create a system of assessment that defines its purpose as supporting and encouraging the needs of learners, whether individuals or groups of individuals, not just in the short-term but over the long-term. Thus, first and foremost, assessment should be designed to provide long-term encouragement, not short-term judgment. Learning needs to be transformed from an act of trying to please others to one of pleasing oneself!

Constructive feedback is the key to helping all parties know how well they are succeeding, helping institutions know whether or not they are accomplishing their educational objectives. If the World Wildlife Foundation wants to enhance public awareness, understanding, and action related to biodiversity, how will they know if they are being successful without feedback? Meaningful institutional feedback is not about giving WWF a grade for their efforts, nor is it about some artificial measure of success such as the number of hits on its Web site or the number of people who heard a particular public service announcement. These measures yield precious little data about value since they provide no feedback of significance; they do not tell the institution whether or not their public education efforts are really resulting in learning and behavior change, and if so, how and to what degree. Feedback is the tool that will enable free-choice learning institutions to achieve their goals, and if they fall short of their goals, it is the tool that will tell them why they have not accomplished their goals. More than good intentions and publicity, free-choice learning institutions need valid and reliable feedback about the impact of their various initiatives on peoples' lives, feedback so they can know how to invest their finite resources today and in the future. Quality feedback is also essential for acquiring and sustaining financial support. Contributors, whether public or private foundations or individuals, all want to know whether the organization is making progress toward achieving its learning goals. If the evidence indicates yes, additional support can be counted upon; if not, then support will inevitably wane, no matter how important the goal. Consequently, quality feedback is vital to the entire process.

Assessment of the success of free-choice learning experiences should be based on how well the five elements of the Free-Choice Learning Bill of Rights are accomplished. Rather than merely counting visitors, subscriptions, or other unrelated measures of satisfaction, those who work within the free-choice sector should be focusing on trying to grapple with the far more challenging task of identifying and measuring a range of meaningful outcomes. Led by Marianna Adams and Jessica Luke, the Institute for Learning Innovation has been trying to develop a list of broad outcomes that result from free-choice learning experiences, recognizing that the implication of the uniqueness of personal learning is that there are many different ways and things one can learn, even when participating with others in a shared experience.

Clearly there is the traditional notion of outcomes being about lea* building or refreshing their knowledge, attitudes, and perceptions about a often subject matter of some kind. But there are many other outcomes t* result. One can learn within the social/cultural domains, such as learning about and increasing appreciation for other people's and other cultures' uniqueness and similarities, as well as learning important life skills such as how to collaborate with others. There are also aesthetic/recreative outcomes such as renewal, refreshment, and restoration, often manifested by wonder, awe, joy, pleasure, and deeper spiritual understandings. Another important outcome is learners' understanding and ability to use resources in the community to fulfill their personal free-choice learning needs. As learners begin to use the entire community as a resource for personal learning, after each learning experience they hopefully better understand how they can do that in the future, an outcome we refer to as free-choice learning literacy. And depending upon the entering knowledge, understanding, and attitude of the learner, on occasion, free-choice learning experiences even result in transformation/connection, significant changes in thinking, attitudes, beliefs, behaviors, or habits-of-mind.

The implication of these broader outcomes is that we need to take a different approach to documenting and "measuring" personal and institutional success. Rather than saying what did someone learn after visiting this exhibition or participating in this program or making this piece of art, we need to be understanding how these experiences are connecting to people's lives and contributing to their personal fulfillment. By necessity the questions we ask are different. Was equal access to learning provided for all participants? Did educational efforts afford opportunities for diverse audiences to access, understand, and construct meaning from learning experiences? Did participants grow and mature as a consequence of their interaction with the institution? Did the experiences support meaningful social/cultural interaction? Did learners enhance their ability to use the institution as a learning tool, not just now, but for the future, and did the experience give learners the tools to extend their learning in other settings and situations? Did learners continue their pursuit of this topic after the learning experience? By assessing such broader outcomes we have a better chance of actually documenting the unique and personal meaning that learners construct from the experiences these institutions offer. We believe these are the true measures of personal and institutional success.

Recommendations for Facilitating Quality Assessment

We suggest that educators consider the following issues related to assessing free-choice learning experiences:

- Take the time to assess free-choice learning experiences—before design begins, during the development of experiences, and after. Such assessment helps to build better, more cost-effective, learner-centered free-choice learning experiences.

- Although assessment adds time and money to the development process, the result is quality education, and quality is rarely too high a cost to pay.

- Before creating any free-choice learning experience, develop clear learning goals and objectives; these goals and objectives should vary based on the need, age, and ability of the learner.

- Free-choice learning goals and objectives should be based on a broad definition of learning and be designed to support learners in their personal growth and development.

- Make sure the personal value and benefits of participating in the learning experience are always apparent to the learner, as are the requirements for participation.

- Strive to continuously collect meaningful feedback; don't neglect the beginning and middle of the process.

- Meaningful assessment of free-choice learning experiences should include both long-term and short-term measures of change and success.

- Don't settle for the easiest and most inexpensive measurements of success; strive for measuring what is meaningful, no matter how challenging.

By utilizing these suggestions for improving practice, it is hoped that free-choice learning institutions will be able to offer ever better learning experiences for the public. Our society would be well served if every part of the free-choice learning sector used the Free-Choice Learning Bill of Rights as a guideline for developing, implementing, and assessing their educational offerings. In this chapter we have emphasized assessment at the institutional level, but we could just as easily have focused on assessment at the level of the individual or at the level of entire communities. The Free-Choice Learning Bill of Rights provides a framework for assessing both personal learning experiences and the quality of community-wide free-choice learning efforts.

Quality free-choice learning experiences are clearly of value to individuals, institutions, and communities; they are also vital to the interests of the whole nation. As we have argued throughout this book, much of what people learn in their lives comes about through experiences in the free-choice learning sector. This has always been the case, but will become increasingly so as America and the rest of the world fully transition into a Learning Society. For these reasons we believe that free-choice learning represents the cornerstone of the new Learning Society, but, although it may be the cornerstone, it is not and cannot be the entire edifice.

iving back to the community: Native American college students mentoring younger ents (Photo by Judith Vergun, Native American Marine & Space Science am, Oregon State University)

CHAPTER 13

BUILDING A 21st CENTURY LEARNING SOCIETY, ONE LEARNER AT A TIME

There is always one unexpected little moment in life when a door opens and lets the future in.

—Graham Greene

No goal should be more important to America than building a Learning Society, a society in which every citizen has the desire, the abilities, and the tools to fulfill their learning needs across their entire life span. It is not just that this is the society we are striving to become, but it is the society we are already deep in the midst of becoming. Free-choice learning is at the core of this effort. Following the guidelines laid out throughout this book and especially in the previous chapter, we can maximize the potential of free-choice learning to contribute to a healthy and vibrant community of lifelong learners. However, even the most fully formed and functioning free-choice learning sector by itself would be insufficient to create and sustain a Learning Society.

As we begin a new millennium and see the dawning of a new economic order based primarily on ideas rather than things, rethinking and reenergizing our educational system seems only appropriate. Our future depends upon having an educational system that can be responsive to the needs of today and anticipate the demands of tomorrow. However, the new educational system of the twenty-first century must be based upon a whole new concept of education, one that says: *Learning is an essential part of every facet of society, and an individual citizen's learning needs are supported every moment of the day, every day of their life.* The current educational infrastructure can be used as a starting point for this new system, but our fundamental approach to education needs to change so that all parts of the current educational system are fully used and integrated. Although our current formal education sector—pre-K through graduate school—is vital to our nation's education, it is not, in and of itself, sufficient. *A successful American education system cannot be based solely upon schooling; it must also include free-choice learning and workplace learning.*

For America to fully transform itself into a Learning Society, the active involvement of all three educational sectors is required. As long as we're all in the same vehicle, we would be well advised to drive in the same direction, but there is no evidence that this is currently happening. Although America possesses the educational capacity to be a world leader in twenty-first-century learning, it is squandering this capacity through a lack of clarity, direction, and purpose. To achieve the promise of a fully functioning Learning Society engine requires that all three cylinders—formal schooling, workplace learning, and free-choice learning—fire completely and in synchrony. Currently, all three are firing, but are functioning largely in isolation, each driven by widely differing perceptions of what their goals and role in society should be. The good news is that the key constituents for change are already in place; America possesses the finest learning infrastructure in the world. The bad news is that the infrastructure is not connected and no one at the top seems to see how the pieces could and should become interconnected. We believe that the greatest challenge to the full transformation of America into a Learning Society is intellectual inertia. Change will require undoing deeply ingrained beliefs and habits and must happen from the bottom up, with vision from the top down. This will not be easy.

One possible approach is to apply the principles of the Free-Choice Learner's Bill of Rights to the entire educational system. This would suggest that all learners in all sectors should be given access to the learning resources of all parts of the community and provided a breadth and depth of educational opportunity sufficient to satisfy their personal curiosity and need to know, insuring they live full and satisfying lives. Likewise, citizens should be given the opportunity to learn in supportive and educationally reinforcing social, cultural, and physical environments wherever they are learning. And at every developmental stage, learning opportunities that promote age-appropriate learning exploration and mastery should be provided in all sectors. These are fundamental rights of all learners and should be at the core of a new twenty-first-century educational system. To achieve these rights will require rethinking and redefining the educational system to accommodate each citizen's learning needs. Throughout this book we have presented myriad ways to begin thinking about the why, where, when, and how of learning, focused mainly on free-choice learning. In this final chapter, we will expand our discussion of these four aspects of learning to the entire educational system, suggesting ways to create a better educational future in America.

Changing Why We Educate

In a Learning Society, the lifelong learning path we choose defines who we are as individuals. Each person's learning path is unique and should be supported by a whole range of institutions and individuals over the course of a lifetime. Although there will be many of these institutions and individuals involved in each learning journey, and many reasons for their involvement (some only distantly related to the learner's personal goals), ultimately all involved in the educational process must accept one premise: *The goal of all education should be individual growth and fulfillment.* This goal should not be driven by the needs and interests of the institution, whether a corporation, a school, a museum, or a television station. The goal of education must always be to support the learning needs of each and every unique learner.

The following story recently appeared in a leading business magazine:

> On a recent trip to Boston, my friend John H. went to a fashionably casual dinner party. The guests were a Gen X crowd—mid to late twenties, affluent, and well educated. They were either employed in the high-tech computer industry or helping their old-economy firms master technology. Much of the evening's conversation revolved around high-tech careers.
>
> Like a fly on the wall, John listened with amazement. All were engaged in some sort of personally guided education program. Some were teaching themselves new computer languages, one was learning Spanish, another was taking a writing course, and two others were learning the art of management on-line.
>
> A few of John's fellow guests were going to night classes. Others simply ordered the manuals, bought the books, and taught themselves. John was shocked to discover that they were doing all of that learning on their own accord. Some courses—especially the more conventional ones—were subsidized partially by employers, but most were not.
>
> "Why spend your limited free time doing all this learning?" John asked his hostess. "You've got to keep yourself marketable at all times," she replied. "You never know when one of these stock market darlings is going to go belly up. You've got to stay on top of everything—you know, keep learning."
>
> The average amount of time these people spent at a job was in the neighborhood of six months to a year. A better job was always around the corner—and said job usually came looking for them. John asked, "By a better job, you mean better money, hours and benefits ... right?"
>
> "Not exactly," she responded. "Of course those things are important, but finding a job that will teach you and grow you is more important. You have to be as marketable as possible. Plenty of 'good jobs' out there are actually dead-end jobs. They pay well and give great benefits, but if they don't grow you, you're vulnerable. If anything goes wrong and you have to reenter the job market with outdated skills, you're up the creek without a paddle."

This story confirms what many have said about Generation X workers, that they are looking for employers who will not only invest in their companies, but will also invest in their workers. However, this growing belief in the need to be better educated does not merely relate to young employees. Certainly for a young employee the emphasis is likely to be on short-term marketability, but what about a middle-aged or older employee?

These employees, too, are increasingly feeling that the workplace owes them more than a salary and benefits package, that they need to be part of the organization in more meaningful ways. For many older workers this is a desire to feel appreciated and respected for the skills and knowledge they possess. They want to work in a place where management allows them to make changes, based on what they know to be a better way to run the organization; they also want to be encouraged and rewarded for helping to train and mentor younger employees. Employees, and in particular managers, should be compensated and rewarded for their role in creating a healthy, happy, and learning-focused work environment. Research from the Society for Human Resource Management indicates that a sense of feeling appreciated and of being supported in achieving a desired career path are the two most crucial factors in job retention today.

All of us are seeking personal fulfillment and satisfaction. Throughout time and certainly today, the path to fulfillment and satisfaction is the road of learning. Whether workplace, school, or the free-choice sector, the public is seeking help in their personal life journey. We can create an educational system that helps people find their own personal path to intellectual, spiritual, and social satisfaction, or we can create an educational system that blocks that path. Today, despite the best of intentions, our educational system opens up pathways to some but not all, while focusing almost exclusively on a narrow sense of the intellectual to the exclusion of the humanist, spiritual, and social.

The key to creating a self-motivated, self-sustaining, self-fulfilled society is redirecting the focus of all education to the individual, rather than the institution, supporting individual learning goals rather than institutional learning goals, and abolishing one-size-fits-all models for one-size-fits-one models. We are in the midst of an economic revolution involving the total transformation of the how and why of the production of goods and services. In the industrial society goods and services were uniformly mass-produced to meet the needs of a large, undifferentiated, "mass" market. In the knowledge society goods and services are custom-produced to meet the needs of niche markets, populated by individual consumers with unique requirements and expectations. Our educational system must undergo a similar transformation, away from a mass production model to one of customized delivery to individual learners. In a Learning Society all citizens are learners.

Changing Where We Learn

In a Learning Society all society is involved with education, so at the core of our vision for transforming education is changing ideas about where learning occurs. America must redefine its educational priorities so that it fully embraces and supports the idea that all parts of society have an important role to play in the educational enterprise. We must abandon the ideas that we can delegate all responsibility for education to a single, monolithic institution such as schooling and that education is something that happens only during a certain stage in one's life—childhood. We also must abandon the idea that education is something that happens only during a particular time frame—fall through spring, 9 to 3, and instead recognize it as a lifetime priority of all parts and all people in society. The solution is not innovative charter schools or allowing families to exercise choice in which schools their children attend or some other school-based reform. Even if we improved schooling in America, it would still be inadequate to meet the needs of learners across the life span. Although redundant, it bears repeating: A successful American education system cannot be based solely upon schooling.

For simplicity, we have subdivided the educational community into three major educational sectors—schooling, workplace, and free-choice—what we call the educational infrastructure of a community. Currently, only one sector in this infrastructure receives full public recognition, utilization, and support as an educational sector. The education of our citizenry suffers as a consequence. Each sector can, and must, play a vital role in the lifetime learning of each individual. As individuals grow and develop, their needs evolve and change. By integrating the capacities and opportunities uniquely embedded within each of the major educational sectors, American society would possess an educational system with sufficient capacity and flexibility to meet the ever-changing learning needs of all citizens throughout their lifetimes. Schooling, working, and free-choice learning are each essential components of a lifetime of educational opportunity; none are individually sufficient. Our goal here is to suggest that the most effective way to meet the learning needs of all citizens, across an entire lifetime, is to utilize all components of the educational infrastructure of a community. We advocate the full utilization of schools, the workplace, and the free-choice learning sector; the learning resources of all three sectors should be available to every citizen, every day of their life. The entire educational infrastructure provides value and support to the nation, and the entire infrastructure needs to be valued and supported.

Currently, there are numerous examples of how this can work. The Smithsonian Early Education Center, housed at the National Museum of American History, allows children free access to the resources of the entire museum community, before and after school. The high school students at the Henry Ford Museum and Greenfield Village High School not only use the objects and documents of the institution to learn about innovation and invention, but the students are taught by curators. In turn, the curators use the students to help with their teaching and educational jobs. In Des Moines, Iowa, an elementary school is located adjacent to a shopping mall and utilizes the mall and all of the downtown businesses as part of normal classroom space. Similar schools exist throughout the country. In Brooklyn, public school facilities are now open nearly twenty-four hours a day to allow the entire community access to the educational resources concentrated there, and the public library has become a major player in both child and adult learning programs in this recently immigrant-dominated community. And some of the largest and most progressive companies in America, such as IBM, Southwest Airlines, and Hewlett Packard, not only allow but encourage employees to volunteer their time and talents in the community, particularly in educational efforts, in schools and in the free-choice learning sector.

Particularly innovative is the "In Their Footsteps/Senior to Senior Program" in Astoria, Oregon, which pairs high school seniors with senior citizens to collect oral histories of community elders that are then turned into multimedia programs for the public (digital videos, CD-Roms, and Web sites). The high school seniors receive the benefits of the collected knowledge and wisdom of their senior citizen partners, as well as insights into history and "on the job training" in multimedia production. Their senior partners are introduced to the latest in multimedia technology and reintroduced to history, while community elders are provided a forum in which to share their stories. All participants in the program benefit by these intergenerational exchanges.

In a transformed educational system, each sector would fulfill its responsibilities continuously. There would be no exclusive responsibility of schools for the education of children, and no exclusive responsibility of the workplace for the education of adults. Responsibility would be equally shared by all sectors, across all time. Schools would play a role in the education of adults, and yes, the workplace would play an active role in the education of children. The free-choice sector, too, would be actively integrated into the educational support of all citizens. We believe that if all three sectors truly pooled their resources, if the lines between school, work, and leisure were sufficiently blurred, there would be ample capacity to provide quality learning experiences for all citizens, all of the time.

One example of what we believe the future could and should look like comes from an unlikely major business, the U.S. Army. A couple of years ago the Army initiated a new advertising campaign. In this campaign there are no guns or soldiers, no tanks or missile launchers. Teenagers share candid stories about surmounting hardships such as pregnancy or a brush with the law to persevere in furthering their education. According to the Army, the goal of the campaign was not just to entice new recruits, but to change the public's view of the military. As the armed forces competed for workers within a knowledge economy, the Pentagon brass appreciated that they needed to proactively insure a suitable pool of recruits AND insure that those recruits arrived appropriately educated to fulfill their roles and responsibilities in the military. The ad campaign was thus equal measure a recruiting campaign and a stay-in-school campaign aimed at twelve- to fourteen-year-olds.

"The Army has a very clear interest in broadening the pool of potential recruits with high school diplomas. But fundamentally this campaign is an opportunity for the Army to gain good will by showing the American people that we do much more than fight and win wars, that we are an educator and trainer of the nation's youth," said then Army Secretary Louis Caldera. According to an article in the Washington Post, "the armed forces are promoting the intangible values of military service in part because they realize they cannot compete with civilian jobs on pay alone, even with enlistment bonuses that commonly reach $6,000." As a result, all branches of the service are expanding programs to allow recruits to earn college credits while in the service, either for military training or through distance learning courses over the Internet. Recruits can not only earn two-year degrees, but can gain benefits that will help to pay for continued education after their stint in the service. The Army and other military branches have come to appreciate that in the twenty-first century, the business they run has an educational responsibility that extends beyond the current needs of their employees. They also appreciate that supporting and encouraging the educational aspirations of their employees is not a distraction, but an integral part of what it takes to run a successful business.

The Native American Marine and Space Science (NAMSS) program at Oregon State University is another example of what we believe the future could and should look like. It is an innovative program pushing the boundaries of where we learn in the formal schooling sector. Now over ten years old, NAMSS has significantly increased the number of Native American students earning B.S. degrees—98 percent of the students in the program graduate—and it has also significantly increased the number of Native American students entering graduate school—40 percent go on to graduate work. Project staff credit success with the fact that students have the opportunity for free-choice learning, through self-selected internships with mentor professors on campus or off campus in the business and scientific research world, and through participation in a strong native community outreach network, serving themselves as mentors for young Native American pre-college students who are considering the study of science, math, and engineering. Presentations of their own original research at professional societies, such as the American Geophysical Union, the American Society for Limnology and Oceanography, the Ecological Society of America, and the Society for Ecological Restoration–Indigenous Peoples' Network, are also encouraged.

During summers, NAMSS students are also required to dedicate a portion of their internship experience to community service or outreach programs to teach, or assist in teaching, younger Native American students and, in some cases, the general public. An important principle requires that learners share what they learn with others, so these opportunities to give back to their community are both personally rewarding and extremely important culturally. Interestingly, NAMSS educational programs have also expanded Oregon State's cultural competency, by supporting the development of new courses, such as Traditional Ecological Knowledge, which provide insight into native ways of knowing. Individual learners and the institution have both benefited.

Changing How We Learn

In a Learning Society all educational efforts should be based upon sound principles of learning. In Albany, New York, deep within an inner-city neighborhood that includes some of the poorest families in America, one school is changing the way they think about what and how they teach. Each student in this new public elementary school is developing his or her own personal learning contract. In collaboration with their teachers and parents, each student gets to figure out not only what they want to learn, but how, in what order and in what ways, and even in many cases where best to learn. In this new model of teaching, the teacher and parents become helpful guides for a student's own personally directed learning journey. The school, as well as the community in which it is situated, becomes the vehicle for helping to launch a lifetime of learning.

It seems too obvious to state, but educational policy and practice in America should be based on the best and most current research on human learning. Currently, educational practice in most schools, universities, work place educational programs, museums, community programs, and on the Internet, suffers from a profound ignorance of the nature of human learning. This must change.

One of the most successful educational efforts of recent years was Ken Burns' television documentary series on the American Civil War. Of course there are many reasons why this show was successful, but without a doubt one of the primary reasons was Burns' skillful ability to transform a distant and arguably abstract period in history into an intensely human, personal story. Unlike most previous efforts to present the Civil War, Burns did not take a textbook approach, focusing exclusively on war strategy, military armament, or even the politics of the period. Instead, he used personal histories, letters, songs, and photographs from the period to bring history alive in a way many had never before experienced; history was presented as the story of real people, powerfully influenced by real events. Burns nailed home this point at the end of the first night's show with a letter from Private Ballou, written to his wife on the eve of the first battle at Bull Run/Manassas, the first major battle of the war. In a style familiar to all moviegoers, mood-appropriate period music accompanied the recitation of the letter. This strikingly poetic letter described the hopes and fears of a man about to face death in battle, as well as his enduring and passionate love for his wife and children back home. The emotions stirred by this letter, and the fact that Private Ballou did in fact die in battle the next day, powerfully touched the viewer, personally and intellectually, in a way no amount of dates, facts, or statistics ever could have. Through the skillful use of emotion, combined with first-hand accounts, photographs, and the judicious use of facts and concepts, Ken Burns successfully taught millions of people about historical events few ever thought they were particularly interested in. Over the course of several evenings, Burns told us a story; he interspersed humor, pathos, surprise, mystery, outrage, and pity as he interwove the events and intrigues of the period. The viewer experienced the events of that tumultuous time through the "voices" of the participants, through their music and photographic images. Burns' use of primary source material was true to the best practices of modern historians, but unlike many historians today who seem more concerned with process than product, Burns did not dilute the impact of the show by attempting to teach people about how to study history. His ultimate achievement was his skillful use of the technology of television to deliver accurate historical information to a lay public. It required a deep understanding of both the needs and interests of the historian, as well as the needs and interests of the general public. In the process, Burns created not just a successful educational television program, but a standard against which all subsequent educational programming is now judged. The take-home message is not to try and mimic his technique, as many, including Burns himself, have subsequently done (with sometimes only marginal success), but to find the unique personal connections and stories in each project that will resonate with users and allow a diverse audience access to the topic.

The success of this television series was not that every viewer ended up knowing at least one specific, predetermined new fact or concept about the American Civil War, rather that the show afforded every viewer the opportunity to connect and learn at least one new thing that was personally relevant. The designers of the show obviously appreciated that an audience of millions of viewers would be entering and exiting the experience with differing learning agendas and purposes, and they strove to accommodate these differences. They also appreciated that learning could occur even if a viewer watched only one segment, or even just one part of one segment. The result was an educational experience that permitted, in fact encouraged, viewers to bring their own unique understandings and interests to the experience, an experience that yielded a wide diversity of learning outcomes.

Educational efforts throughout America would do well to emulate this model. This does not mean that we always create a television program to teach what we hope to share with learners but that education must be predicated on an appreciation that each human experiences and finds meaning in the world in a unique, highly personal way. Knowledge and understanding are not absolutes, but personally constructed views of reality. Learning is an ancient process, molded by millions of years of evolution, designed to enable the organism to have a safer, longer, and consequently more satisfying life. All learning is about finding meaning in the events of the world in such a way that each individual can make current and future decisions that enhance and extend his or her life. The power of the Ken Burns series was that it connected to people in highly personal ways, allowing them to experience and understand the Civil War as never before. In the course of this experience viewers also learned something about themselves.

Whether in school, at work, or while involved in free-choice learning, the purpose of education must be just that—to connect personally with learners in order to meet and facilitate their learning needs. Individuals are unique, not only in how they look and act, but also in how they think and make sense of the world. Thus efforts to facilitate learning need to be geared toward supporting the uniqueness of each individual, rather than targeted at some imaginary "typical" student. Education needs to take advantage of personal needs and motivations, rather than trying to force learners to learn things they are neither ready for nor motivated to learn.

We also now understand that all learning is highly contextual, strongly influenced by what someone already knows and understands, what they feel and believe, and their unique view of the world. We know, too, that learning is strongly influenced by the social and cultural relationships of that individual and the physical environment in which the learning occurs. Learning is not some kind of abstract event that happens in the vacuum of the mind, but quite the opposite: Our minds work very hard at making sure that every bit of new information, experience, feeling, or thought is firmly anchored and attached to other bits of information, experience, feeling, and thought in our brain. Everything is connected, and the greater and more appropriate the connections we construct, the easier it is to remember and use that newly constructed learning. Humanity's greatest evolutionary advantage over all other creatures was our ability to use language to facilitate learning, enabling us to use other humans to help make learning connections.

Humans are highly social creatures, and we learn much if not most of what we know in the company of others. Parents instruct their children, and more often than we would like to acknowledge, children teach their parents. Adults teach each other, children teach each other. All of us, every day, interact and learn from the people in our world. Most of the time, we don't consciously think of these interactions as being educational experiences, but they are. In a transformed educational system, even our everyday encounters would be appreciated for the important educational function they play. Once consciously elevated to the status of "important," these everyday interactions with others would become more frequent and more productive.

America must embrace the fact that not only is every citizen a lifelong learner, but every citizen is also a lifelong educator! Whether we are three or 103 years of age, each of us has much to learn, and each of us has a role in helping others to learn. For years we have been bombarded with rhetoric about a teacher shortage, but in actuality there is no teacher shortage in America. If we think about education as encompassing more than schooling, there are 285 million learners in America, and by a wonderful coincidence, there are 285 million teachers, a perfect one-to-one ratio. We need only to figure out how best to support and encourage each and every one of us to be both learners and teachers. The deficiency in the system is not the human resources, but the commitment to and knowledge of how to convert our human resources into effective practice.

If every mother and father better understood how important their interactions with their infants and young children were, and how to facilitate those interactions, more children would grow up in intellectually stimulating environments. At present, large segments of our population grow up deprived, not because of a lack of interest or desire on the part of their parents, but due to a lack of parental experience and knowledge about how to optimize the educational home experiences of their children. In our current system, economic disadvantage is perpetuated through educational disadvantage. In a transformed educational system, priority would be placed on helping each and every American parent better understand their roles and abilities as their children's first and most important educators, rather than trying to compensate entirely with schooling. Every parent would be provided the support necessary to perform these educational functions rather than made to feel inadequate, as is often currently the case, and every child would be not only a learner, but also a teacher to their parents, rather than erroneously being told and shown daily that only adults have any knowledge worth communicating. Imagine how wonderful it would be if our children were encouraged to help adults learn how to explore the world with fresh eyes so that we too could discover that even everyday phenomenon and experiences are full of wonder and surprise. No educational gift could be more precious!

The parent-child relationship is only one facet of the social and cultural context of learning. A wealth of research documents how important mentors and facilitators are in most people's lives. Sometimes that mentor is a professional educator, but often the mentor is a family member, a friend, an acquaintance, or co-worker. All of us benefit from the guidance of others when learning and, ultimately, none of us can be taught anything, we can only have our learning facilitated by someone willing to share his or her knowledge and experience with us. Many of us are fortunate enough to have found a mentor in our lives, someone who has been willing to help us achieve our potential, someone who, through the sharing of their experiences, shortens our learning journey even if only slightly. All three educational sectors should strive to increase the number of mentors and facilitators they support, ultimately trying to help each participant experience the joys of being both a learner and a teacher.

Learning is a process of making connections between the internal/mental world of the mind and the external/physical world. Not surprisingly then, being in the world helps with these connections; being in appropriate physical contexts facilitates learning. In other words, it is easier for children to learn about animals at the zoo or in a wild place, where they can actually stand face-to-face with real animals, for adolescents to learn about the world of work while actually doing a job, and for adults to learn mathematics through solving real problems in the real world rather than by doing exercises in a book. It is why all of us benefit by traveling and talking to all kinds of people in order to understand that the ways we Americans live and think are not the only ways for people to live and think. This is why doing new things with hands and mind, trying strange foods, manipulating unfamiliar objects, and seeing curious sights are so intrinsically motivating and enjoyable, as humans we are pre-adapted to derive pleasure from some novelty. The most important take-away message from all of this is that facilitating learning in appropriate physical contexts is not a waste of time;

in fact, it is the opposite that tends to be a waste of time. Learning in appropriate settings is likely to be long remembered and easily transferred to new situations. Learning in irrelevant or inappropriate settings is likely to be little remembered and difficult to generalize to new situations. Children need to be out in the world, adolescents need to be doing real things that really matter, and adults need to have access to multiple experiences and information sources. All individuals need to be able to experiment with different roles and responsibilities, to investigate the unknown in a safe and secure way, and to live life in physical environments that appropriately support and reinforce our learning needs, whatever the stage of our learning journey.

Changing When We Learn

In a Learning Society, learning is a journey, not a destination, a journey with peaks and valleys, breakthroughs and letdowns, a continuous cycle of never-ending exploration, followed by a few, deeper periods of mastery. Such mastery opens up opportunities for further exploration. Every stage in life involves gradations of exploration and mastery and each stage has its own unique needs and requirements, opportunities and challenges.

Prenatal infants are in deep preparation for all of life's journeys, including learning. By the time of birth, the infant is well primed to learn and the stage is appropriately set for a lifetime of learning. In recent years much has been made about the importance of the early childhood years for learning. This is absolutely true, but as we've tried to emphasize, all stages of life are equally important for learning; none should be ignored or given short shrift. A quality education system should support learning throughout a person's lifetime in all kinds of settings.

Let's take adulthood. As suggested earlier, mastery is one of the most fundamental aspects of adulthood. Nowhere is this more prevalent, and more satisfying, than in the workplace. In recent years, considerable attention has been placed upon those few business leaders who have become masters themselves at supporting and nurturing learning and personal mastery among their staff, collaborative teams, and entire organizations. In these increasingly competitive times, organizational learning is perceived as essential to a corporation's viability and sustainability. And clearly, it is only through the personal learning of individuals in an organization, and the collaborative learning of teams, that the organization itself learns. A number of visionary business leaders have come to believe that over the long term, the more they encourage educational growth and mastery among their staff, individually and collaboratively, the more economically successful they will be.

For instance, Kazuo Inamori, founder and president of Kyocera, a world leader in advanced ceramics technology, is one of a small number of organizational leaders recognizing the importance of individual and team learning. It is his belief that if his employees themselves are not motivated to grow and develop technologically, there is no way that the organization can grow intellectually, become more productive, or develop technologically. He teaches his employees to "look inward as they continually strive for perfection, guided by the corporate motto: 'Respect Heaven and Love People.'" The corporation provides a multitude of opportunities for personal and spiritual growth, even allowing meditation time during the workday.

Another notable example is business leader Bill O'Brien, president of Hanover Insurance. O'Brien also passionately believes that the total development of his staff is essential to achieving corporate excellence. He believes that there is no fundamental trade-off between the higher virtues of life and economic success. In fact, he and his managers believe that over the long term, the more they encourage personal growth and mastery, the more economically successful they will be. After all, people with high levels of personal mastery tend to be more committed, take more initiative, have a broader and deeper sense of responsibility in their work, and ultimately learn faster. For all these reasons, Hanover Insurance encourages personal growth among their employees because they believe it makes the organization stronger.

Learning does not stop at retirement, though, even at the age of sixty, seventy, eighty, and beyond, there are new sights, smells, tastes, sounds, and feelings to be discovered. Getting older does not exempt us from the need for, or the pleasure of, exploration and mastery. Every stage in life should be filled with the challenges of learning—challenges, as discussed earlier, that are appropriate to the skills and abilities of the learner, agreed upon by the learner, and attainable as well. Historically, because the opportunity for self-selection and choice has always been present and possible, the free-choice learning sector has been a model of age-appropriate learning. Unfortunately, because of externally imposed criteria of success and productivity, schools and the workplace have sometimes not afforded all learners equal opportunities to explore and master their learning at a level appropriate to the needs and motivations of the individual. But this, too, as we've suggested, is beginning to change. In the future, we should all have the opportunity, regardless of our age, to discover the joys and intricacies of biology, chemistry, physics, geology, history, geography, political science, art, music, and many other topics at the core of the human experience. The site for learning these topics may be a school, but just as likely the setting will be our places of employment or our homes, and the vehicle a technology such as the Internet.

Then again, perhaps the best model we can provide for an organization that supports continuous, age-appropriate, multi-entry learning is that stalwart of the Industrial Age, the public library. In communities large and small, in buildings new and old, Americans of every age, ability, and income have equal access to the collective knowledge of the world. There are books for toddlers, written at appropriate levels of complexity, using only single syllable words, in large print and amply illustrated to accommodate the needs of early learners. For the young child there are stories, biographies, and materials on every topic guaranteed to spark the imagination of even the most curious child. There are books for teens and young adults, many explicitly designed to explore issues and concerns of those coming of age. For adults there are vast collections of materials: books, periodicals, folios, and, increasingly, virtual texts, on a range of topics, including how-to books, travel guides, reference books, fiction, and nonfiction—something for everyone. And for older learners there are materials designed for their needs; coming full circle, many are written in large type to accommodate diminishing physical abilities. In all of these libraries are readily available staff, willing and able to assist the learner in finding just the book or resource to satisfy their unique, personal interests and needs. Not a bad model for a successful educational organization!

So as we proceed into the twenty-first century, let us rethink our education system, but let us not abandon that which has been successful. We can build a new and better tomorrow. As we build the future, clearly there is much that must be abandoned and rebuilt, but there is also much that is worth preserving and reusing.

Creating a Twenty-First-Century Learning Society

Reforming education in America and fulfilling the promise of a fully functioning Learning Society, though daunting, is not an impossible task. In broad strokes we have attempted to paint a vision. Many of these suggestions require time, careful thought, and much restructuring. However, before we conclude, we would like to make a few very specific recommendations which could be implemented sooner, rather than later, and would in our opinion significantly speed America's transformation into a Learning Society.

- Focus educational reform efforts upon individuals rather than institutions. Make the lifelong learning success of each citizen the focus of educational policy, regardless of age, income, race, ethnicity, gender, or religion.

- Restructure all Departments of Education at the national, state, and local level into Departments of Learning to encompass all types and degrees of lifelong learning in the schooling sector, but also the free-choice learning and workplace sectors.

- Insure that federal, state, and local support of education is more equitably distributed to all parts of the educational infrastructure. The free-choice learning and workplace learning sectors deserve and require as much attention and financial support as the formal schooling sector.

- Establish a lifelong learning budget for every citizen and provide structures that will enable each individual to wisely and carefully invest that budget. Individuals should be able to spend their learning budgets at any time in their lives, and within any part of the educational infrastructure.

- Create, train, and support a cadre of personal learning coaches who can assist parents, children, teens, adults, and seniors with the development and assessment of their own personal learning goals and objectives. Make access to these personal learning coaches a right of all citizens, not the privilege of a few.

- Develop new models of assessment that focus on individual growth and development rather than group averages and standards. This shift in focus will facilitate intrinsic motivation, reward initiative and improvement, and encourage personal responsibility. Such assessment needs to start at the very beginning of the learning process and support the learner throughout their entire personal learning journey. We need to begin developing and implementing these new assessment models *now*.

Our future requires that we have a better-educated citizenry, but being well educated does not mean being able to pass multiple-choice tests, or jump through meaningless academic hoops. A well-educated citizen possesses the basic skills necessary to have a successful career in our modern work world, and if he or she chooses to be a parent, he or she needs to possess the skills necessary to competently facilitate the learning of their children and others in their immediate family. This new citizen also has an awareness of the rich worlds of experience and knowledge that represent the collective million-plus years of human history, as well as the skills and capacity to explore their own personal, intellectual, and spiritual growth and enrichment—in other words, to continually learn wherever he or she is, whenever he or she chooses, throughout his or her lifetime. These are the learning goals that, if fulfilled, will result in a well-educated citizenry.

Many may read this chapter and say that in principle this all seems fine, but how can we possibly make it work? Maybe this would work for a few individuals, but what about a whole society? How can we take these few examples and scale them up so that they work for everyone? The answer is, you cannot. This is the point—you cannot take what works for a few individuals and scale it up for everyone; that is the mass production model. Meaningful education is a process that starts with learners at the grass roots, with vision and leadership from the top. What we need to do is find not one strategy, but thousands if not millions of strategies that work, and scale them out so that ultimately all citizens are involved. If the history of educational reform has taught us anything, it is the wisdom of this approach. So let's stop trying to find large-scale solutions.

We need to change our strategies, and invest our resources in insuring that all citizens have equal access to the educational opportunities that work for them. Just as individual learners construct meaning from each educational experience they have, we as a society must construct an educational system that develops the learning skills and potentials of each and every unique citizen. From the ground up, we must support each and every citizen in applying their potentials and using their acquired skills on their own unique educational journey. This is a challenging task, but we believe it is possible. To do so will require tremendous changes, and for many a significant reordering of priorities. We will have to break down some systems, but we will find in doing so that we have the capacity to truly achieve meaningful educational reform and meet the educational needs of all twenty-first-century learners. The raw material exists, the know-how exists, and certainly the need and desire exist. What we have lacked is a vision of what meaningful educational reform could and should look like, a vision we hope we have begun to elucidate. What we need now is the leadership and the will to make change happen.

Everything you can imagine is real.

Pablo Picasso

REFERENCES

CHAPTER 1

p. 2 Sheppard, B. (2001). *Museums, libraries and the 21st century learner.* Washington, DC: Institute for Museum & Library Services.

p. 3 Christoffel, P. 1978. *Toward a learning society: Future federal funding of learning.* Princeton, NJ: The College Board; Sakata, B. 1975. Toward lifelong learning. *Educational Perspectives,* December, 14.

p. 3 Dizard, W.P. (1982). *The coming information age.* New York: Longman, Inc.

p. 3 Machlup, F. (1962). *The production and distribution of knowledge in the U.S.* Princeton: Princeton University Press.

p. 3 Pine II, B.J. & Gilmore, J.H. (1999). *The experience economy: Work is theatre & every business a stage.* Boston: Harvard Business School Press.

p. 3, 4 Shenk, D. (1997). *Data smog: Surviving the information glut.* New York: Harper Collins Publishers.

p. 4 Clifford, G. (1981). The past is prologue. In: K. Cirincione-Coles (Ed.) *The future of education: Policy issues and challenges.* Beverly Hills, CA: Sage Publications.

p. 4 Cremin, L. (1980). *American education: The national experience.* New York: Harper & Row Publishers.

p. 4 Harris, N. (1979). The lamp of learning: Popular lights and shadows. In: A. Oleson and J. Voss (Eds.), *The organization of knowledge in modern America, 1860-1920.* Baltimore, MD: The Johns Hopkins Press.

p. 4 Hilton, W.J. (1981). Lifelong learning. In: K. Cirincione-Coles (Ed.) *The future of education: Policy issues and challenges.* Beverly Hills, CA: Sage Publications.

p. 5 Lewington, J. (1998). More Canadians pursuing informal learning, survey reveals. *The Globe and Mail,* November 11, A13.

CHAPTER 2

p. 12 Falk, J. H. (Ed.) (2001). *Free-Choice science learning: How people learn science outside of school.* New York: Columbia Teachers College Press.

p. 12 Falk, J. H. & Coulson, D. (2000). *Los Angeles science education research (LASER) project: Telephone survey report.* Annapolis, MD: Institute for Learning Innovation.

p. 13 Rosenweig, R. & Thelen, D. (1998). *The presence of the past: Popular uses of history in American life,* New, NY: Columbia University Press.

p. 15 deCharms, R. (1968). *Personal causation: The internal affective determinants of behavior.* New York: Academic Press.

p. 15 Deci, E.L. (1992). The relation of interest to the motivation of behavior: A self-determination theory perspective. In: K.A. Renninger, S. Hidi and A. Krapp. (Eds.) *The role of interest in learning and development.* Hillsdale, NJ: Erlbaum.

p. 15 Deci, E.L. & Ryan, R. M. (1985). *Intrinsic motivation and self-determination in human behavior.* New York: Plenum.

p. 15 Deci, E.L., Schwartz, A.J., Sheinman, L. & Ryan, R.M. (1981). An instrument to assess adults' orientations toward control versus autonomy with children: Reflections on intrinsic motivation and perceived competence. *Journal of Educational Psychology,* 73, 642-50.

p. 15 Deiner, C.I. & Dweck, C.S. (1980). An analysis of learned helplessness: The process of success. *Journal of Personality and Social Psychology,* 31, 674-85.

p. 15 Dewey, J. (1913). *Interest and effort in education.* Boston: Riverside Press.

p. 15 Harlow, H.F. (1954). Motivational forces underlying behavior. In: *Kentucky symposium: learning theory and clinical research,* pp. 36-53. New York, John Wiley & Sons.

p. 15 Herbart, J.F. (1965). Umriss padagogischer vorlesungen [Lectures on pedagogy]. In J.F. Herbart (Ed.) *Padagogische schriften,* Vol. 2, pp. 9-155. Dusseldorf: Kupper. (Original work published 1806.)

p. 15 Maehr, M.L. (1984). Meaning and motivation: Toward a theory of personal investment. In: *Research on motivation in education Vol. 1. Student motivation.* New York: Academic Press.

p. 15 McCombs, B.L. (1991). Motivation and lifelong learning. *Educational Psychologist* 26(2): 117-127.

p. 15 Paris, S.G. (1997). Situated motivation and informal learning. *Journal of Museum Education,* 22(2 & 3), 22-27.

p. 15 White, R.W. (1949). Motivation reconsidered: The concept of competence. *Psychological Review,* 297-333.

p. 16 Covington, M.V. (1992). *Making the grade: A self-worth perspective on motivation and school reform.* Cambridge: Cambridge University Press.

p. 16, 18 Csikzentmihalyi, M. (1990a). *Flow: The psychology of optimal experience.* New York: Harper Collins.

p. 16 Gottfried, A. (1985). Academic intrinsic motivation in elementary and junior high school students. *Journal of Educational Psychology,* 77, 631-45.

p. 16 Paris, S.G. & Cross, D.R. (1983). Ordinary learning: Pragmatic connections among children's beliefs, motives, and actions. In: J. Bisanz, G. Bisanz and R. Kail (Eds.) *Learning in children,* pp. 137-69. New York: Springer-Verlag.

p. 16 Pintrich, P. & DeGroot, E. (1990). Motivational and self-regulated learning components of classroom academic performance. *Journal of Educational Psychology,* 82, 33-40.

p. 16 Rohrkemper, M. & Corno, L. 1988. Success and failure on classroom tasks: Adaptive learning and classroom teaching. *Elementary School Journal*, 88, 297-312.

p. 16 Schiefele, U. (1991). Interest, learning and motivation. *Educational Psychologist* 26(3-4), 299-323.

p. 17 Csikzentmihalyi, M. (1975). *Beyond boredom and anxiety.* San Fransisco: Jossey-Bass.

p. 17 Csikzentmihalyi, M. (1990b). Literacy and intrinsic motivation. *Daedalus*, 119(2), 115-40.

p. 17 Csikzentmihalyi, M. & Hermanson, K. (1995). Intrinsic motivation in museums: Why does one want to learn? In: J. Falk & L. Dierking (Eds.) *Public institutions for personal learning.* Washington, DC: American Association of Museums.

p. 17 Csikzentmihalyi, M. & Nakamura, J. (1989). The dynamics of intrinsic motivation: A study of adolescents. *Research on motivation in education Vol. 3 Goals and cognitions.* New York: Academic Press.

p. 17 Falk, J.H. & Dierking, L.D. (1995). *Public institutions for personal learning: Establishing a research agenda.* Washington, D.C.: American Association of Museums.

CHAPTER 3

p. 22 Leibovich, M. & Stoughton, S. (1998). When keeping up isn't child's play. *Washington Post*, December 15, Business, p. D1.

p. 22 Milner, B. (1997). Play centres dress up downtowns. Report on Business, Toronto, CA: *The Globe and Mail*, September 15, p. B1.

p. 22 Robinson, J. & Godbey, G. (1997). *Time for life – The surprising ways Americans use their time.* University Park, PA: Penn State Press.

p. 26 U.S. Bureau of the Census (1999). *Statistical abstracts of the United States, 1999* (119th Edition). Washington: Government Printing Office.

p. 27 Godbey, G. (2001). The use of time and space in assessing the potential of free-choice learning. In J. Falk (Ed.), *Free-Choice science education: How we learn schience outside of school*, pp. 64-76. New York: Teachers College Press.

p. 27 Haggerty, M. (1997). Developers offer plans for Tariff Building: Housing, stores, museum among proposed uses. *Washington Post*, September 2, Business, p. D9.

CHAPTER 4

p. 35 Cajete, G. (1975). *Look to the mountain: An ecology of indigenous education.* Skyland, NC: Kivaki Press.

p. 36 Dewey (1938). *Experience and education.* New York: Macmillan.

p. 38 Calvin, W. H. (1997). *How brains think.* New York: Basic Books.

p. 38 Rosenfield, I. (1990). *The invention of memory.* New York: Basic Books.

p. 38, 39 Sylwester, R. (1995). *In celebration of neurons.* Alexandria, VA.: Association for Supervision and Curriculum Development.

p. 39 Albjerg Graham, P. (1998). Educational dilemmas for Americans. *Daedalus,* 127(1), 233-247.

p. 39 Amabile, T.M. (1983). *The social psychology of creativity.* New York: Springer-Verlag.

p. 39 Amabile, T.M. (1985). Motivation and creativity: Effects of motivational orientation on creative writers. *Journal of Personality and Social Psychology,* 48, 393-97.

p. 39 Csikzentmihalyi, 1995

p. 39 Csikzentmihalyi & Hermanson, 1995

p. 39 Csikzentmihalyi and Nakamura, 1989

p. 39 Damasio, A. R. (1994). *Descartes' error: Emotion, reason, and the human brain.* New York: Avon Books.

p. 39 deCharms, 1968

p. 39 Deci, E.L. (1972). Intrinsic motivation, extrinsic reinforcement, and inequity. *Journal of Personality and Social Psychology,* 18, 105-115.

p. 39 Deci & Ryan, 1985

p. 39 Lepper, M.R. & Cordova, D.I. (1992). A desire to be taught: Instructional consequences of intrinsic motivation. *Motivation and Emotion,* 16(3), 187-208.

p. 39 Lepper, M.R. & Greene, D. (1978). *The hidden costs of reward: New perspectives on the psychology of human motivation.* Hillsdale, NJ: Erlbaum.

p. 39 McGraw, K.O. (1978). The detrimental effects of reward on performance: A literature review and prediction model. In: M.R. Lepper & D. Greene (Eds.) *The hidden costs of rewards.* Hillsdale, NJ: Erlbaum. pp. 33-60.

p. 40 Csikzentmihalyi, M., Rathunde, K. & Whalen, S., (1993). Talented teenagers: The roots of success and failure. New York: Cambridge University Press.

p. 40 Dierking, L.D. & Pollock, W. (1998). *Questioning assumptions: An introduction to front-end studies in museums.* Washington, D.C.: Association of Science-Technology Centers.

p. 40 Gottfried, 1985

p. 40 Hidi, S. (1990). Interest and its contribution as a mental resource for learning. *Review of Educational Research,* 60, 549-571.

p. 40 James, W., ([1890]1950). *Principles of psychology, 2 volumes.* P. 237. New York: Dover.

p. 40 McCombs, 1991

p. 40 Pintrich & DeGroot, 1990

p. 40 Schiefele, 1991

p. 40 White, 1949

p. 43 Gardner, Howard. 1983. *Frames of mind: The theory of multiple intelligences.* New York: Basic Books.

p. 44 Goleman, D. (1995). *Emotional intelligence.* New York: Bantam Books.

p. 45 Freud, S. (1959). Inhibitions, symptoms and anxiety. In *The Standard Edition of the complete psychological works of Sigmund Freud*, vol. 20. London: The Hogarth Press and The Institute of Psychoanalysis.

CHAPTER 5

p. 48 Barkow, J., L. Cosmides & J. Tooby. (1992). *The adapted mind: Evolutionary psychology and the generation of culture.* New York: Oxford University Press.

p. 48 Cashdan, E. (1989). Hunters and gatherers: Economic behavior in bands. In S. Plattner (Ed.) *Economic anthropology*, pp. 21-48. Stanford: Stanford University Press.

p. 48 Lee, R. & Devore, I. (Eds.). (1968). *Man the hunter.* Chicago: Aldine.

p. 48 Weissner, P. (1982). Risk, reciprocity and social influences on !Kung San economics. In E. Leacock & R.B. Lee (Eds.) *Politics and history in band societies.* Cambridge: Cambridge University Press.

p. 49 Falk, J.H. & Amin. (1998). Unpublished dialogue recorded in the *World of Life* exhibition at the California Science Center.

p. 50 Bruner, J. (1996). *The culture of education.* Cambridge, MA.: Harvard University Press.

p. 50 Calvin, W. H. (1997). *How brains think.* New York: Basic Books

p. 50 Comte, A. (1855). *The positive philosophy of Auguste Comte.* Translated by Harriet Martineau. New York: Calvin Blanchard.

p. 50 Durkheim, E. (1895). *Les regles de la methode sociologique.* Paris: F. Alcan. Reprint, *The rules of sociological method.* New York: The Free Press, 1938.

p. 50 Falk, J.H. & Dierking, L.D. (1992). *The museum experience.* Washington, DC: Whalesback Books.

p. 50 Falk, J.H. & Dierking, L.D. (2000). *Learning from museums: Visitor experiences and the making of meaning.* Walnut Creek, CA: AltaMira Press.

p. 50 Hudson, J., and K. Nelson. (1983). Effects of script structure on children's story recall, *Developmental Psychology* 19: 525-635.

p. 50 Nelson, K., and A. L. Brown. (1978). "The semantic-episodic distinction in memory development," in *Memory development in children.* (Ed.). P.A. Ornstein. Hillsdale, N.J.: Erlbaum. pp. 233-41.

p. 50 Schauble, L., Leinhardt, G. & Martin, L. (1998). A framework for organizing a cumulative research agenda in informal learning contexts. *Journal of Museum Education*, 22(2 & 3), 3-8.

p. 50 Sylwester, 1995.

p. 50 Vygotsky, L.S. (1978). *Mind in society: The development of higher mental processes.* (M. Cole, V. John-Steiner, S. Scribner & E. Souberman, Eds.) Cambridge, MA: Harvard University Press. (Original work published in 1930, 1933, 1935).

p. 53 Ceci, S.J. & Leichtman, M. (1992). Memory cognition. In: S Segalowitz & I. Rapin (Eds.) *Handbook of neuropsychology*, pp. 223-240. Amsterdam: Elsevier.

p. 53 Ceci, S. J., & Roazzi, A. (1994). The effects of context on cognition: Post-cards from Brazil. In: R.J. Sternberg & R.K. Wagner (Eds.) *Mind in context.* Cambridge, UK: Cambridge University Press. pp. 74-101.

CHAPTER 6

p. 63 Barkow, Cosmides & Tooby, 1992

p. 63 Calvin, 1997

p. 65 Csibra, G. *Science.* November 24, 2000.

p. 65 Gallagher, W. (1993). *The power of place: How our surroundings shape our thoughts, emotions and actions.* New York: Poseidon Press.

p. 65 Gibson, E.J. and Walk, R.D. (1960, April). The "visual cliff." *Scientific American. 202*(1): 64-71.

p. 65 Held, R. and Hein, A. (1963). Movement-produced stimulation in the development of visually guided behavior. *Journal of Comparative & Physiological Psychology.* 56, 872-876.

p. 65 van Heteren, C. & Nihuis, J.G. *The Lancet.* September 30, 2000.

p. 65 White, B and Held, R. (1966). Plasticity of sensorimotor development in the human infant. In J.F. Rosenblith & W. Allinsmith (Eds.), *The causes of behavior.* Boston: Allyn & Bacon. pp. 60-70.

p. 67 Dancy, R.B. (1989). *You are your child's first teacher.* Berkeley, CA: CelestialArts.

p. 67 Hudson & Nelson, 1983.

p. 67 Nelson & Brown, 1978.

p. 67 Piaget, J. (1952). *The origins of intelligence in children.* New York: International Universities Press. Originally published in 1936.

p. 69 Bettelheim, B. (1975). *The uses of enchantment.* New York, NY: Alfred A. Knopf. p. 46.

p. 69 Britz-Crecelius, H. (1986). *Children at play.* New York, NY: Inner Traditions International. p. 32.

p. 69 Fein, G. (1984). The self building potential of pretend play. In T.D. Yowey & A.D. Pellegrini (Eds.). *Child's play: Developmental & appliEd.* Hillsdale, NJ: Erlbaum.

p. 69 Fein, G. (1986). Pretend play: Creativity and consciousness. In D. Gorlitz & J. Wohwill (Eds.). *Curiosity, imagination & play.* Hillsdale, NJ: Erlbaum.

p. 69 Smilansky, S. & Shefatya, L. (1990). *Facilitating play: A medium for promoting cognitive, socio-emotional and academic development in young children.* Gaithersburg, MD: Psychosocial & Educational Publications.

p. 71 Falk & Dierking, 2000

CHAPTER 7

p. 78 Adelman, L., Dierking, L.D., and Adams, M. (2000). *Summative evaluation year 4: Findings for Girls at the Center.* Technical report. Annapolis, Maryland: Institute for Learning Innovation.

p. 79 Artz, K., Bartow-Melia, A., Glassman, B. & McCray, K. (1999). *Intergenerational experiences and the OurStory Program: History through children's literature program*, evaluative survey report. Washington, DC: National Museum of American History.

p. 79 Berk, L.E. (1989). *Child development*. Boston: Allyn and Bacon.

p. 79 Büchner, K., Dierking, L.D., & Soren, B. (1999). *The Story in History summative evaluation, National Museum of American History*, Washington, DC, technical report. Annapolis, MD: Institute for Learning Innovation.

p. 82 Bandura, A. (1964). Behavior modification through modeling procedure. In Krasner & Ullman (Eds.) *Research in behavior modification*. New York, NY: Holt, Rhinehart & Winston.

p. 82 Bandura, A. (1977). *Social learning*. Englewood Cliffs, NJ: Prentice Hall Inc.

p. 82 Bandura, A. & Walters, R. (1963). *Social learning and personality development*. New York: Holt, Rhinehart & Winston.

p. 82 Canale, J. R. (1977). The effect of modeling and length of ownership on sharing behavior of children. *Social Behavior and Personality*. 5: 187-191.

p. 82 Elliot, R. & Vasta, R. (1970). The modeling of sharing: Effects associated with vicarious reinforcment, symbolization, age and generalization. *Journal of Experimental Child Psychology*, 10, 8-15.

p. 82 Gray, R. & Pirot, M. (1984). The effects of prosocial modeling on young children's nurturing of a 'sick' child. *Psychology & Human Development*, 1, 41-46.

CHAPTER 8

p. 91 Berk, 1989

p. 91 Elkind, D. (1984). *All grown up & no place to go*. Reading, MA: Addison-Wesley.

p. 91 Erikson, E. (1950). *Childhood and society*. New York: Norton.

p. 94 Institute on Education and the Economy. (2001). *School-to-work: Making a difference in education*. New York, NY: Teachers College, Columbia University.

CHAPTER 9

p. 104 Jacobi, J. 1973. *The psychology of C.G. Jung*. New Haven: Yale University Press.

p. 104 Maslow, A.H. 1968. *Toward a psychology of being*. New York: D. Van Nostrand.

CHAPTER 10

p. 114 Knowles, M.S. (1970). *The modern practice of adult education*. New York: Association Press.

p. 114 UNESCO, *Final Report, Fifth International Conference on Adult Education*. 14-18 July 1997.

p. 115 Clark, P. (February 18, 2001). An artist's harvest. *Washington Post.*

p. 117 Groer, A. (August 30, 2001). Want a vintage toaster? Bring lots of bread. *Washington Post.*

p. 118 Senge, P.M. (1990). *The fifth discipline: The art and practice of the learning organization*. New York: Doubleday.

p. 119 Newman, D.F, Griffin, F. & Cole, M. (1989). *The construction zone: Working for cognitive change in schools*. Cambridge, England: Cambridge University Press.

p. 120 Lave, J. (1990). The culture of acquisition and the practice of understanding. In: J.W. Stigler, R.A. Shweder, & G. Herdt (Eds.) *Cultural psychology: Essays on comparative human development*, pp. 309-327. Cambridge: Cambridge University Press.

p. 120 Lave, J. (1991). Situating learning in communities of practice. In L.B.Resnick, J.M. Levine, & S.D. Teasley, (Eds.) *Socially shared cognition*, pp.63-82. Washington, DC: American Psychological Association.

p. 120 Lave, J. & Wenger, E. (1991). *Situated learning: Legitimate peripheral participation*. Cambridge: Cambridge University Press.

p. 120 Matelic, C.T. 2001. Mentoring tradition. *Museum News* (November/December), p. 44-49.

p. 120 Matusov, E. & Rogoff, B. (1995). Evidence of development from people's participation in communities of learners. In: J. Falk & L. Dierking (Eds.). *Public institutions for personal learning*. pp. 97-104. Washington, DC: American Association of Museums.

p. 120 Roche, G.R. 1979. Much ado about mentors. *Harvard Business Review*, January-February, p. 14-28.

p. 120 Rogoff, B. (1990). *Apprenticeship in thinking: Cognitive development in social context*. New York: Oxford University Press.

Taylor, K. (August 30, 2001). Live and learn. *The Washington Post.*

Tharp, R.G. & Gallimore, R. (1988). *Rousing minds to life: Teaching, learning, and schooling in social context*. Cambridge: Cambridge University Press.

CHAPTER 11

p. 125 Jennings, G. (2001). Museums and the aging revolution. *Journal of Museum Education*. 26(1): 2.

p. 128 Barlow, R. (2001). One for the books. *US Airways Attache*. September.

p. 129 Hart. J. (1992). *Beyond the tunnel: The arts & aging in America*. Alexandria, VA: Museum One Publications.

CHAPTER 12

p. 146 Borun, M., & Dritsas, J. (1997). Developing family-friendly exhibits. *Curator*, 40(3): 178-196.

p. 146 Borun, M., Dritsas, J., Johnson, J.I., Peter, N., Wagner, K., Fadigan, K., Jangaard, A., Stroup, E.& Wenger, A. (1998). *Family learning in museums: The PISEC perspective*. Philadelphia, PA: The Franklin Institute.

p. 146 Borun, M., Chamber, M.B., Dritsas, J. & Johnson, J.I. (1997). Enhancing family learning through exhibits. *Curator: The Museum Journal*, 40/4: 279-295.

p. 137 Dierking, L.D. & Adams, M. (1996). *Spirit of the Motherland Exhibition: Summative evaluation*. Annapolis, MD: Institute for Learning Innovation (at that time Science Learning, inc.).

p. 140 Falk, J.H. & Holland, D.G. (1993). *What about AIDS? Traveling exhibition: Remedial evaluation*. Annapolis, MD: Institute for Learning Innovation (at that time Science Learning, inc.).

CHAPTER 13

p. 165 Packer, Arnold. (2000, August). Getting to know the employee of the future. *Training & Development*, pp. 39-43.

p. 168 Suro, R. (September 21, 2000). Army ads open new campaign: Finish Education. *The Washington Post*.

p. 174 K. Inamori (June 5, 1985). The perfect company: Goal for productivity. Speech given at Case Western Reserve University.

p. 174 Senge, 1990

About the Authors

John Falk and **Lynn Dierking** arc founders and directors of the Institute for Learning Innovation in Annapolis, Maryland. Their books include *Learning from Museums*, *The Museum Experience*, and *Free-Choice Science Education*.